ENJOY THE RIDE

ENJOY THE RIDE

Timeless Principles for Building
a Successful Business and Family

FRITZ GRUPE
With Tory Swim Inloes and Veronica Rossi

Copyrighted Material

Enjoy the Ride: Timeless Principles for Building a Successful Business and Family

Copyright © 2019 by Shady Oaks Publishing. All Rights Reserved.

No part of this publication may be reproduced, stored in a retrieval system or transmitted, in any form or by any means—electronic, mechanical, photocopying, recording or otherwise—without prior written permission from the publisher, except for the inclusion of brief quotations in a review.

For information about this title or to order other books and/or electronic media, contact the publisher:

Shady Oaks Publishing
PO Box 207007
Stockton, CA 95267
enjoytheridebyfg@gmail.com

Library of Congress Control Number: 2019901324

ISBN: 978-1-7328218-0-4 (softcover)
       978-1-7328218-1-1 (hardcover)
       978-1-7328218-2-8 (eBook)

Printed in the United States of America

Cover and Interior design: 1106 Design

Publisher's Cataloging-In-Publication Data
(Prepared by The Donohue Group, Inc.)

Names: Grupe, Fritz, 1937– author. | Inloes, Tory Dawn Swim, author. | Rossi, Veronica, author.

Title: Enjoy the ride : timeless principles for building a successful business and family / Fritz Grupe, with Tory Swim Inloes and Veronica Rossi.

Description: Stockton, CA : Shady Oaks Publishing, [2019] | Includes bibliographical references and index.

Identifiers: ISBN 9781732821804 (softcover) | ISBN 9781732821811 (hardcover) | ISBN 9781732821828 (ebook)

Subjects: LCSH: Grupe, Fritz, 1937– | Success in business. | Entrepreneurship. | Interpersonal relations. | Work-life balance. | Real estate development. | Planned communities.

Classification: LCC HF5386 .G78 2019 (print) | LCC HF5386 (ebook) | DDC 650.1--dc23

To my family, friends, and business partners who lived the stories I memorialize in this book.

Table of Contents

Introduction

Part One Foundations

Chapter 1
    Daring to Dream   3
    Digging In: *John Carsten Grupe: The Legacy
    of a Nineteenth-Century Entrepreneur*   12

Chapter 2
    Values Worth Their Value   17

Chapter 3
    Learning Financial Responsibility   37

Chapter 4
    Getting Curious: Learn How to Ask
    the Right Questions   51

Chapter 5
Becoming a Lifelong Learner   67
Digging In: *Learning to Create Solutions—My First Big Deal*   73

Chapter 6
Listening and Communicating Effectively   79

Chapter 7
Having the Courage to Take Action   99
Digging In: *Where's the Next Stoplight? Anticipating Change and Taking Action*   107

Chapter 8
Building Confidence and Trust Through Action   111

Chapter 9
Practicing Patience   131
Digging In: *From Sharing to Selling the Dream: A Closer Look at Creating a Sense of Urgency and Marketing a Master-Planned Community*   138

Chapter 10
Valuing Relationships   153

Chapter 11
Prioritizing Relationships   169
Digging In: *When a Dream Comes to Fruition: Creating Shady Oaks*   180

Part Two Being Resilient

Chapter 12
   Accepting Consequences 205
   Digging In: *Dealing with the Unforeseen, Unforeseen with Integrity and Confidence: Rebounding from the Savings-and-Loan Crisis* 224

Chapter 13
   Embracing Change 233

Chapter 14
   Making Difficult Decisions: When It's Time to Pull the Pin 247
   Digging In: *When Surviving Is Success: Withstanding the Great Recession* 263

Chapter 15
   Leaning on Your Values 277

Chapter 16
   Keeping Balance 289
   Digging In: *Our Horse Habit* 297

Chapter 17
   Banding Together to Bounce Back 309

Part Three Life Is Better When It's Shared

Chapter 18
   Building Teams That Execute   319
   Digging In: *Teaching Teamwork*   338

Chapter 19
   Helping Others Succeed   343

Chapter 20
   Giving Back   357

Chapter 21
   Having Fun and Being Thankful   369

In Conclusion   373

Acknowledgments   375

Notes & References   377

Index   393

Introduction

*I*F YOU'VE GOT A LITTLE TALENT and you're willing to put in the work, you can go a long way.

I was just twenty-five when I developed my first shopping center. For weeks, I'd been driving past a residential property on a great corner lot that was for sale. I just knew it would make a great commercial site if only I could overcome a few hurdles. The land needed to be rezoned and curb cuts secured to make the property commercially viable, tenants needed to be found, and leases needed to be negotiated. Only then would it be possible to get financing on the property as I personally had no substantial capital to fund the deal.

Rather than dwelling in "if only" thoughts, I gave it a shot after completing my research and took action toward implementing my vision. Many people had to be convinced—and I found ways to convince them. With a $5,000 investment that a good friend matched—far from chump change to two twenty-five-year-olds just getting started in life—we were able to tie up that residential property for a year. Now I had the time to face all the challenges—the rezoning, the curb cuts, and leases—and I was on my way to becoming a commercial real estate developer.

Sounds simple, doesn't it? Have an idea, figure out how to make it happen, and you're done. Easy, right?

Not quite. There are lots of people out there with good ideas. And there are lots of people out there with money, too. What's harder to find are people with good ideas that they're able to implement.

Which brings me to this book. It's my hope that by sharing both my accomplishments and my mistakes, this book will help you achieve your goals and attain true fulfillment, personally and professionally.

In order to put my experiences into perspective, I have tried to tie events into a historical context, where appropriate. I am a fourth-generation Californian with forefathers from all over Northern Europe. I never met my great-grandfather Grupe, who left Germany for the United States at sixteen years old, but I wish I could have seen his perspective on California when he arrived in 1849. Back then, it wasn't yet a state, the population was 165,000 (a far cry from today's 40 million people), and life was very different. For my three great-grandchildren, I expect their future will be just as different, but as much as the world changes, solid principles remain the same. I hope they will learn from my journey when they're ready.

From a business perspective, most people find it interesting that my training began at nine years old, when I began my first business selling eggs to family members and neighbors. By fourteen, I was moving onto the cattle business and then onto real estate in my twenties. At twenty-eight, I began my first master-planned community, which brought a whole new way of lakeside living to Stockton, California, and by the time I was forty-five, I was managing a company with

INTRODUCTION

more than one thousand employees and developing in thirty-five cities and seven states.

It might sound like a ride with only upside, but it hasn't been. I went from having a goal of making $10,000 *per year* in 1962, to losing $10,000 *per hour* in 1986, 1987, and 1988 because my lender went broke and was taken over by the Resolution Trust Corporation (RTC), an arm of the federal government that refused to honor their written loan commitment. Those were tough years, but I survived the emotional ups and downs through my faith, and the support of my wife, family, friends, and the great outdoors.

My failures have taught me as much as my successes. I have seen firsthand the value of keeping a positive attitude and of not falling into the role of victim. And I have learned the importance of maintaining balance in life, even when the business world is in chaos. Amazing things can be accomplished when you embrace change. Who would have thought I'd take up a horse sport at age sixty and just eight years later win the U.S. title—and then go on to represent the U.S.A. at the World Equestrian Championship in Salzburg, Austria?

At eighty-one years-old, I am still enjoying my work. I still drive horses, my family is together, and I have great, supportive friends and partners. It fulfills me to drive through the communities, office parks, and shopping centers we've created and hear from satisfied residents and tenants.

It's been a great life! I feel truly blessed, yet I still feel excited to go after new dreams—and excited to help others achieve their dreams, too.

The title of this book, *Enjoy the Ride,* was chosen because most goals and dreams can't be achieved in a single day. Some take years, and still others take a lifetime. Getting married might be a good goal, for example, but building an enjoyable, loving relationship happens continuously—forever. By focusing on the process of *achieving* as much as *achievement,* we ensure we're not just thinking about the destination, but finding fulfillment along the way.

    This has been my journey so far. I hope you'll come along for the ride.

Part One

Foundations

Chapter 1

Daring to Dream

I GUESS I HAVE ALWAYS BEEN A DREAMER. Plenty of time for that when you're a kid irrigating a walnut orchard from sunup to sundown or plowing a hundred-acre field ten hours a day. There's nothing like a long day alone under the hot sun to get your imagination going. In those days, I'd dream about the plans I had for my herd of cattle or the future farm I envisioned owning. I sure wasn't dreaming about doing *everything* I've done. I just had no way to see that far ahead.

My dreams have unfolded as I've discovered my passions. When I started out as a developer at the age of twenty-eight in 1965, it wasn't with the intent to grow what became one of the largest privately held real estate companies in the United States in the 1980s. I wanted to make a profit by building better homes that made people happy because it improved their quality of life. When I began to compete in combined (carriage) driving at the age of sixty, it wasn't with the goal to make the U.S. Equestrian Team and win national titles. I've always loved horses, and it looked like a fun pastime to share with my wife. But it really is amazing what can happen if you follow your passions, work hard, and live your life with the attitude, "Why can't it be me?"

Along the way, I've tried to stay true to my ultimate goal of leading a joyful, balanced life, focused on giving back and making meaningful connections with family and friends. I've worked to educate myself, to create beauty, and to enjoy the ride. These values and passions, combined with hard work and the principles you'll read about in this book, paved the way to each one of my life's achievements.

I haven't done it alone. My wife, Phyllis, has journeyed with me through every success, setback, decision, and celebration since we married in 1960. Many others have also played important roles in my life, both personally and professionally. To me, the process of achieving, especially as a team, is where real satisfaction can be found. As one of my former executives, Ann Quinn, fondly reminisced on her twelve years with The Grupe Company, "How did we do all of this? I mean, it's incredible what we all did together. There was magic."

Are you still searching for your dream? You might start by taking a close look at your values and your interests. What draws you in? Where do you naturally choose to focus your energies? Asking these questions might not necessarily reveal the *grand* vision, but you'll begin to see a direction—and that will enable you to take your first steps. Dreams are achieved by those who fan the early sparks—and take action.

Finding the Dream Through Small Steps

For me, it all started with eggs. When I was nine, I started my first business at the encouragement of my father. About three years earlier,

DARING TO DREAM

we had moved from Stockton, California, to a farm in Bellota, twenty miles east, near Linden, California. There was a big pen where I could raise chickens—that was the beginning of my "egg business." My main client was my mother. At that time, a dozen eggs sold for 75 cents in the city, but I sold my "farm fresh" eggs for 54 cents a dozen.

It was a good product, and I had a loyal customer base. I kept solid records in my "Egg Book." It was a great way to make some money and learn business skills as a kid. By the time I was fourteen, the money I'd earned allowed me to make my first investment: an eight-month-old Hereford steer that weighed around four hundred pounds. I called him "Big John" in public, but you can imagine the sorts of names my teenage self called him as he'd step on me, knock me aside, or drag me around until I halter-trained him and started taking him to livestock shows.

Though I had no way to predict it then, purchasing that first steer was a major milestone in my life. I already knew I loved being outdoors; that steer taught me I could make a business from a passion. I sold him not long after, and, with the money I made, I bought a cow that was expecting a calf. Soon, I became focused on growing my herd. It was the first dream I was determined to pursue.

My parents knew little about raising cattle, but that didn't stop me. I eagerly reached out to a wide range of resources for guidance, from my high school agriculture teacher, Chet Pierce, to successful cattle ranchers.

I also didn't let limited teenage finances deflate my ambition. I saved every penny I made and poured those savings back into my cattle operation. One by one, my herd grew. It never felt like a sacrifice to be so frugal or disciplined with my finances. Later in life, I would learn that I was practicing "deferred consumption." It was the way to reach my goal since I couldn't afford to buy an entire herd right off the bat. By the end of my sophomore year of high school, I was seeing visible progress. I owned six cows and calves, and one dogie—a calf whose mother has died. By the time I married at the age of twenty-two, I owned about twenty-five head of purebred cows.

My love for those cows was pretty apparent to everyone who knew me. In order to afford the engagement ring for Phyllis, I sold some cows. As she likes to tease, "My goodness! That was when I knew he really loved me. I was even more important than his cows!"

Selling that first egg and purchasing that first steer were initial steps that would lead me to recognizing a *lifelong* dream: to own a farm one day and raise purebred cattle.

After college—which began at University of California, Davis and finished at University of California, Berkeley with a degree in agricultural economics—Phyllis and I returned to my childhood home in 1960. In her, I'd found a partner who shared my love for farm life. *My* dream had become *our* dream, and we put everything we had into chasing after it. It didn't take long, however, for us to realize that being tenants on my father's ranch limited our ability to achieve it. We wouldn't reach our dream as things stood. We needed—and wanted—our own property. And, in order to have the farm we hoped for, it would take money and have to be a sizable piece of land.

Around this same time, I had the opportunity to gain retail experience at a drugstore located in my father and his partner's shopping center, which had almost thirty stores then. The position was temporary, just to offset the hustle of Christmas shopping. I started in the back, inventorying and building shelves, but once I got out on the floor to wait on customers, I noticed the stuffed teddy bears that lined the drugstore's highest shelves just weren't selling. I was bored to tears just standing around and began to wonder . . . could I sell those bears? It was a challenge I couldn't resist.

First, I recommended we move them lower, where they could be better seen. Then I focused on the customers. I quickly learned how fun it was to build rapport with people browsing the store and to identify potential teddy-bear buyers. It was great training in what I would later learn is called "qualifying the prospect."

Who was my target customer? The fathers and grandfathers—who seemed so old to my twenty-three-year-old self—waiting around while their spouses shopped. They were being good sports, but they were not the ones with the mission. It was easy to put myself in their shoes (I wasn't the only one feeling idle), strike up a conversation, and help give purpose to their wait.

"Have you thought about what you're going to get your grandkids for Christmas?" I'd ask, placing a teddy bear in their hands. Once you've got someone holding a teddy bear, it's pretty easy to close the deal.

To make it even more fun, I gave my commission to whichever clerk sent the prospect my way. It became a team effort, those bears flew off the shelves, *and* I got to enjoy watching the men return to their wives victorious and happy.

It was at that moment that I realized selling was a way to earn an income. Even more significantly, I realized I loved it! Selling made people happy—and it made *me* happy, too. But it was going to take *a lot* of teddy bears to buy a ranch. There had to be a better way to reach my goal.

When I looked, the answer was right there.

Making the Dream Happen Through Bigger Steps
Real estate has always been a common theme in my life. My dad was one of five partners in a successful real-estate and insurance-brokerage

firm in Stockton and was quite a visionary developer in the 1940s and 1950s. At his suggestion, I transferred to UC Berkeley in my final year of college to finish my degree so I could take advantage of one of the first real estate programs of its kind, now expanded to be the Fisher Center for Real Estate and Urban Economics.

After my experience selling teddy bears that Christmas season, I began to see how real estate might allow me to tap into the same passion I'd discovered for selling and move me toward my goal. It wasn't long before a plan began to take form. We would still make our living from the land, however, in a very different way than we had envisioned it! Phyllis and I would move to Stockton temporarily so I could sell houses, thereby earning enough to buy the cows and property that would complete our dream of having a farm and cattle ranch. Our plan was perhaps a little naïve, but we had a good dream and were hungry for it!

We knew what we had to do, but that didn't mean it was easy. Leaving the security and beauty of my family ranch for Stockton was scary and devastating for both of us. Phyllis sometimes reminds me of how we sat on the lawn in front of our house and cried because we didn't want to go. We did it anyway. It was a necessary step in creating the life we envisioned, and a **tipping point**—one of those moments that truly makes a difference even decades later. Leaving Bellota for Stockton wasn't the first tipping point I'd experienced—marrying Phyllis and discovering our shared love for ranch life were tipping points as well—but the move to Stockton *was* a major one. Without a doubt, that decision affected the course of our journey.

From there, things began to unfold in ways I never could have imagined. I started as a real estate salesman for Sims & Grupe, the firm from which my father had since retired. I fell in love with it. I studied to get a real estate license, worked long hours, and learned *a lot* just by having my antenna up and being observant. It was no longer just a means to an end. It satisfied me professionally like nothing I'd done before. I was now making people happy on an entirely new level as I helped them find their perfect home. I never lost sight of the dream to own a farm and a cattle ranch. That, too, would come true, but my aspirations now straddled two worlds, personal and professional.

When we first moved to Stockton, my goal was to make $10,000 a year, about $3,000 more than what my dad could pay me. This was at a time when a public school teacher earned about $5,000 per year, a movie ticket cost 70 cents, and a gallon of gas hovered at 30 cents a gallon. But in three years, I wound up blowing past my goal and earning $36,000 that year. And I was gaining valuable experience and knowledge that would prepare me for future endeavors. The same approach that had proved successful in growing my cattle operation had worked yet again.

How did I do it? I worked hard. I deferred consumption. I asked questions. I listened. I collaborated with others to find answers. I took action and developed confidence by building from small steps to bigger ones.

After spending five years as a real estate salesman driving prospective buyers around looking for their ideal home, I gained confidence in my instincts for giving people what they wanted. The hard work paid off. After two years at Sims & Grupe, I won the company's incentive trip to Hawaii for being the top salesman. It was a big deal at the time because the trip had gone unclaimed for a couple of years. Nobody thought anyone could do it. I proved them wrong—and got a nice vacation out of it!

The happiness of my customers and the recognition of my team at Sims & Grupe helped me build the confidence that would propel me into building homes—another example of how one step leads to another.

For me, the dreams have come through pursuing my passions. Everything I've ever done has unfolded through having fun, doing my job, making people happy, and honoring the powerful connection I have to the outdoors. Much like in science, where one discovery leads to another, my smaller dreams laid the foundation for my bigger dreams.

Dreams Worth Chasing

Many people can't see something before it's created, especially if it's new and bold, so if you can visualize your dream, you're halfway there. That said, it's the *second* half—the doing—that's the key. **A dream without the ability to execute it has no value.**

I don't want to discourage dreaming just for the fun of it, or suggest that every dream has to be chased. I think that would be bad advice.

> *A dream without the ability to execute it has no value.*

Dreams *can* be just for fun. I've dreamt about going after plenty of things I never did anything about. But when a dream turns into a vision that's backed up by a belief—that's when I decide to take action. My dream of owning a herd of cattle, for example, was based on my love of working with animals and being outdoors.

Successfully executing a dream comes down to developing a plan, daring to go after it, and sticking to it. If you study people who have made huge strides in their respective fields, their success often comes down to their talent, their ability to visualize what was possible before others could, *and* their courage to move forward and *keep* moving forward even when things get tough. Don't worry. We're going to get to all of that, and the conflict between being tenacious (a must in business) and being willing to pull the pin (pushing yourself to make a difficult decision) and let go.

For now, think about where you stand. Be honest! Are your dreams coming true, or are you continually giving up? If your dream has grown into a vision you feel passionate about, it's time to have courage, be tenacious, and take action. It's easy to get overwhelmed by all that it will take to accomplish your dream or held up by the many decisions you'll need to make. But most decisions aren't life threatening. There aren't many things that are unchangeable—most things you *can* change—so why not get on with it?

I like to say that **a half-assed decision now is better than a perfect decision never.** A more polite way I have heard this said is, "Perfection can be the enemy of progress." The important thing is to make sure you have a dream and go for it!

Digging In: John Carsten Grupe
The Legacy of a Nineteenth-Century Entrepreneur

I was fortunate to grow up with many inspiring examples of family members who not only dreamed big but succeeded at turning their dreams into reality. My childhood was filled with stories of my grandparents' and great-grandparents' ingenuity, commitment to hard work, love for education, and the budding entrepreneurial spirit that many of them shared.

My great-grandfather John Carsten Grupe (1828–1889) always stood out as a model of somebody who had a dream and willed it into reality. From his example, I learned at an early age that no dream is too big to chase if one is willing to put in the work and adapt as circumstances change.

In 1844, great-grandfather Grupe, who went by his middle name of "Carsten" on legal documents, left his home of Hanover, Germany, at the age of sixteen in pursuit of opportunity and the dream of a better life. He was one of the two million people who immigrated to the United States between 1841 and 1850, a time when it took weeks rather than hours to travel from Germany to New York.

In the 1840s, the United States was reaping the rewards of technological advancements in transportation, communication, industry, agriculture, urbanization, and the economy alike. It was an exciting time. However, while many benefited, a significant portion of the population remained marginalized, disenfranchised, or enslaved. Women couldn't vote and, according to the 1840 U.S. census, nearly 15 percent of the 17 million U.S. population remained in the institution of slavery—an institution that was not abolished until 1865.

Once news arrived that gold had been discovered in California, my great-grandfather wasted little time. He made the necessary preparations for the small, corner grocery store he had bought in New York after working as a clerk for a year to be managed in his absence and boarded a schooner for a six-month journey to the gold fields of California. He would be one of the eighty thousand prospectors who would head to California in 1849 and as a result participated in the largest mass migration in U.S. history up to that point. Many more would come—by 1860 the population of California was more than 360,000 people, with women making up about a third of that number.

When my great-grandfather stepped off the *Joseph Hewitt* in San Francisco in July 1849, California had been ceded from the Mexican Republic only about sixteen months prior and looked very different compared to today.

Although not yet a state, it was certainly not without a history of its own. For thousands of years, California had been home to a dense network of diverse, innovative, and vibrant indigenous civilizations—sometimes referred to collectively as the California Indians. In 1848, the indigenous population totaled 150,000. The non-indigenous population before the Gold Rush totaled approximately 15,000 and primarily included Mexican citizens, American citizens, Californios (those of Spanish descent but born in California), Europeans, and Russians.

When my great-grandfather arrived, law, government, and education were in flux, lacked oversight, or didn't exist in some areas. Ideologies grounded in domination and racism formed the basis for nineteenth-century settlement and brought disastrous results for the indigenous populations, which dropped to around 30,000 by 1860. Yet at the same time, there was cultural collaboration as, in the words of American historian J.S. Holliday, the "world rushed in."

Upon arriving in San Francisco, my great-grandfather immediately headed by boat to Stockton. The infrastructure that existed then paled in scale to what twentieth-century development would bring, but change to the California landscape was well underway. Stockton had already developed into a major transportation hub, supply depot, and trade center for the Southern Mines by 1849. On July 23, 1850, Stockton became incorporated—the seventh city in California to do so.

John Carsten Grupe Freight Line.

To keep pace and do well, my great-grandfather adapted as needed. When mining didn't yield enough success, he began to work as a driver on a pack train. Within four months, he had saved up the necessary capital to start his own business—a freight line between Stockton and Angels Camp, Sonora, and Mokelumne Hill.

He remained opportunistic. When the price of lumber was high, he turned to whip sawing and sold lumber for $1 per foot. He partnered in a store in Mokelumne Hill but eventually sold it, as he would his one-room store in New York.

Before setting down roots in California for the long haul, my great-grandfather returned to New York to set things in order there. On April 30, 1852, he became a naturalized citizen, listing New York City as his home. On that same day, he obtained a passport with the intent to travel abroad to Germany.

My great-grandparents John Carsten Grupe and Catherine (Behnke) Grupe and their first home.

When he returned from Germany in the fall of 1852, he married Catherine Margaret Behnke (also from Hanover, Germany), and set down roots in the San Joaquin Valley. In November 1853, he became a father. Seven more children would follow. When he passed away in 1889, he had ingrained himself in the San Joaquin Valley as a businessman and farmer and was known as a man of morals.

While I was aware of my great-grandfather's story as a child, it was not until I grew up that I saw his journey as unique and consequential. I feel a deep sentimental attachment to him as I still farm 170 acres of his original homestead along Jack Tone Road in Linden—land that has been in the family since November 11, 1867, when he acquired title by patent.

Through big and small steps, John Carsten Grupe was willing to change his strategy and tactics in order to make his dream come true without compromising his values. As a young immigrant, he dared to dream. In the process, he led an adventurous life and left a meaningful legacy.

Chapter 2

Values Worth Their Value

*T*HERE ARE VERY FEW overnight successes. And you know what? You may *want* to be an overnight success, but you don't *need* to be. Don't fall into the trap of thinking that things should come quick and easy. Walk on the right path, and you'll get where you want to go in due time.

Early on, my parents instilled in me the value of a strong work ethic. They modeled how fundamental values, such as accountability, thrift, and morality bring success and joy. Adhering to these values worked well for them, just like it did for my great-grandfather in the nineteenth century. Some principles are just timeless. Tried and true.

When I have put these principles into practice and paired them with a good attitude, they haven't let me down. My values-based upbringing was so formative, I consider it another tipping point in my life. The principles I learned laid the foundation that's helped me turn my dreams into realities.

The Value of Love

My parents, Greenlaw Grupe and Anne Dervin, were five years apart. They got engaged after just two weeks of dating and married only six months later in 1936. Though they were very different, they complemented each other, adored one another, and were demonstrably affectionate. If they ever argued, I never saw it. Where my father was strategic, rigorous, and stern, my mother was easy-going, vivacious, and compassionate.

When they married, my dad, who was twenty-four, owned a gas station and worked as a realtor in Stockton. In 1943, when I was about five, my parents moved to a 250-acre hill ranch in the greater Linden area, just ten miles east from the homestead of my great-grandfather John Carsten Grupe. The ranch bordered the Calaveras River and had its own 50-acre reservoir. The lake was abundant with fish, and the river edge teemed with wildlife: skunks, possums, raccoons, coyotes, an occasional deer, and lots of feral cats.

Moving to the ranch was a dream come true for my mom, who always had a deep love for animals. As a child she would return home with injured cats or puppies in the basket of her bicycle. Once, she even brought home a turtle with a hole in its shell. Once home, she patched the shell, hand-fed the turtle flies, and enjoyed its company in her parents' yard for another fifteen years. That attentive tradition continued on our ranch as she nursed many animals back to health, such as the deer she named "Bambi."

My mother would start her days feeding the animals by hand. In the afternoons, she was often off, modeling for the Junior Aid or department stores, playing bridge, or volunteering. She had incomparable energy, loved to be social, and yet the only appointment she

VALUES WORTH THEIR VALUE

would commit to in her day was a formal cocktail hour with my dad after he arrived home from work.

The Bellota ranch sat on top of a hill, and from their porch you could see clear to Mt. Diablo, seventy miles away to the west, and clear down to the Calaveras River to the north. My mother called Diablo the Diamond Head (Hawaii) of the Valley. My parents' home overlooked 100 acres of what they called "bottom land," which my father rented out to Filipino farmers who grew row crops, like tomatoes, lettuce, and cabbage. The reservoir occupied 50 acres. Of the remaining 100 acres, about 20 of it were walnut orchards that my dad farmed himself, and 50 acres were permanent pasture to run cows on.

My two younger sisters and I had a great childhood on that ranch. There were cats for my sister Luanne to dress up and push in her buggy and a playground for my sister Sue to hold circuses for the family to watch. Because of my mother's love for animals, we were surrounded by cats, dogs, horses, sheep, deer, cattle, rabbits, and chickens.

Wild animals, too. At a young age, I learned how to run a trapline. Our property was fertile grounds for fox, raccoon, and possum. When I trapped any of these, I would heal them and put them in a cage, adding to our collection. I had such an eclectic bunch, my dad recommended we attempt a small zoo at his shopping center in Stockton—an idea which *did not* pan out the way we'd hoped.

When I wasn't at school or working on the ranch, I spent hours riding my horse, Babe, with my rescue dog, Buster, running alongside as we roamed the foothills. On some summer evenings and weekends, you could find me swimming in our lake while my parents barbecued.

There was plenty of time to think. I spent a lot of time alone working in the field, the nearest neighbor was miles away, and kids

Feeding Nino the lamb at Bellota farm with sisters Luanne and Sue.

didn't use the phone in that era like they do today. In fact, we had a wall crank telephone that was on a party-line system that we shared with ten other households. We learned to recognize our distinct ring, two long and one short bells. Sharing the line with so many other people, we did not use the phone unless it was really necessary.

Considering all of that, there was a lot of time for me to dream, which included coming up with some pretty good pranks. I enjoyed tricking the farmhands, especially Leo, our Filipino chief irrigator. One time, I found him asleep in the field, and I quietly drove a wheel tractor over him, put it in neutral, revved the engine, and scared him.

I wasn't afraid to try out pranks away from the farm, either. While on a fishing trip with some classmates hosted by our great agriculture teacher, Chet Pierce, I put a dead water snake in his sleeping bag. Despite

Riding Babe, with Buster alongside, at the Bellota ranch, 1946.

that dumb move and him subsequently throwing me in the river, we remained very close. Mr. Pierce saw potential in me and told me on my graduation to keep him in mind as a potential partner if I went into the cattle business. Unfortunately, the opportunity never arose as he left education to become an administrator for the Port of Stockton.

Even my parents didn't escape my pranks. Once after I'd killed a gopher snake by throwing a rock, I put it in my shirt to go scare my mom and her friends while they played bridge. I got a little piece of my own medicine that day, as the snake had only been knocked unconscious and spontaneously slithered out of my shirt and onto the table.

In childhood I learned to work hard, but I also discovered what brings joy to healthy relationships and sustains them. One of my favorite boyhood pictures—which I chose as the cover for this book—is of me, riding bareback on Babe, with Buster at our side, eager for our next adventure. We don't have much in that picture—I don't even have a saddle—and the old cattle chute can be seen in the background. But the three of us are distinctively happy, scrapes and all. It's a picture that's worth a thousand words to me, as it illustrates just how simple happiness can be when you're doing what you love.

The Value of Accountability

I was raised to accept responsibility and not to place blame or to think of myself as a victim. My mistakes are mine. I don't shy away from them or try to pass the buck.

When you fail to own your mistakes, you give up the power to learn and grow. You transfer that power to whomever (or whatever) you blame. Why would you ever want to limit yourself like that?

A dedication to personal accountability has run through my family for generations. My father graduated from Stockton High School in

VALUES WORTH THEIR VALUE

1929, just months before the start of the Great Depression. Within my father's yearbook, there is a congratulatory send-off written by the principal, W. Fred Ellis, to the graduating class. While he had no way to foresee the harsh future that awaited his students, his message and advice was all too fitting.

"In the years to come," Ellis wrote, "you members of this class of 1929 will win some successes and in all probability meet some failures. In either case the responsibility will be yours. . . . Stand on your own feet; be humble in your successes; accept the responsibility for your shortcomings."

Surely, as the Great Depression unfolded, his students must have felt that everything was against them. And they were right—they had been dealt a devastating hand. But through resourcefulness, creativity, collaboration, and resilience, *many* found ways to pull through. It didn't happen in a day or even a month, but it did happen.

In my dad's case, he went to college and then, struggling to find work, took matters into his own hands by starting a small service station with his friend Bob Weaver. Totally committed to it, they worked hard and ensured that their enterprise excelled. In time, they were able to open a larger, updated service station. My father didn't wallow in the difficulty of his situation but focused on finding a creative solution instead.

My parents expected no less from me. When I was teased in grammar school, they expected me to face my lot head on. I attended school in a small, one-room schoolhouse in Bellota. The student body totaled about twenty-two students and was almost entirely composed of the children of Italian, Catholic immigrants. At that time, the U.S. was at war with Germany, and the other kids didn't like that I was Protestant, and they resented my German heritage even more. With a

German nickname on top of it (my given name is "Greenlaw" and it was not until high school that I was called "Fritz" both at home and at school), I was an easy target for endless teasing. They called me a "Nazi" and didn't let me sit with them at lunch. I wasn't the only one snubbed. The "Okies"—a derogatory term used at the time for those who had migrated west to escape the destruction of the 1930s Dust Bowl—sat alone as well.

The taunting was upsetting, to say the least, and it would've been easy to wallow in negative feelings, but I was determined that one day others wouldn't just let me sit with them at lunch, they'd *want* to sit with me. With that attitude, I took control and fixed my sights on *changing* the situation.

I shared what was happening with my Irish grandfather, who, in response, bought me some boxing gloves and taught me how to box. You could say that times were a little different then. But I did find that once I was willing to stand up for myself, which in this case meant being willing to fight back, the teasing ended.

> *Life has unfair moments, but if you focus on what you can control—your attitude, for example—then setbacks don't have to make you a victim.*

Life has unfair moments, but if you focus on what you can control—your attitude, for example—then setbacks don't have to make you a victim.

I've faced a lot of unfair moments, especially in business. This book is filled with them. Early on I decided to embrace an attitude of gratitude. When things get tough, I don't blame myself, and I don't blame others. Instead, I acknowledge the hand I've been dealt and ask: *Now what am I going to do?*

Great-grandpa Jon Nickols from the Netherlands and Grandpa Val Dervin (holding me) from Ireland.

The Value of Morals

I was fortunate to grow up in a very stable family, where ethics and morals were extremely important. I've always wondered why we wait until college to have a class in ethics in our society. If you're in your twenties and they still have to teach you ethics, it's a little late, isn't it? How many people do you think change their ethics at that stage of life? Instruction should start at home with kids observing their parents' actions. In other words, ethics should be, as they say, "caught, not taught."

I had an interesting balance in my moral upbringing, as my dad didn't go to church—although he had as a child—and my mom began to go to church *after* having children. My father's religious upbringing never left him, though, and my mother's desire to protect, provide, and care for her children motivated her to become active in the Methodist church in Linden.

What I was taught at home was reinforced in the classroom. Today, I'm not sure that happens as often as it should. If schools don't take part in teaching ethics, when will it be learned for those who don't learn it at home? I recently read a statistic about early American education that caught my attention: In the 1770s, "90 percent of the educational thrust was of an ethical, moral, religious nature." Think of the leaders who came out of that tradition. I was fortunate to have an excellent teacher in Elsie Armanino and to have her through several grades. She was strict, but she taught me respect and other values—all *in addition* to the curriculum.

As my siblings and I learned early on, we each have the ability to make choices for good or evil. We also learned that it's human to sin. My parents took the time to work with us when we got into trouble and to instill in us tools to deal with our setbacks. For example, my sister Sue wrote in our family history about a time she stole from another child's rock collection. She didn't really like the kid—and liked even less how much he bragged—but the longer the rock was in her possession, any gratification she may have initially felt was replaced by feelings of shame.

In an attempt to get rid of the guilt, she tried hiding the rock in our bed of camellias but grew fearful that our dad would find it while gardening. So, she took her pony and galloped out to a field and disposed of her loot there. Still, she was haunted by the fear that somebody would find it and, as she put it, "tell her how bad she was." Eventually, she could no longer bear hiding what she had done and admitted everything to our dad.

He met her confession with understanding and guidance. "We have to do something about it," he told her, "but it sounds like you learned your lesson. It was good of you to tell me." While my sister had to write a letter of apology to the child's parent and buy an entire new rock collection for the child, her misdeed was addressed with compassion and turned into a true teaching moment.

Having parents who genuinely cared for my well-being and loved me unconditionally instilled trust and strengthened my self-esteem. That model was something I wanted to replicate for my own children. Phyllis and I also wanted our kids to attend Sunday school so that they could benefit from its teaching and have a basic belief system.

The Value of Discipline and Hard Work

As I mentioned in the last chapter, my start as a businessman came at the age of nine, when I began selling eggs to my mother and my neighbors. One egg at a time, I built an impressive savings. Yes, I worked a lot, but I *wanted* to. I had a goal of buying a steer, which cost about $200 (which would be about ten times that today), so I could participate in Future Farmers of America (FFA).

All the while, my father was there, insisting that I develop the training to do well in business. He required that I keep a meticulous record of how many eggs I sold and the time I worked, down to the exact minute. This was all done in my Egg Book—a green, cloth-covered ledger. He saw the book as an essential training tool and a way to track how my business was doing.

My Egg Book and earliest business records, here showing entries back to February 1948. I even noted when eggs broke.

It was a priority for him. He spent a lot of time looking over my records with me—but he never made it to *any* of my high school football games, even though I was captain and the only player to go on to play college football! But that was my father for you. He focused on what was important to him—the rest, he didn't bother with.

At the time, keeping such strict records felt unnecessary and taxing to say the least, but, in hindsight, I see that as early training in math, time management, accountability, and discipline. While my father's demand for exactness irritated the hell out of me, the lessons I learned in running my egg business have transcended *every* business I've started—and I've started more than forty businesses. The Egg Book taught me to know my business, track my costs, and make sure there was a demand.

In time, keeping such precise records *did* become easier, and I began to reap the rewards of my efforts. By high school, the practice had become second nature, and I saw a direct correlation between *the quality* of my records and my ability to *make progress* toward my goals. As Aristotle said, "We are what we repeatedly do. Excellence, then, is not an act, but a habit."

As my records improved, I could turn to them to analyze and track how certain decisions panned out, as well as compare my business decisions to those of others. Because I had been measuring my output for so long, I had developed a keen awareness of my abilities, which gave me confidence to take on bigger tasks and responsibilities.

My father took it upon himself to make sure I was developing habits that would serve me in the long run, so I would ultimately be able to stand on my own two feet.

The Value of Trust

I grew up with a lot of autonomy for getting the job done and getting it done right. I was allowed, encouraged, and made to solve difficult problems with little help. Some of that independence came with growing up on a farm, but my parents were also pretty hands-off—at least compared to a lot of today's parents.

Ultimately, they trusted me with a lot of responsibility. I started driving a tractor when I was ten, got my driver's license when I was fourteen, and was responsible for keeping my personal commitments and completing key duties on the farm.

One day, I was driving my dad's big beet truck down the road to Linden and pulling a large tractor trailer behind it. It was an old military truck with wheels turned by chains—and it was noisy as hell. Somewhere along the way, I no longer heard the familiar clang of the ball mount going up and down in the trailer hitch. I looked in the rearview mirror, and I saw that I was no longer pulling the trailer. As soon as I could, I turned around, retraced my path, and began looking for the missing trailer.

Much to my horror, it had crashed through a walnut tree (cutting right through it, so that the tree sat on top of the trailer) and stopped about ten feet in front of Solari's Inn. Now, Solari's Inn was *the* place to be. From the shuffleboard and the soda fountain, to the fresh raviolis ready for pickup, it was an institution. Luckily, the matter was sorted out pretty easily. I told my father what happened that night, and he went down to talk to Mrs. Solari, who said, "Give me $250 bucks for the tree, and we'll forget it." But to this day, I hate to think of what could have happened if that trailer had gone another ten feet.

It was through situations like that I learned trust brought freedom to act independently. And freedom to act independently sometimes brought accidents—*and that was okay.*

As management expert Stephen Covey (author of *The 7 Habits of Highly Effective People* and former consultant for The Grupe Company) taught, "Trust is the highest form of human motivation. It brings out the very best in people. But it takes time and patience, and it doesn't preclude the necessity to train and develop people so that their competency can rise to the level of that trust." I was very fortunate to have been given that by my parents.

The Value of Attitude

I have learned the importance of having a positive attitude that centers on *achieving* more than *achievement*. If you aren't enjoying the ride, trust me: the destination won't be rewarding enough.

The easiest way to keep a good attitude is to pour yourself into things you feel connected with and inspired by. As they say, if you love your work, then working is easy.

When work brings joy, it almost seems wrong to even call it "work." People sometimes use different words to describe it, like a *passion* or a *calling*, but it's still hard work. The only difference is how you feel about it.

Phyllis's life provides a great example of this sort of heart-driven work. While I'd saved every penny to build a herd of cattle while growing up, Phyllis had saved nickels to buy a horse. She started at the age of five—that's right, *five*—and did whatever she could to add to the nickel jar that sat on top of the refrigerator, whether it was watering people's gardens or babysitting. After seven years of hard work and saving, Phyllis finally bought her first horse in 1952 with her saved $67 and an $18 loan from her parents (which she paid back). She purchased her first horse from the slaughter yard and named her "Desba."

Now, Desba wasn't very pretty. She had a big split ear and had obviously been captured and marked for slaughter. But Phyllis didn't care. She felt she had hit the jackpot with her little wild mustang from the desert.

Because Phyllis lived in the city, she had to board Desba at a stable three miles away. To afford the cost of feed and boarding, Phyllis continued to work odd jobs such as babysitting and yard work to support her horse. Of course, by the age of twelve, Phyllis was already a regular at the stable—she'd been working there for a year to earn money to buy a horse. Every summer morning at 5:30 a.m., Phyllis would pedal to the stable on her bicycle. She'd ride Desba the entire day—bareback, since all her money went to feed—and then pedal back home before her sunset curfew. At night, covered with dirt, horsehair, and sweat, she'd take a shower and head to bed, eager to do the very same thing the next day.

That is a perfect example of a great attitude and work ethic—*and* of the enjoyment of achieving as well as the achievement. I can brag because I married her!

The Value of Time

Time is often a more finite resource than money. People lament that there aren't enough hours in the day, but there are a perfect number of hours if you know how to manage and administrate them.

As my children recall from childhood, whenever a homework assignment seemed big, I advised them to make a list (a process I detail in Chapter 7). It's a practice that worked for them as teenagers and has always worked for me whenever I'm faced with a business project or decision that feels too big or overwhelming. As you're looking to manage your time, make a list of what needs to be done and then ask yourself: *What's most important?* Do that first. Because you only have so much time in one day.

For the rest of it, *delegate* if you can. Part of time management is giving people the opportunity to help you reach your dream. If you don't truly delegate and give others the freedom to act (meaning you're not second-guessing them all the time), then you will not get the job done—and you'll have wasted your time and, likely, someone else's.

Some years ago, Phyllis taught me an important lesson about delegating and its clear correlation to time management. We were celebrating our 25th wedding anniversary in Mexico, and she was having a tough time. She was suffering from a bad bout of bronchitis and swamped with a myriad of responsibilities—raising our teenage children, competing nationally with our Belgian horses, and giving endless support to me, The Grupe Company, and our education-focused nonprofit.

In the spirit of celebrating such a milestone anniversary, I asked, "What is it you *really* want?"

She thought about it and resolved, "I want four more hours in every day."

Hesitantly, I admitted, "Well, I can't give you that."

She didn't miss a beat. "You can, and I have it all figured out," she said. "I would like to hire an assistant who can help me do the things that I need to have done."

So we hired Phyllis her first assistant and, in the process, *added* four hours to her crowded days.

Part of delegating is allowing others to make decisions on your behalf. I try to always assess where my time is best spent. Do I go to Phoenix to look into an apartment deal worth about $2 million, or head to Sacramento to explore a $20 million hotel deal? With the way my schedule stacks, it's often impossible for me to do both, but both need to be done, and time is of the essence. As Benjamin Franklin observed, "You may delay, but time will not."

In a scenario like the above, I'd obviously pick the $20 million deal. The *magnitude* is what makes it an easy decision. It's not that the other isn't important—it is. But, faced with a choice, I have to rely on my partners and key executives and have confidence they will make good decisions. Would I have written the offer a little bit differently? Maybe. Or maybe they would do it better. Or maybe it wouldn't make any difference at all! But the decision still needs to be based on the optimal use of my time. And, perhaps even more importantly, if I keep going over to Phoenix to make the $2 million deal, I'll never get out of going.

That doesn't diminish the importance of walking around and seeing delegated work up close, when possible. It's not uncommon for me to check on details of execution, to model behavior I expect (such as picking up trash on the ground at a work site), to get to know all the people in my organization whenever it's possible. This doesn't mean I assume the responsibility of those in charge or disrespect their position as the boss. It's an opportunity to provide support and set an example, not to undermine their efforts.

The Value of Thrift

I was careful with how I spent my money so that I could continue growing my herd of cattle. My parents took care of paying for my school and clothes, but I was responsible for the rest. I was pretty set on my goal, so I weighed possible purchases against how that money could benefit my herd instead.

Perhaps saving came a little easier to me—or perhaps I just wasn't as tempted since our little town didn't really have anywhere to spend money. Either way, I learned what a difference it made to just *save*.

I had a solid (and perhaps a little extreme) example of thrift in my dad. During my third year of college, my dad asked me to build what we lovingly called the Poverty Hills Duck Club on my parents' ranch. He *loved* to duck hunt and include relatives in the hunt. I learned a lot about thriftiness as I built that club.

VALUES WORTH THEIR VALUE

I'm not kidding when I say he saved bent nails. He saved *everything*. All the lumber and windows I used came from years of him holding onto every bit of scrap lumber from his shopping center, including material that had been in fires. Driving nails through scorched wood was a good workout, but eventually I had to talk him into letting me get an electric saw.

That duck club was the first building I ever built, and you could tell. Doing all the labor by myself, it was hard for me to lift the six-by-eight-foot windows into the openings that were five feet off the ground. I thought it would work just as well to install the windows from the inside by reversing the window sill, until it rained and the windows leaked—as they did every time it rained thereafter. It was a good lesson to learn *before* becoming a professional homebuilder!

Startling statistics have been published about the number of Americans who fail at the important practice of being thrifty. Many

Building Poverty Hills Duck Club, 1961.

can't write a check to cover a $500 emergency—63 percent, according to one survey. To me, that's unbelievable. I've been able to do that since I was a teenager. I'll grant that financial security can be a difficult goal to reach for many. There are extenuating circumstances and stresses, but irresponsibility *is* preventable. So where do so many people go wrong?

It's really pretty simple: there's more money *going out* than there is *coming in*. Financial security comes when you live within your means. This may seem obvious to you—and I hope it is—but how often do people buy a car, or a house, or run up credit cards, spending more in the year than they can possibly pay off? Unfortunately, all the time. They fall into the trap of using short-term money for long-term obligations, something that will get you in trouble personally as well as in business. The surest way to increase your net worth is to *spend less than you earn*.

Once you're in the right mindset regarding how you want to manage your money, a lot of it then comes down to discipline. Budgeting—and sticking to it—is crucial. Maintaining control when it comes to money has opened a lot of doors for me, and it has also saved me from some serious heartache.

I feel so strongly about the importance of learning to manage your finances that I'm focusing in on the principle of financial responsibility next.

Chapter 3

Learning Financial Responsibility

𝒫HYLLIS AND I HAVE always made managing our finances a top priority. For us, being responsible about our spending is a foregone conclusion. Especially because, being in real estate and farming, we were often living on an inconsistent income. Our answer to that fluctuating variable was to set a household budget that remained constant regardless of whatever income came in that particular month or year. To accomplish that, we had to *defer consumption*, something both Phyllis and I had been practicing since our youth.

What is **deferred consumption**? Well, put simply, it's waiting for the right time to spend. It's learning to hold off on buying the shiny thing that's got your attention until you can truly afford it. You don't have to spend every damn dollar you make. Saving is a habit; overspending is one of the worst habits you can have. Think about smoking. What do you think when you see someone smoking, considering all we know about the terrible long-term effects of that

Our first home in Bellota. Our automatic dryer was the clothesline, 1961.

habit? I feel the same way when I see someone using a credit card for borrowing versus the temporary use of credit to be cleared monthly.

The foundation of financial responsibility is based on restraint. When it comes down to it, it's not just how much you *make*—it's how much you *save and invest*. There are schoolteachers who end up millionaires and millionaires who go broke.

A Test of Self-Reliance

In college, when I was ready to expand the herd I'd been growing through high school, I saw an opportunity that required more cash than I had on hand. At that time, I was working hard in my studies during the weekdays and returning to the ranch on weekends to take care of my cows and check on the alfalfa-hay business I had started during my junior year of college.

LEARNING FINANCIAL RESPONSIBILITY

By growing my own alfalfa hay, I cut part of the expense related to my cows as well as brought in an additional stream of income. I rented 100 acres on my father's ranch—the "bottom land" he had once rented out to Filipino vegetable farmers. Not having the time to irrigate the acreage or bale the hay on my own, I teamed up with a neighboring rancher, Elliott McCombs, who owned a hay baler. It was my first business partnership. Elliott was a towering man about seventeen years my senior, and most people were scared to death of him. But I had purchased hay from him and felt comfortable enough to ask him if he'd like to partner with me. We rented the land together, hired someone to irrigate it for $1 an acre, and then I paid Elliott to do the baling. He was a good partner, and I gained valuable experience in business and delegation (being some one hundred miles away at college). I was not only making money by working for my father at $1.50 an hour and selling calves, I was also making money by selling hay. Pretty good for a twenty-year-old.

With my businesses operating smoothly, I was ready to increase my herd. I went to my dad in the hopes he'd give me a loan to buy some really good purebred Herefords from the Orvis Ranch, the oldest and finest herd in the state, located in Farmington, California. I thought I was a safe bet. I didn't need much, and I had equity that far surpassed the amount I wanted to borrow. But Dad wouldn't do it. He was confident that, due to the size of my existing herd, the bank would give me a loan, so off to the bank I went.

There, I learned that he was right—the bank *would* give me a loan, but only if my father guaranteed the note. I argued that this wasn't necessary, as I could easily pay back the loan amount by selling just two cows, but the banker wouldn't budge. I left discouraged but proud that a solution for increasing my capital was just one signature away.

I went back to my dad and told him how the meeting had gone. All he needed to do was co-sign the loan, and I'd be on my way. No problem, right?

Wrong. He informed me he would *not* guarantee my loan. In response to my obvious disappointment, he reasoned, "If I start signing your notes now, you'll be coming to me the rest of your life." Then he took me to another bank that would lend me the money *without* his guarantee.

I left that experience with an awareness of the financial self-reliance expected of me. It annoyed me initially, but it also gave me a valuable sense of independence—confidence that I could build my accomplishments, my very *life,* on the strength of my own merits. Now, I see my father's *I won't help you* for what it really was: *you can do this yourself.*

Phyllis and I have tried to teach that same principle to our children and grandchildren. We want them to know that they can build their dreams on their own merits.

We prioritized teaching our children the value of money. We didn't give allowances. They didn't wear designer clothes (our daughter Bonner still remembers desperately wanting an IZOD shirt and K-Swiss tennis shoes). They didn't even fully grasp the magnitude of my business growing up. Bonner told people her dad "built houses." She saw me as *respected* rather than as successful.

The way we raised them, *wanting* to do something didn't always result in *getting* to do something. When they did want something, we'd ask that they come up with a list of pros and cons so that they were part of the decision-making process. We were careful not to overindulge them *except* if they were chasing a passion and applying

LEARNING FINANCIAL RESPONSIBILITY

themselves. Then, we wanted to be their biggest cheerleaders and supporters.

In the same tradition, Phyllis and I have made it a priority to teach our grandchildren the importance of deferred consumption. We don't want them to miss out on the opportunity to build their own dreams. I think deferred consumption is best taught when the reward is seen early on. When we give our grandkids money or they earn it, we offer them the chance to deposit it into "Papa's Bank," which pays a healthy 20 percent interest. I don't think 5 percent is a big motivator, but 20 percent is tempting. I tell them, "Just think, in three and a half years you'll have twice as much money as you do now." Papa's Bank has helped build their awareness in investing as an alternative to consumption. Just recently, my youngest grandson stopped by to deposit $225 he had earned—that takes a lot of time at age nine!

Once my grandchildren are out of college or equivalent training for their chosen profession, and on their own economically for two or more years, I invite them to participate in a cousins' investment fund. I started this idea in 2014 because of a concern I had about "trust fund babies." I lend my grandchildren money individually at a cheap rate to invest in The Grupe Company projects. I help them learn how to read pro formas, study market research, and decide what percentage of the fund they want to risk in a deal. While I am there to help train and guide them, it is their collective and final decision. So far, they have done very well over the past few years, earning rates of return of more than 20 percent per year.

It's been very gratifying to see my grandkids learn such important skills. Here are a few others I feel are important that I've tried to pass on to them as well.

Every Financial Decision Is a Choice

Instead of having the attitude, "He's got it, and I don't," I believe it's better to focus on the freedom you have when it comes to your own money. You get to choose if you have money in the bank or if you spend it. When Phyllis and I married, her first car was a fifteen-year-old Desoto, for which I paid $175 cash. Our savings went into cattle. You decide how much you're going to spend on rent or a home payment. You decide how much you're willing to spend on car payments (I always paid cash). All of these things are decisions.

You Don't Have to *Have* Money to *Make* Money

There's more to being financially successful than how much money you make in a year, or how much money you personally have to put toward your dream. The successful execution of creative ideas is far more lacking in our society than money. I've learned you don't need a bunch of money *before* you can be successful. There's money out there and people looking to back individuals just like you, who want to work hard and turn ideas into reality. As American businessman Henry Ford observed, "Thinking is the hardest work there is, which is probably the reason why so few engage in it."

Later, we'll look at some of the creative ways I started with limited capital, because what it really does come down to is having a good plan—something people will *literally* buy into—and having the ability to execute it.

Economical Savviness Adds Up

The choice to rent or own is not new, but the options available are rapidly expanding. There are often much cheaper alternatives to owning an asset. Millennials particularly like the trend of sharing or renting rather than owning. Look at the popularity of Uber (ridesharing service) or Airbnb (hospitality service). They are two of the biggest companies in their industries despite being barely ten years old and not owning a single car or room. For many Millennials, sharing what they own is an easy way to make additional income. To my great-grandchildren, this will be a way of life.

Avoid Borrowing Against Your Credit Cards
If the bank will lend you money at 6 percent, why would you pay 20 percent interest for the ease of using a credit card? And yet, most Americans do. Make the switch, and you could set aside that 14 percent into your savings account. If you can afford to pay a credit card, you can afford to save.

Have Multiple Streams of Income
You've heard the warning: "Don't put all of your eggs into one basket." As a young egg salesman, I learned what literally happens when you do that! Don't rely financially on just one source *especially* if you're in businesses with cycles that last for years.

Over time, develop **multiple streams of income (diversification)** so that, if one comes under strain, the others are still there. For me, I have three: real estate development, ownership of income-producing assets, and farming. I've found that when any one of those incomes is under strain, the others carry me through until things—such as bad weather or economic downturns—stabilize once again. This was one of the ways I was able to withstand the collapse of the savings-and-loan industry and the housing bubble of 2006. Having cash flow coming in is more important than having cash in the bank.

Don't Save Just for the Unexpected

Some things are unforeseeable but pretty likely to happen. Crops get rained on. Droughts happen. Booms and busts are part of the real estate cycle. We don't know when these unforeseens will hit, but they're on the radar. But there are also events that happen that are completely unanticipated, or what I like to call the *unforeseen, unforeseen*. Things will happen in your life that you do not see coming and have no way to predict. The only way to plan for the *unforeseen, unforeseen* is to prioritize saving and investing so that when it hits and unfolds, you can rest assured you've saved just for that moment, and you'll be better off than if you hadn't.

Put Your Money Where the Value Appreciates

When faced with a choice, ask yourself: *Which purchase will hold more value in two years?* As a teenager, when I had to choose between buying a new car and growing my herd of cattle, the better economic choice was to invest in the herd. The moment I drove away with my car, that asset began to depreciate in value, as cars do. So I bought a car that was used and didn't have air conditioning. I still got to keep my cows, and I could go anywhere I wanted. I just had to roll the windows down to stay cool.

Leverage Your Resources

How are you going to leverage your resources? Capital leverage—the ratio of debt to equity—can be a springboard forward or an anchor.

Real estate development is a poster child for both. If you borrow money at 5 percent and invest it at 10 percent, that's wonderful. If you borrow money at 5 percent and invest it at 0 percent or a negative, that can sink you. That's why it's a good rule not to take on debt for non-income-producing assets.

The concept of leverage applies to human resources, too. How are you going to use your team members (their knowledge, their creativity, their energy, etc.) to their maximum advantage? A big staff is necessary when you are growing and have a lot to manage, but it's a killer when the market dries up.

Look for Alternative Uses of Time and Money
When you're not doing something that's earning you money, it's costing you money. When you're doing something for *less* than you can otherwise earn, it's costing you money. When you're doing tasks that you could delegate and *still* make a profit, that's *also* costing you money.

One of the best financial tips I can offer is to always weigh the **opportunity cost** of a decision. This principle has influenced every business decision I've made since I was a teenager. There are *always* alternative uses of your time and money.

While I didn't know the term "opportunity cost" at the time—and wouldn't learn it until a real estate class at UC Berkeley—I first observed the concept at play as a teenager. My cows required time, but they didn't need me daily and certainly didn't need me hourly. And, though my cows brought in money when I sold them, in the meantime, I had to carry the cost of their feed, vaccines, and general health. Even as a teenager, I had several options. In any given hour, I could:

- take care of my cows, which saved me from paying someone else.
- work for my dad for $1 an hour (the hourly wage for farm labor at the time).

▸ work for someone else who might pay me more. At that time, I had started a sheep-shearing business. I charged $1 a sheep and could shear *four* sheep in an hour. That was a very good hourly rate—comparable to making about $38 an hour in 2019—and I was a teenager.

What was the better economic choice and use of my time?

When I had the option to work for my dad or shear a sheep, the better choice was to shear. If the choice was between working for my dad and doing nothing, the best use of my time was to work for my dad.

As you make decisions, be sure to define the *opportunity cost* and weigh its impact. Or, put another way, Are you satisfied with what you're giving up in exchange for what you're getting?

Let Your Money *Make* Money

This may seem simple, but how many people do it? How many people save enough money or save for long enough to benefit from compounding interest? If you start rat-holing money at a young age, all of a sudden, you've got money. If you take that money and invest it, your interest can actually start to earn interest. Now you're making money because you *had* money. Everybody can learn from that; very few people do.

To help you focus on the value of the earning capability of money, reflect on the "Rule of 72," which I learned from Jim Klingbeil, who for the past forty-five years has been one of my closest friends and is one of the largest apartment developers in the United States and chairman of UDR, a large apartment real estate investment trust (REIT). If you want to learn how long it will take to double your money, divide 72 by the annual return you earn on your investment. For example, if you have money invested at 12 percent, every six years, it will double.

LEARNING FINANCIAL RESPONSIBILITY

Or, to figure out at what interest rate you need to invest your money for it to double, divide 72 by the number of years you have to invest. For example, if you want to see your money double in ten years, you need to invest at 7.2 percent. If you want to see your money double in five years, you need to invest at 14.4 percent.

In my experience, people are often afraid to open up about their financial difficulties because they are embarrassed about decisions they've made. Just because you've made bad decisions, that doesn't mean you have to keep paying for them. Financial responsibility is like a diet. Through consistency and discipline, it *can* become a habit.

For everything there is a season. . . . a time to keep, and a time to cast away (Ecclesiastes 3:1, 6 RSV)

After Phyllis and I moved to Stockton in 1962, we kept my treasured herd of cattle (which I started as a teen with my purchase of Big John) for four more years. At least once a week we would leave the kids with the babysitter and take the hour-long drive to Bellota to check the fences and the gates and make sure the cattle had plenty of feed and water.

One evening, I got home late from a long day at the office, and we drove out to the ancient and dilapidated hay barn in Bellota to give the cows their yearly vaccinations. We used an old cattle chute built in about 1920. A chute is a long, narrow, wooden tunnel that culminates in a squeeze where cattle can be immobilized. It keeps cattle moving in an orderly fashion so you can give them the treatment they need—in theory. It's hot, dusty, and dangerous work, and things don't always go as expected.

That particular night, it was close to dark, and everything was going pretty well, when all of a sudden, one old cow decided she wasn't going to have anything to do with the squeeze. She began backing up. As she backed into the cow behind her, *that* cow went up on her hind legs—then all hell broke loose! The cow in back crashed over backwards, and lay upside down in the tight confines of the chute, stuck tight, unable to move, and suffocating from her own weight. Phyllis ran to the car to shine the headlights so I could better see the poor upended cow struggling in the chute. Time was critical if I was to save her.

I used every cussword I could think of and made up a few new ones as I beat the boards of the chute to free the cow before she died. Finally, I yanked off enough of them and freed the cow. She stood up and walked calmly over to join the herd, but I was left shaky and covered with dirt, sweat, and manure.

I went right to the car and exclaimed to Phyllis, "I'm going to sell those damn cows until I can afford to get some help!" Man, I was mad at those cows that night!

I'd had it. I ran an ad in the *Western Livestock Journal* and sold the herd to another purebred breeder.

As hard as it was to sideline such a symbolic component of my dream, it was absolutely necessary, and it paid off. It was the responsible and smart thing to do. I was overextended, and I knew it. The opportunity cost was simply too high. I needed to focus my time and energy where it counted most—building my company without sacrificing family dinners and making time to give back to the community. While I couldn't afford for someone else to care for my cows, that didn't mean *I* could afford to care for them.

But I also trusted that I could work my way back. Ten years later, in 1977, we finally had the means to bring cattle back into our lives at the level we wanted and within our budget when we purchased a cattle ranch in Mariposa, California, along with the previous owner's herd of cattle.

As I'll share in the next chapter, that ranch has been a dream come true, the ultimate reward for our hard work, financial responsibility, *and* curiosity—an indispensable trait I'll turn to next.

Chapter 4

Getting Curious: Learn How to Ask the Right Questions

I'VE NEVER BEEN TIMID about asking questions. As a child I was always peppering my mother, who had a high school education, with endless questions. My inquisitive nature exhausted her to the point that she purchased a set of encyclopedias. From then on, her tired "I don't know" was replaced with the assured and relieved "Look it up!"

I've had practice asking questions since I was a child—and thankfully had parents who took the time to validate my curiosity. I've learned that there is a tremendous amount to discover in the world and that it pays off to observe and listen. By asking questions, you confirm that your decisions are sound and that you're making the most of your opportunities. If you can't do that, you had better reexamine your plan. Curiosity is *great* fuel for realizing your dream.

It Can All Start with a Question

For my high school graduation present, I wanted to learn how to water ski. True to form, my dad gave me a motor—but no boat. So, I sold a cow and bought a boat.

It was a little plywood boat, but paired with the twenty-five-horsepower engine—which was the largest outboard they made in 1955—it went fast enough to pull a person on water skis. I *loved* being out on my family's 50-acre reservoir on the ranch. I'd spend two or three evenings a week on that lake.

Water skiing on my parents' lake at Bellota, 1959.

During our courtship, Phyllis and I spent many hours doing just that. After we married, we would host a big Fourth of July party at the Bellota ranch, with swimming, boating, and water skiing on that lake—an event we continued to host even after Phyllis and I moved to Stockton.

Phyllis and I play at the lake on my parents' ranch during our courtship, summer 1959.

I never forgot my love for that lake. I went back as much as time would allow. So in 1965 when I was a twenty-eight-year-old responsible for the development of the remaining 750 acres of the Benjamin Holt estate, I saw an opportunity for others to enjoy living by a lake, too. This resulted in the development of my first master-planned community, Lincoln Village West, a $75 million development in 1965 dollars.

Many things set Lincoln Village West apart at the time, but its defining feature remains the 57-acre freshwater lake and its accompanying 3-acre beach. I had been selling houses for only five years when I had the idea to create it, and my idea simply broke precedence with what had been done to that point in Stockton. The city didn't even have a zoning ordinance to allow the type of lake community I envisioned, so I had a lot of research, proving, and convincing to do. And, at the age of twenty-eight, where was I going to get $75 million to do it?

Later, I'll share more details about how I executed my vision, particularly the last piece—how I was able to finance the deal. But by taking that first initial desire and developing it through commitment, curiosity, and effort, I was able to create a dream neighborhood for thousands of people—and one of my proudest achievements.

Asking the Right Questions

So how do you get to the questions that will help you find what you're looking for?

First, you've got to get comfortable with *asking*. And as with most things, the more you do it, the better you get at it. Make the quest for information part of every day. What have you got to lose by gaining knowledge?

Next you need to zero in on what makes a *good* question. There may be no such thing as a bad or stupid question, but a question that doesn't get you an honest answer isn't very useful.

To get honest answers, you need to ground your questions in compassion and be sensitive to timing and privacy. You need to ask the question to people who represent a variety of perspectives and, when you get an answer, you need to listen. If that foundation is in place, then asking is worth the bravery required.

What is a *good* question? Well, it's got several traits:

Good questions come when you do your homework. If you become an expert at zeroing in on *exactly* what you're trying to figure out, you'll have a phenomenal tool for moving your dream along. Research is a good way to prepare beforehand. The more you know going in, the more you'll be able to get to specifics that will have a real impact on your goals.

Good questions are based on honest intent. Why are you asking? Do you *really* want to know, or are you just looking to start an argument? If you want people to talk to you openly, they deserve to be received with an open mind. Avoid leading questions that are statements rather than genuine questions. Leading questions communicate that you've already made your mind up and *do not* invite meaningful conversation.

Good questions are sensitive to timing. Asking questions that put employees on the spot in front of others does *not* help the situation and probably won't get you an honest answer. You want to cultivate a culture that allows people to feel comfortable enough to take risks. To do that, you can't make them look bad when they fail. They will already feel bad enough. You have to discuss what went wrong while still being respectful of that person's feelings. Be mindful of when things should be asked in private, when something might be too sensitive to talk about, or when there is not enough time to appropriately discuss an important matter (like when an employee is already heading out the door to make a prior commitment).

Good questions are asked more than once. I always go to more than just one source. I believe you can learn from everybody and that it's good to hear different points of view. Also, if things don't feel right to me, I assume they aren't, and I keep asking.

My tendency to ask the same question of multiple people drives one of my oldest and dearest friends, Dino Cortopassi, crazy. Dino is a very successful Central Valley farmer and agribusinessman, and we've been close friends and business partners for more than sixty years, since our days at UC Davis. Often I'll go to Dino with questions about farming. By now he's figured me out: "Are you asking me that question because you really want to know?" he'll say. "Or are you asking me because you want to compare my answer to what the three other guys you've asked have said?"

The first source may be spot on—as Dino always is, of course—but it never hurts to ask for more perspectives. Even when I *think* I've got an idea all figured out, I'm always surprised by how much can be gained just by asking others. When you ask a question, and keep an open mind, you are initiating an educational experience, regardless of the answer.

You'll find most people are eager to help. People are more approachable and willing to mentor than we might think. They were once there, too, and haven't forgotten the role others played in their own journey. Every age has its advantage in business, and when you're young, there are many businesspeople ready to help a young, start-up businessperson. As you get older, you've got a little track record behind you and are at the prime of your career. At that point, people love to exchange information so all parties can learn. Then, by the close of your career, you have a great network of folks who enjoy sharing old stories as well as new concepts, and it's your turn to give back.

I've always been impressed by my long-term friend and hunting companion Preston Butcher's willingness to share information with other people. He heads up the Legacy Partners in San Francisco, which is one of the largest developers of multi-family, office buildings, and industrial projects in the western United States. He is an active YPO'er (an organization I'll soon introduce), trustee of the Urban Land Institute, and has served on our friend Charles Schwab's board. I share this to show he knows a great deal.

I once asked him, "Why are you so willing to share all your techniques and financial numbers on your projects?"

His answer was, "Sharing helps all of us build better communities, *plus* very few people can execute even if you tell them how you did it."

Remember what I said about the hard part of building a dream? It's the second half—the doing—that often stops people. And there it is, right there, in Preston's words.

Like Preston, I have found that sharing information for the good of the team, or the industry, far outweighs any risk. And it feels good to do. I've been on the other side plenty of times.

Comparing Notes with Those in the Thick of It
While I like to study both what succeeds and what fails, I've found that experts in the field and those in the thick of it—and learning right beside me—give the best advice. Especially in today's world of rapid technological advances, there is always someone else who's trying to figure out a similar process or problem.

As the answers start coming in, the job becomes figuring out which ones to listen to and which to discard. One of the things I tell our team members is that, while I may not know the right answer, I can usually spot the wrong one. Whether a question leads to something you expect, or something surprising, it's almost always worthwhile. Sometimes answers help you figure out what you *don't* want to do. That's valuable knowledge, too.

You can learn from the mistakes of others as well, or by sharing your own mistakes, for that matter. I often compare numbers with friends and colleagues. Sometimes we'll shoot the breeze about who's had the biggest setback. We hold nothing back. Sure, we commiserate, but then we move on to brainstorm and troubleshoot.

Even at the professional level, organizations exist for the purpose of supporting well-intended discussions about what works and what does not. My career would have had a totally different path had I not been involved in the Urban Land Institute (ULI) and Young Presidents' Organization (YPO). Involvement in those organizations has allowed me to network, introduced me to new ideas, helped me stay current in my field, and brought great friends and business associates into my life.

I've been a member of ULI—which is composed of developers, builders, architects, bankers, brokers, and city officials, to name a few—since the late 1960s and was president of the organization from 1987 to 1989. When I was starting out, I benefited tremendously from getting to know others in real estate and land use. I have relied on that network multiple times in a variety of ways. It was through ULI that I became aware of experts in the field, such as land planner Bob O'Donnell, who I hired for the development of Lincoln Village West. As our company began to build out of state, I found local leadership for our offices through my ULI connections. Because of the organization, I knew a few developers who were very successful in their cities and states, but I was convinced they would be better off as part of our team, taking leadership roles for the region.

Central to that organization's culture is offering opportunities to share experiences gained, "mistakes made, and lessons learned." *That's* how you learn: not by avoiding pitfalls but by turning them into growth opportunities—in this case, through dialogue and exchange.

Likewise, my involvement in YPO, an organization founded in 1950 and dedicated to the continued education and networking of chief executives, helped me develop a different set of skills—managing a fast-growing company. I discovered YPO while attending a ULI conference. I was talking with Colorado real estate developer Walter A. Koelbel, Sr. about issues I was having specific to being an executive and expanding a company. He asked me some questions about my operation and, after determining that I met the qualifications to join YPO—which has an age-limit cap for its membership and accepts only presidents of companies that meet certain employee- and dollar-volume thresholds—he recommended I look into it.

And I did. After joining YPO, I saw so much value in it that I went on to become the chairman of the only chapter in Northern California at the time and chaired a YPO area conference at Pebble Beach as well as a YPO university held in Phoenix, Arizona. While chairing the conference at Pebble Beach, I began the process of forming a second chapter in Northern California with other members of the committee. Our goal was that each chapter would be smaller and have a more intimate feel. This was also the beginning of YPO forums—small groups of about eight to twelve company presidents—which was later established nationally by my close friend and former international president of YPO, Charles "Jiggs" Davis.

Participating in forums was the highlight of my YPO experience. It's safe to say they've been one of the best things that has ever happened to YPO members, providing an opportunity to meet monthly and talk in a confidential atmosphere about anything—personal or professional—with others going through similar challenges. That sort of trust and fellowship is invaluable, and I'm grateful to have had it.

Asking Questions to Check Your Course

I had *a lot* of questions after I purchased Big John, my first horned Hereford steer, at the age of fourteen. I bought from the oldest herd in California and chose that breed because they were the best quality and grew the biggest in size. I was new to the business, and the learning curve was steep. While I managed my operation carefully, I was filled with questions, especially when the decisions of my competitors didn't make sense to me.

I remember once returning from a bull sale preoccupied by the price my neighbor was asking for his bulls. He'd been in the business a long time and was at least three times my age—and he was *selling* bulls cheaper than I could *raise* them. How'd he do that? It bugged the hell out of me.

The story could have stopped there. I could have assumed he had a leg up or knew something I didn't. He had a lot more experience—that was a given. But I couldn't shake my curiosity and had to know what I was doing wrong. I told him I couldn't compete with what he charged.

"What do you mean, 'You can't raise them that cheap'?" he asked.

My question—and undoubtedly my young age—perplexed him. I offered to show him my records so he could see how I came up with my costs. I had exact figures on all my expenses (the Egg Book had prepared me well) and tracked everything from food, to vaccines, to labor and transportation.

As we talked, my neighbor realized he didn't count the *non-cash* costs that I had tracked. He was taking *opportunity cost* for granted. For example, he didn't track his feed because he just turned his cows out to the pasture he owned. I explained that feeding his cows was still costing him the opportunity to make rent money on that land. Same with labor—if he was working for himself for free, it meant he couldn't work for someone else for a wage. In short, while our *cash* costs were similar, my selling price included *non-cash* costs, which he failed to include.

The discrepancy was indisputable. "I'll be damned," he said. Then he got on the phone, called his brother, who was his business partner, and told him to drive over. "Look at Fritz's costs here," he said. "We don't count any of this stuff."

I'm pretty sure they changed how they ran their business after that—and I had the confirmation I wanted that I wasn't missing a critical piece in my own business.

If you see people around you succeeding, ask them about it. If you see others doing what you're doing but going about it completely differently, ask them why.

A lot of people are scared to test what they know or reveal what they *don't* know. Many ignore their curiosity because they're afraid it will expose their lack of knowledge, but it's a Catch 22. How will you learn if you don't ask? What are you afraid of?

Whatever the reason, find a way to cope with the discomfort you're trying to avoid. Remind yourself that short-term discomfort is worth it. Who knows? The answer you receive might just change your life.

The Day the Cows Came Home

The story of how we found our cattle ranch in Mariposa, California, in the foothills below Yosemite is a great example of how asking a single question can have a huge impact. In 1977, Phyllis and I were on the hunt for a ranch to bring us closer to fulfilling the dream we had been chasing for sixteen years. We had been looking for several years but hadn't found anything yet. We wanted a place we could have adventures with our four kids—a place to hunt, raise cattle, and ride horses.

One afternoon, I learned about a ranch that was for sale but outside of our price range. I drove the two-hour distance to Mariposa to take a look with my son, Mark, who was sixteen at the time. We looked at it as purely an educational trip.

While we were looking at that ranch, I told the broker that the 10,000-acre ranch he was showing me was out of my price range. The broker mentioned, "Well, the ranch next door is going to come up for sale next year."

So I asked, "Well, why is he waiting a year to sell it?"

"He's building a home up in Midpines," replied the broker, "and he wants his kids to finish school here. Once his home is done, he's planning to sell."

It would have been easy just to accept that answer, right? It wasn't for sale yet, after all. Instead, I asked myself, *Is there a way to make a deal now?* I thought about what I wanted—a ranch—and what the owner wanted—to stay a little longer so as not to disrupt his children's schooling.

On the spot, I created an offer. "Would he sell it to me if I let him stay there until his new home is done? I'd own it, but he could stay for free and continue to run his cows for free."

The broker called the owner, who immediately wanted to meet. I'll never forget the drive to what would become *our* ranch. There was quail everywhere, and a four-point buck ran right in front of our jeep. For avid hunters like my son and me, we saw endless opportunity over the course of that short drive. Even though there had been three years of drought and it had been overgrazed, the beauty of the ranch couldn't be hidden.

Before going over, I had already called Phyllis to tell her about the ranch. We were committed to our budget. We were in the market only for what we could afford.

"Make him an offer," she encouraged. "You know what I would or wouldn't like, and if you think it's *that* special and fits our criteria, buy it."

Upon seeing the ranch and speaking with the owner, I fell in love. It was tree studded, had a lot of game, and it had an airstrip, which was a huge plus for me. My time was increasingly becoming stretched as my company was building out of state. I knew that if I was going to spend weekends away with my family, distance couldn't be an obstacle.

And it fit our budget. Because of its location and higher elevation, which we liked, it was cheaper for me to buy that 2,600-acre ranch *and* an airplane than to buy a ranch of equal size closer to Stockton. None of these details were lost on me. We made a deal that day.

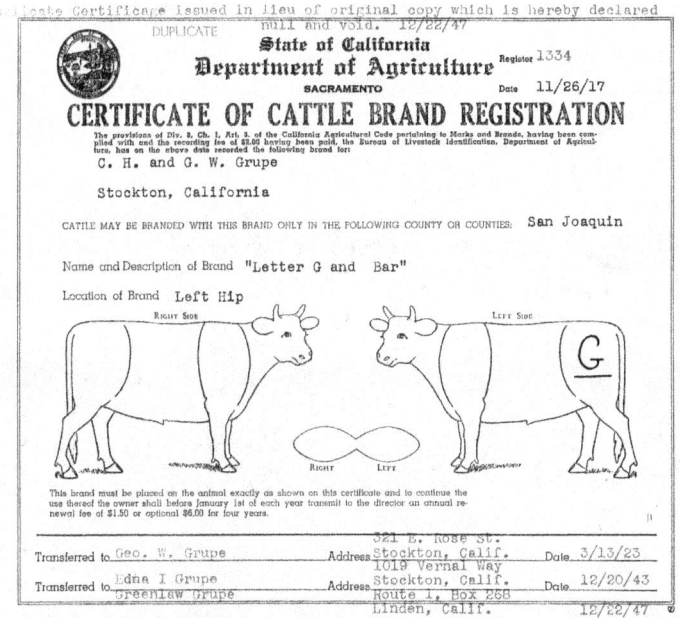

In 2017, we celebrated the centennial of our cattle brand's registration.

From 1977 on, Phyllis and I started spending most weekends with our family at the ranch, which we named the G Bar Ranch after our family's cattle brand (G), which dates back to my great-grandfather John Carsten Grupe. Once the ranch was ours, Phyllis and I brought over a used 500-square-foot, single-wide mobile home onto the run-down property, where we stayed when we visited. Getting the mobile home up to such a remote property was a feat in itself. It survived all the hairpin turns, but we couldn't find a level place to put it once we got there. We ended up putting it on stilts on a steep hill, one side on the ground and the other propped over a seven-foot drop—and man, did our kids get a kick out of making that modular *rock!*

Our temporary Mariposa home. The kids made it "rock"! *ca.* 1978.

For about a year or two, we stayed in that small trailer every weekend we went up. After the previous owner moved out, we still had the remodeling of the home ahead of us. We didn't care. We were cramped—our three daughters slept in one room, while our son slept on the pull-out couch—but it was so much fun. The kids rode horses, we hiked and hunted, and we went down to the Chowchilla River and just explored. In place of watching TV (it was *years* before we got one at the ranch), we'd listen to music and play games.

Eventually, we let our kids bring their buddies. On weekends, you'd find Phyllis religiously packing up the big van we'd nicknamed Big Bertha, filing in the eight kids (each of ours bringing a friend, of course) and two dogs, and packing in all the food we'd need for the weekend. It was chaotic, but *great* fun.

The next year, in 1978, I hosted our first annual dove hunt—held on the opening day of dove-hunting season—a tradition that continues to this day and is just one of the many wonderful ways we are able to enjoy the ranch with our friends.

In 1980, the neighboring ranch Mark and I had visited when we were first looking for a ranch dropped its selling price and was again on the market. Business was picking up for us, and now we could afford to buy it and add 10,000 acres to our property. As we've experienced time and time again, when we *defer consumption* until we can truly afford something, we get much more than we would have by *not* waiting.

It has been a profitable land-investment strategy for us. At a subsequent date, we sold off 4,600 acres for three times as much as we paid for it. Our herd of registered and commercial Angus cows—at its peak about six hundred mother cows—has carried the cost of keeping the 8,000-acre ranch. Again, deferring consumption until we were financially ready paid off. The ranch has increased six times in value since we purchased it.

Most importantly, the ranch has brought immense joy and an immeasurable positive influence on our family. The purchase provided a place for us to spend uninterrupted time together having fun, creating memories, and learning to work together as a team. On that ranch, our children, grandchildren, and great-grandchildren have gotten a taste of the lifestyle that means so much to Phyllis and me.

The herd has been a *wonderful* source of happiness, creativity, and collaboration for Phyllis and me, and now our daughter Sandy, as we've studied the nuances of genetics and how best to grow our herd. Considering all of this, I'm so glad I asked the realtor if the owner would sell his ranch earlier than planned. While it *does* take courage to ask—especially depending on what you're asking—you'll never know what could be unless you do. Sometimes, one question sets you on a path to making a dream come true.

Chapter 5

Becoming a Lifelong Learner

*W*HILE CURIOSITY INSPIRED ME to ask questions, pairing it with a dedication to *learning* helped me stay on course. Education has been the tool I've used to find answers and fulfill my dreams.

Phyllis and I absolutely value education and have encouraged our family to pursue formal training that complements and supports their passions. We have also focused our philanthropic efforts on education since the early 1980s, and we've seen firsthand the direct correlation between success and the willingness to learn.

For me, education started at home. My parents took an active role in teaching me about the world around me. My grandmother Grupe had a fierce love of learning, being a former teacher, and she loved to play games with my sisters and me that had an educational objective. My dad was especially invested in how I did in school. Not only were good grades expected, but so was thorough comprehension. Once, after helping me figure out a math problem, my dad tore up the equation and had me replicate it on the spot to make sure I truly understood how to get the answer.

Only a portion of my education has taken place in classroom settings—from a one-room schoolhouse in my youth to lecture halls at UC Berkeley—but I believe educational opportunities are everywhere if you just look.

Even in the classroom, I learned much more than just the subjects being taught. In the 1940s, my grammar school had two buildings with approximately eleven students in each building—grades 1 through 4 in one room and grades 5 through 8 in the other. The school was about four miles west of the ranch, and I had to walk or run one mile just to catch the bus. The school was heated by a wood stove that the boys were required to keep going in the winter. If you wanted a drink or needed to use the restroom, you had to go outside to the tank house, which was about twenty yards away.

With only three kids in my class, it perhaps heightened our level of interaction, but it also limited extracurricular activities. We'd attempt soccer, but with so few kids, we'd end up just kicking the ball around the mud puddles. Since we didn't know better, it worked for us—we had fun, and we learned about teamwork, communication, and how to deal with confrontation.

Inside the classroom, things were a bit tougher for me. I struggled with some parts of learning, like reading and spelling. I became aware of my tendency to transpose letters and numbers, but it wasn't until I was in my forties that I learned I was dyslexic. I grew up at a time when the symptoms were written off as being a lackadaisical, lazy student.

While dyslexia made learning more challenging, it also made me very careful in my calculations. I had to know my figures inside and out, understand the *logic* behind them, and be able to do them in my head—a skill that made a tremendous impact as I matured as a businessman. Ultimately, this ability became a strength that outpaced what I'd felt as a weakness earlier in life.

My high school was bigger, with 350 kids. A larger student body brought new opportunities, especially in leadership and teambuilding. I was thrilled I could now play sports in a team environment. I became captain of the football team, threw the shot put, and ran track (my one-mile run to the bus throughout grammar school had prepared me for that!). I was elected class treasurer and class president. I loved leadership. Vocational training was my favorite subject. I received the award of state farmer (meaning I got recognition beyond my own school). Shop felt like home to me. It was there that I built a horse trailer and learned to work on my car.

My goal after high school was to be a farmer. I didn't want to go to college. I knew what I wanted to do, so why take a detour? Not only that, but all of my friends from school and through FFA were going to work on farms. *Nobody* was going to college. I not only knew what I wanted to do, but I was passionate about it, so it frustrated me to be plucked out of my dream and put into what seemed like a nightmare of more school, but my father was determined.

My dad was a college graduate of the 1930s, and both of his parents were educators. The chaos and uncertainty of the Great Depression had further reaffirmed his belief that a college degree brought security. "Just go and have fun," he told me. "They want you to play football. You like doing that. Go, and maybe you'll like it."

My mom's family was more cavalier, you might say. They were hardworking entrepreneurs and didn't see education past high school as necessary. But my mom *had* wanted to go to college and regretted she hadn't had the support, so she was very supportive of my going.

My parents' belief in higher education extended to my sisters, Luanne and Sue, who both completed college educations as well.

So I went to UC Davis, which ended up being a big tipping point in my life, though in the beginning I found a university of that size and prestige intimidating and scary. But soon enough, I found that I did like it. Maybe too much. My grades that first year didn't quite cut it for UC Davis—even though by the end of my freshman year I actually *wanted* to be there. I had realized that going to college wasn't a detour but a necessary stop. I was sent home with an invitation to return after demonstrating I could raise my grades at a community college.

I was upset and worried that I had compromised my future, but my father told me not to dwell on the disappointment. Instead, he pushed me to work toward the goal of reentry and involved himself in the process, asking daily how many pages I had left to study and hiring a tutor to help me. I was readmitted into UC Davis and then later graduated from UC Berkeley, which I transferred to in 1959 in order to take advantage of their real estate program.

I continued my education after graduating from college. After deciding to become a real estate salesman, I began to study and passed the test to get my real estate license. Learning a trade has brought great comfort and peace of mind to my life. Knowing I always had a solid trade to fall back on was empowering. It gave me the courage to try as many businesses as I did. If they didn't work out, I knew how to sell houses and could always return to that.

My experience taught me that *how* I applied myself counted as much—or more—as *where* my education took place. My somewhat humble beginnings in a one-room schoolhouse didn't mean I couldn't end up at a prestigious school. That said, what good is going to a great school if you're not making the most of what it has to offer?

But you don't *have* to go to a prestigious school, either. From those early days of caring for my cows, to running and owning a multimillion-dollar company, every question I've asked has rounded out my knowledge base. We are the sum of all our experiences, after all. And it's as important to figure out what you *don't* need to know as much as what you *do*.

Sometimes, the best education happens in the saddle. You can't ask your way through everything. You have to go through certain experiences firsthand. When I entered the equestrian sport of combined driving at the age of sixty, I discovered quickly the value of hands-on learning. I didn't get a carriage and a team of horses working together successfully in rhythm solely by asking my trainers questions. When I compete with my twelve-year-old horse and win, everybody says, "Oh, boy, you sure did a nice job driving that horse." But that horse has been in training since he was three years old. That's nine years of effort, five days a week. That's a lot of work! Experience is one thing that can be gained only through . . . yep. Experience.

My younger self would probably be astonished that, even at eighty-one years old, I'm still eager to learn new things. I meet regularly with innovative farmers to discuss the best techniques, participate in YPO Gold meetings, and attend events sponsored by the Fisher Center for Real Estate and Urban Economics.

A wonderful forum for learning over the past forty years has been my participation in the Bohemian Club, which was formed in San Francisco in 1872. The private club originally consisted of artists and newspaper people and, later, accepted members who shared an appreciation for its pillars—literature, art, and music/drama.

Every summer, more than 2,500 members and guests stay spread out in more than a hundred "camps" meeting at "the Grove," a 2,700-acre redwood grove owned by the Club on the Russian River, north of San Francisco, for educational lectures and live entertainment. The membership of my camp, Pelican, is very diverse, consisting of many different professions: college professors, Nobel Prize winners, surgeons, actors, decorated war heroes, presidents of Fortune 500 companies, U.S. senators, leading world winemakers, a movie producer, a priest, even a farmer turned real estate developer. I refer to many of these friends as "campmates" throughout the book, and some of the best knowledge I've learned is from them.

Although the motto of the Bohemian Club is Shakespeare's "Weaving spiders, come not here," and we don't talk shop, we can't help but learn from each other.

A person's beginnings do not have to limit where they end up. I went from building a leaky, makeshift building for my dad's duck club to being inducted into the prestigious California Homebuilding Foundation's Hall of Fame in 1991. I started out by helping at my kids' school district and progressed to being a regent at University of the Pacific (UOP) and founding chair on the UC Merced Foundation Board of Trustees. When it came to leadership positions in the field of real estate and land development, I went from being president of the Stockton Board of Realtors to president of the Urban Land Institute.

Becoming a lifelong learner has provided me with endless possibilities. I think physicist Albert Einstein might have said it best: "Intellectual growth should commence at birth and cease only at death."

Digging In: Learning to Create Solutions
My First Big Deal

I made my first big deal a few years out of college. It was around 1965, and I had been working as a house salesman in Stockton for only about two years when I learned that my parents' neighbor, Albert Anderson, wanted to sell his 150-acre walnut orchard in Bellota so that he could retire and move to Stockton.

I'd known Anderson since I was a little kid and wanted to sell it for him, but I was only about twenty-six, and he wanted to list it with a very reputable farm broker instead of me. I don't blame him now. In hindsight, why would you list it with somebody who had just moved to town to be a house salesman? But it disappointed me at the time.

I still kept his walnut orchard in the back of my mind, though. I saw it as a problem to be solved—one that I knew I could turn into an opportunity. *Somebody* was going to sell it. Why not me?

I kept looking for ranch deals and came across a guy, Clancy Camps, who was looking to buy a walnut orchard. I took him out to Anderson's orchard to see if he would be interested—and he was. The only holdup was that he had to sell his 200-acre piece of land to get the necessary cash.

So now I knew someone who wanted to *buy* a walnut orchard and someone who wanted to *sell* a walnut orchard. Now I just needed to find someone who wanted Clancy Camps's 200 acres of bare land—and I knew where to start for that.

My friend Dino was living with his wife, Joan, and kids on a 30-acre peach orchard that his dad owned, but he was looking to expand. His dad had told him he could use it as equity for buying a bigger piece of property if he could ever find one.

The wheels started turning. I had a friend (Dino) who wanted to expand; a neighbor (Albert Anderson) who wanted to sell his walnut orchard and retire; and a local (Clancy Camps) who wanted an orchard because he was tired of growing row crops. I knew the motivations and objectives behind each of these scenarios and wondered: Could I solve *all* their problems by solving *each* of their problems?

I was convinced that I could figure out a way to meet all of their objectives—and I did. I came up with a three-way exchange that allowed me to help everyone reach their goal (i.e., be happy) and make what, at the time, was a huge commission. How did the deal play out?

Dino traded his 30-acre peach orchard as a down payment for the 200 acres of bare land that Clancy Camps owned.

Clancy Camps bought the 150-acre walnut orchard from Anderson with cash and the 30-acre peach orchard.

Now, Anderson had cash and a peach orchard he *did not* want. He was selling his walnut orchard, after all, because he wanted to retire. But I needed all of these parts to work simultaneously to pull off the deal.

The peach orchard was only 30 acres, and I knew that would be much easier to sell later for Anderson than his 150-acre walnut orchard. Until I could find a buyer for the peach orchard, Dino and I leased it back from Anderson so he didn't have to even worry about it. We continued to farm it for about a year and paid rent to Anderson. Once I found a buyer for the peach orchard, Anderson had the capital to retire and move to Stockton. As that time approached, I was only too happy to sell him his house.

It was a big hit for me, and I was grateful. My friends at the time were making $7,000 a year, and I made more than $30,000 on that one deal.

I see curiosity as having interconnected parts—asking and searching, listening and finding answers, *and* acting. To complete the process of wondering, you've got to act. Remember, that's what sets apart those who succeed: they don't just *talk* about their goals at cocktail parties; they get out there and start working to make them happen.

Taking action *is* a big step. I've always enjoyed seeing a problem others missed (or didn't want to touch) and being creative and courageous enough to try solving it. Meeting the challenge of solving a problem can be very rewarding. With a little creativity and innovation, some problems can actually turn into tremendous opportunities.

As my friend Dino says, "Great opportunities are often cleverly disguised as insurmountable problems."

Tips for Creating Solutions

Coming up with the farm exchange not only increased my capital, but it also built my confidence because I had achieved something few others do by figuring out how to help all three parties reach their goal. **Make people happy. It's possible.**

Curiosity is key to the creative process. How did I make the leap from being curious to actually creating something that others would buy into? Well, I followed a process. I have found that many of my projects have followed a similar path:

1. **I let myself wonder.** I ask myself, *Why do things work the way they do?* and *Is there a better way?* Innovation requires challenging the status quo. Once I figure out what I want to improve or solve, I am on my way.

2. **I do my homework.** Sometimes it requires a lot of research to really understand a problem. As I become convinced that something should be done, I learn everything I can by identifying why it *hasn't* been done and what creative work remains to find a solution.
3. **I fill a need.** If you can create solutions to other people's problems, they will pay you. Another person's problem can be *your* opportunity. Some of the best advice I've heard is from Christian minister Robert H. Schuller: "The secret to success is to find a need and fill it." There are unmet needs all around and, as my farm-exchange deal proved, solving a problem can be very financially rewarding.
4. **I take time to think.** I sit back and *really* think about the specifics of execution, the very details that make all the difference. As I said in Chapter 1, once you visualize something in detail, it's like you've already done it.
5. **I don't do it alone.** I turn to friends, associates, professional networks, or experts in the field to test my solutions. Those conversations always trigger something that either motivates me to take the next step or to go back to the drawing board. Different people can help solve different parts of a problem.
6. **I look toward creating value.** There are two types of value— demonstrable and perceived. When you go to buy a car, there's a *demonstrable* value—something you can see—for the car that has fewer miles on it and is not worn out. Now, you may or may not see *perceived* value; you may *feel* it instead. The strength of our company's solutions is often found in the details because we bring both types of value to the projects

we touch. For example, in our Brookside development, the sidewalks are 50 percent wider. The crosswalks have different kinds of pavement. The stop signs are custom-made. We'll go to great lengths for these details. We spent an extra $600,000 and three years of research on the custom-designed lampposts. Why would we do that? Because residents and visitors *feel* the difference. They feel that it's just *better*.

7. **I give it my all.** As Phyllis likes to say, "Don't just do it somehow; do it triumphantly." When we watch others succeed, we don't see all the effort and dedication that led up to the moment of accomplishment. If you're working hard and putting in the time, solutions and ideas are building inside of you somewhere—sometimes they just take a while before they come out.

8. **I make time for rest.** Sometimes, the best solutions come when you're not looking for them. It might be more productive to take a break, clear your mind, and step away from demands. My most creative ideas often come when I'm outdoors and in nature and not even thinking about the problem at hand. I can't remember ever going on a vacation where I didn't think of a creative business idea that more than paid for the trip—all because I had time to think about how to better solve a particular problem.

As you test the solutions that you've created, ask yourself:

▸ Is it filling a need?
▸ How will my product be perceived?

- Am I offering something unique?
- What details will set my solution apart?
- Does it have value to someone? (i.e., profitable?)
- What expertise do I need to bring into production?

Chapter 6

Listening and Communicating Effectively

*A*ROUND MY JUNIOR YEAR in high school (1954), my Agriculture class went to a neighboring ranch to learn how to vaccinate, castrate, de-horn, and brand the cattle. I was one of the more experienced students. By then I had been showing steers at the San Joaquin County Fairgrounds for a few years. I really got in the middle of the procedures, and by the end, I was bloody and filthy and asked the teacher if I could borrow the school bus to drive the three miles home and change my clothes.

Believing I had received permission, I jumped into the yellow school bus. As I drove away, people were hollering. I thought they were just saying goodbye, so I just waved back and kept driving. Well, they were trying to stop me.

My parents' house was up on a hill, and you had to go under a cypress tree arch, which my mom had worked years to grow. Somehow

I managed to drive the school bus up the narrow lane, but not without losing the bus's mechanical stop arm and wrecking the arch.

I changed my clothes and headed back to the job at hand. When I returned the school bus, my teacher, Chet Pierce, exclaimed, "What the hell are you doing, taking the school bus?"

I replied, "Well, I asked ya!"

"But I was *busy!*" he threw back. "I didn't know what the heck you were asking me. You should never have taken the bus."

What went wrong in that conversation? Well, it wasn't a conversation in the first place. I *thought* I had heard permission from my teacher but overlooked everything else that indicated that he had not really heard me and that he would never dream of giving me such a liberty.

Communicating effectively is challenging, and maybe that's why so many misunderstandings and miscommunications happen on a daily basis. It's much more than words spoken. Effective communication requires making sense of tone and nonverbal cues such as facial expressions (eyes always tell a story) and body language. It takes judgment to know what to say and when to say it, when to compromise or stand firm, or when a little boldness or humor might help the conversation along. Those are decisions that take practice and experience.

Being able to express one's thoughts and have productive conversations are essential skills for turning any idea into a reality. When all parties in a negotiation benefit, not only is it easier, but the deal lasts. As I often say to my teams: *Good thoughts in your head, not transmitted, aren't worth squat.*

While communication may come more naturally to some, everybody can improve at it. From decades of managing teams, I've seen how compassion, respect, listening, trust, wisdom, open-mindedness,

LISTENING AND COMMUNICATING EFFECTIVELY

and even a little humor can improve the outcome of our daily interactions and conversations. As the Bible teaches, "it is best to listen much, speak little, and not become angry." (James 1:19 TLB)

The Necessary Ingredients of Compassion and Respect

When it comes to having meaningful and effective conversations, one's attitude is a good place to start. I try to approach communication with the following attitude, which my dear friend and campmate, The Very Rev. Dr. Alan Jones, author and dean emeritus of the historic Grace Cathedral in San Francisco, sums up with this statement: "I care about you, and we're in this together." Think about how that mindset could change the way you communicate. What type of criticism would that keep you from saying? Would you be more patient? More invested in how the conversation turned out?

I think how people want to be treated is pretty straightforward and universal. We all want to be respected and understood. We want our contributions to be acknowledged. None of us likes to be treated unfairly. Yet, we often forget these basic principles when we're talking about a sensitive subject or a heated topic.

In the effort to be a compassionate communicator, I try to start by simply understanding that those I talk with have battles, backgrounds, and burdens I don't know about—and that they have feelings which may be neither right nor wrong, but just are. How we deal with others around us reveals our compassion or caring about their point of view. I like to give people the benefit of the doubt. Communication becomes easier with a little bit of grace.

People also communicate differently, and the gaps in those differences can cause a lot of frustration. Have you ever had a friend come talk to you for advice, and half an hour later, you're still really unclear on the problem? To you, it feels like they are just rambling all over the place, and you can't help but feel annoyed.

I've brought in business consultant Devora Zack, author of *Networking for People Who Hate Networking: A Field Guide for Introverts, the Overwhelmed, and the Underconnected* (2010), to teach my associates how introverts and extroverts communicate and process information differently. In a nutshell, introverts think to talk; extroverts talk to think. When the two personality types get together, the difference in how each communicates can drive the other nuts and lead to frustration and misunderstanding.

For an introvert, when somebody keeps talking and talking, it can be hard not to wonder, "What is their point? Where are they going with this?" On the other hand, from the extrovert's point of view, they might wonder why the introvert is quiet and not asking questions. "Why don't they participate more? Aren't they interested in what I'm saying?"

Learning to understand and tolerate the different ways people communicate frees you up to actually solve the problems at hand rather than being distracted by the delivery.

If communication isn't approached with some open-mindedness and compassion, people are bound to misjudge and could miss out on the opportunity to work with someone who has a lot to contribute—not to mention that good communication is satisfying and fun.

The Art of Listening

Some of my earliest memories go back to when I was a boy, duck hunting with my dad, grandpa, and their friends, and just listening to the guys talk. Those conversations influenced me a great deal. I learned that listening builds trust and strengthens friendship, and

LISTENING AND COMMUNICATING EFFECTIVELY

that it's healthy to prioritize time for companionship. Those male outings had such an impact on me as a child that I have continued the tradition of hosting annual all-male hunting trips with family and friends throughout the years.

Working as a house salesman in Stockton in the early 1960s, I quickly learned how valuable it was to just listen. It didn't take long to learn how different my perspective could be from my customers'. What I thought of as a nice house could easily differ from what they thought was a nice house. Making the customer happy was my goal—that's what had won me over to sales—and that meant learning to be more open-minded. I really did have to put myself in their shoes.

What were they looking for? What type of home would make *them* happy?

As a salesman, I found that the more people trusted me and my intentions, the more honest they'd be about what they were looking to find. But I also had to be willing to listen to what they were saying. For five years, as I drove women around in my car—they were usually the ones doing the house shopping and making the decision to buy—I observed that many of them were looking for open floor plans that would allow them to be part of the action.

That knowledge, and everything else I learned from my customers, was extremely important when I began to think of ways I could set my master-planned communities apart. Not only could I improve quality of life by introducing waterfront living, I could create an open floor plan in response to the unmet needs of many of my female customers.

Listening doesn't come easy to everyone. Most people are borderline disasters at it. How many of us have heard parents say, "I don't understand my kids. They just don't listen to me!" This bears repeating. The parent says, "I don't understand my kids. They won't listen to me." But how can you understand the other person if you're doing all the talking?

To *really listen* is to engage in a conversation so that others feel validation, trust, compassion, and interest. Here's a closer look at the qualities I find essential in a good listener:

1. **Engage.** *Good* listeners engage in whatever way they can. They follow up with questions that are non-threatening, genuine, and relevant. They make eye contact. They show empathy. They know when to talk and when to listen. They are as involved in the conversation when they're listening as when they're talking. They're not just listening to the words that are being said. They're paying attention to the gestures and tone of voice—the complete picture. If you listen only with your ears, you miss 80 percent of the conversation.
2. **Prioritize understanding.** Listening is difficult, especially when you think you have all the answers. My goal as a listener is to understand what the other person is trying to say, not to show them how smart I am. As bestselling author Stephen Covey, who at one time consulted with our executives and their spouses, said, "Seek first to understand, then to be understood." A good listener tries to stay focused on what is being said rather than thinking about what his or her response is going to be. Agreement is not required to be a good listener!
3. **Reserve judgment.** Being a good listener (or a good person, for that matter) requires that you have sensitivity. If people believe you care about them and that you won't be quick to judge, they'll share more. As the well-known scripture advises, "First take the log out of your own eye, and then

LISTENING AND COMMUNICATING EFFECTIVELY

you will see clearly to take the speck out of your brother's eye." (Matthew 7:5 RSV)

From managing teams, I've learned that people are more willing to be forthcoming if they're not worried about how the boss is going to react. If someone is telling you about a mistake, you're better off shifting the focus to lessons that can be learned and then ending the conversation by thanking them for their honesty. As my friend and fellow YPO'er James C. Morgan says in his book *Applied Wisdom* (2016), "Bad news is good news if you do something about it."

4. **Be trustworthy.** People are not going to tell you something that's sacred if they don't trust you. If you have a problem, you're not going to tell somebody who is going to blab it all over. I follow the Golden Rule: *Do unto others as you would have them do unto you* (Luke 6:31). We all appreciate having a friend with whom we can share confidences. I have been very fortunate in that regard.

   I think I've been successful in asking people some penetrating questions and even in butting into their business, if you will, a bit more than others because people believe that I do care about them and that I'm trying to help them—not further my own cause or make them look foolish.

5. **Try to see the other side.** We all approach things a little differently. That doesn't have to be an issue. I have some friends who have very different views than I do on certain issues. One of my closest friends is Congressman John Garamendi, with whom I've hunted on the opening day of dove season every year for the past forty years. John is out of central casting as a political figure: handsome (according to his wife, Patti), big

(All-American football and wrestling champion from Cal), Harvard MBA, Peace Corps volunteer, and most importantly, to me, he has a great eye for cattle and buys from one of the best herds in the United States. It bears the "G" brand, and I'll give you a hint—it's not "G" for "Garamendi."

Sharing good times with Congressman John Garamendi at Brookside Farm.

John is a "go-to" guy in California for his knowledge on water and trade issues. He was ahead of his time on suggesting solutions to our out-of-control healthcare costs in America. In addition, he's invested *pari passu* in a real estate investment with me. As accomplished as he is, he still listens to counsel from the wine-drinking experts who gather around the dinner table at our dove hunt. Quite a few complex problems have seemed easier to solve after a couple glasses of wine.

John and I have some political and philosophical differences on how to solve certain problems. We discuss them at liberty, and those conversations are *always* positive because we stay focused on the issues. We can talk about any subject because we respect one another, trust each other, and enjoy being together. John was kind enough to share his thoughts on how I moderate these "Dove Hunt Policy Debates":

> Fritz has a wide range of friends who hold firm views on everything, especially about hunting, cooking, and politics, in that order of priority. That being the case, politics always seems to come up late in the evening following an exceptional and much debated dinner of dove, polenta, and wine. Therefore, the timing is not propitious for a thoughtful and factual discussion. Here is where Fritz's skill of negotiation, leadership, and personality are displayed in fullness as he steers the debates away from too vigorous an offense or a defense by suggesting, "That's an interesting argument. Let's consider this." When that does not slow things down, he'll announce that everyone is expected to be up for breakfast at 5:00 a.m.

We can all benefit from listening to views different from our own. I believe this so strongly I once hosted a small luncheon in the dining room of our home to raise funds for both a Republican *and* a Democratic congressman from different districts. As far as I know, it may be the first and only time this has ever been done.

It was so unique it sparked the interest of a major television network that showed up unannounced, wanting to find out why the congressmen would agree to such a thing. I did not want to put the congressmen in an awkward position, so we declined the interview.

So then, why did I host the luncheon? I did it to show that both sides of the aisle could get together, have a meaningful discussion, and benefit from exchanging ideas.

It was a very positive experience and solution-driven. The politicians learned from the constituents, and the constituents learned from the politicians. By staying focused on the issues and not the personalities involved, each left with better insight into his community.

Learning to Be Sensitive to Timing

Compassionate communication extends to being sensitive about timing. It's important to consider when and where you share information. If somebody came into my office and began to tell me all the problems they had at home, that wouldn't be the time to bring up that they're over budget. I mean, why pounce on somebody when you can see they're already struggling? It's important to be able to read people and understand where they're coming from. With that, it's easier to know when to say something, when not to, and how.

LISTENING AND COMMUNICATING EFFECTIVELY

I was reminded of the importance of this lesson when Phyllis and I decided to go for a romantic getaway when we had four young kids at home. I was working too hard, traveling all over the United States, and I'd been gone quite a bit. So I suggested, "Let's just get away for a couple of days and get somebody to watch the kids." Friday came, and we were excited to head to Heritage House in Mendocino. Despite my anticipation, I got home late. Screw-up number one.

I knew that unless we could make it to the restaurant by eight, they wouldn't serve us dinner. The entire drive I was nervous, speeding, and wondering if we'd make it. We didn't. We got there about ten or fifteen minutes after eight. We took a chance and went into the restaurant, but the host informed us we were too late and would have to go down the road to the Little River Inn if we wanted dinner. Screw-up number two.

So we went down the road, both of us feeling uptight. We chose a table by the window, ordered a drink, and I start offloading all the stuff that had been on my mind to Phyllis. I had recently attended a YPO meeting where they talked about the importance of being open with your wife and telling her the things on your mind. They also advised, if anything was bothering you, not to hold back and to tell your spouse about it. As we were waiting to be served, it felt like the opportune time to put that advice into practice. So, I started telling Phyllis all the things she was doing that were irritating me. Screw-up number three.

She started to cry. It was the final straw in a long line of screw-ups. A guy came over from the bar, not knowing what was going on, and said, "Sir, will you please just marry this girl?"

We've told this story to our kids and other people because it taught me such a valuable lesson. When you have something you need to talk about, you can't just blurt it out when the other person is not ready or the timing is wrong. In your marriage (or business), it is good to be open and candid and say what's on your mind. But you have to be careful with your timing and with how you say it. *How* you communicate what you have to say is as important as *what* you have to say.

Life Is a Negotiation
From buying a car to choosing a restaurant, life is filled with negotiation and compromise. It's a lot faster and easier when people agree with you. We all know that. But on the other hand, sometimes when people disagree with you, it turns out to be a better stew. I don't claim to have all the knowledge on a particular subject and enjoy other people's input because I usually learn something.

At our company, we view positive disagreements as good and healthy. They help us improve our products and give better service to our customers. In addition to being a good listener, there are several ways to improve the outcome of negotiations:

1. **Try to figure out how to make everyone involved better off.** What do you want? What does the other person want? How can you satisfy both? It's usually not good when somebody gets the short end of the stick. The goal is for everybody to benefit—or at least enough people so you'll get the level of support you need to succeed.
2. **Does the difference make a difference?** To my Irish grandfather Papa Val Dervin, it was always win or lose, black or white. One day my mother, who was used to arguing with him, came to me sobbing, "Papa Val thinks that I stole all of his gold. He says he went to Alaska as a young man, and he

got a bunch of gold. He believes he gave it to me to take care of, and now he wants it."

This didn't make a lot of sense to me. My grandfather had never been to Alaska, and he didn't have any gold, either. He was quite old by this time and struggling with Parkinson's disease and its effect on his memory. I went to talk to him and said, "Papa Val, Mom put your gold in the bank, so it's safe." He quickly replied, "Oh. Okay. Thanks." In that situation, I just agreed with him, and he was happy. The difference didn't make a difference—the gold was totally fictional, and, an hour later, nobody remembered even what the argument had been about. This solution may seem obvious, but it was not to my mother. She was distraught that her father thought she was stealing from him. We all have our blind spots. To me, in almost all cases, relationships are more important than who wins the argument.

3. **Be selective when sharing information.** Choose your words carefully. Telling a woman "You have a face that makes time stand still," comes across differently if you say, "You have a face that would stop a clock."

    Learn when you're ready to share information, and with whom. When I am explaining my vision for a new community to a planning commission, I do not bring the engineer with me and have him explain how complicated the entire infrastructure would be.

    This principle also extends to what you say about others. It does no good to put people down or make others look bad so you can look good. It can also hurt your cause if you share too much about the misdeeds of others. My friend, the late Masud Mehran (developer of the prestigious Bishop Ranch business park in San Ramon, California), gave me some advice I've never forgotten. We were at a meeting in Pebble Beach for the Advisory Board of the Real Estate Graduate School at UC Berkeley. I was telling him of my plans to tell the group how one of the largest banks in the United States (whose agent would be in attendance at the conference) had been totally uncompromising in our dealings when the savings-and-loan industry collapsed. Masud listened and then said, "Fritz, don't tease the alligators while you're crossing the swamp."

In other words, venting wasn't worth the risk. It wasn't going to get me closer to the solution I was after, and it could have made the bank that I was doing business with angry, or even scared off others from wanting to work with me.

In evaluating how much to share in situations, Phyllis likes to say, "When in doubt, leave it out."

4. **Prepare for the difficult questions.** I'll sometimes ask my team, "How are you going to answer a difficult question when you're interviewed on television by an investigative reporter?" This situation isn't just hypothetical. At times, tough questions have to be answered in high-pressure, high-visibility circumstances. While you can't anticipate every single question you'll be asked, you do need to be ready to handle difficult questions.

I start by acknowledging the question and thanking whoever asked it. Next, I weigh how much to share. If it's controversial and asked with the sole purpose of hurting my cause, I'll engage the interviewer. "Are you familiar with the background?" I'll say. "Why don't you tell me what you know, so I don't tell you what you already know?" From there, I'll give background information on the situation and invite the interviewer to weigh in on the controversial points with questions, such as, "What would you do?"

Which leads to my next point—

5. **Let others discover when they're on the wrong path.** I participated in a YPO session where we had to critique a forum member's problem without giving any direct advice or suggesting any solutions. We were to ask questions that helped the proponent think up alternate solutions. This was not a time to show off your genius at work. It was a wonderful exercise in allowing *others* to find their own way to a solution.

When a person discovers the path they're going down is wrong on their own, they're more apt to correct it. If you point out a solution before they're ready to hear it, they might continue on down the same road once you're gone. My father used to often share Benjamin Franklin's quote, "A man convinced against his will is of the same opinion still."

6. **Focus on the votes that count.** Part of negotiating is understanding who needs to be happy, otherwise it's easy to get overwhelmed and distracted. If you're going to buy a house, it would be nice if your mother liked it. But it would be even nicer if your *spouse* liked it. You don't need to make everybody happy. That's all part of negotiation—understanding whom you need to please.

In 1979, our company purchased a beautiful historic building—at that time known as the Bank of America building—in downtown Stockton. Built in 1915, the ten-story building was our first redevelopment project. We negotiated the purchase for nearly half of the asking price in exchange for taking on the responsibility of bringing it up to code.

When you have a problem to solve, it's important to identify who needs to be part of the solution. It just so happened that the head of code enforcement for the fire department went to our church. Before closing the deal, I asked him to help me figure out what I needed to do to comply, which he readily did. After all, it was in the city's best interest to have sustainable redevelopment in the downtown area, and that occurs only when the economics work.

7. **Stay focused on the issue.** Negotiations go more smoothly when participants stay respectful and remain interested in the other side's problems. As I mentioned regarding my friend John Garamendi, we can have great conversations because there is a level of trust and an understanding that we're discussing the issues—not our personal morality.

One way to stay respectful is to avoid going over people's heads. I rarely went to a planning commission meeting without having gained full support of the staff. I just don't do that. I try to work with people who are closest to the problem and go over their head only in very rare circumstances, such as outright negligence, an unwillingness to do their job, or consistent and total incompetence.

There's also no need to antagonize other people's anger or minimize other people's feelings. To solve issues, you don't have to straighten out everybody in the world in the process. Why spend time arguing about something that's not going to

LISTENING AND COMMUNICATING EFFECTIVELY

make any difference in the long run? If others don't want to change their mind—move on.

8. **Take advantage of the power of humor.** The ability to laugh and have a good sense of humor, especially about my mistakes, has been important to me—and helpful. Humor can make otherwise stressful situations feel a little more relaxed and help to build consensus among diverse interests.

For example, water is one of the most contentious issues within the state of California. The reality is that, in many years, supply falls short of demand and that the various entities with an interest in water rights—urban consumers, farmers, environmental organizations, governments (local, state, tribal, and federal)—each have different thoughts about how it should be managed and allocated. As you might imagine, The Metropolitan Water District of Los Angeles (the largest distributor of treated water in the United States, providing water to nineteen million people and three hundred cities), the Westlands Water District (the largest agricultural district in the U.S.), and the Nature Conservancy each have their own opinion about how water should be paid for, allocated, stored, and transported. So, how do you create agreement when there are so many unique needs, many of which are conflicting?

Let me tell you—it's not easy.

I decided to host a meeting at my home to see what headway could be made on the matter in a nonthreatening place. As a farmer and businessman, I care deeply about California's water system and want to see the entire state succeed. I'm affiliated with a lot of people who feel the same way through my former appointment as the deputy chair of the California Partnership for the San Joaquin Valley, where I worked alongside Sunne Wright McPeak (former secretary of the California Business, Transportation and Housing Agency under Governor Arnold Schwarzenegger) and Peter Weber (a retired corporate executive who lives in Fresno and is dedicated to moving San Joaquin Valley and the state of California forward economically). Both Sunne and Pete have been instrumental in crafting statewide policies on water, transportation, and governance, and their knack for being inclusive and sensitive to the various constituencies has been a great example to me.

Although this was not an official meeting, I was able to attract the head of major entities, such as those mentioned above, in addition to congressmen from two different districts because they had enough respect for the goal of the meeting and knew that I was not going to be biased.

Thinking I might try something creative (although perhaps not polite) at the start of the meeting, I said, "Our job today is *not* to talk about water issues as they pertain to your own individual region. Our job today is to talk about a state-wide water plan and what we can do to try to come up with a plan that will help everybody. So, if I can tell where you're from and you start representing your region, I'm going to give you this card." I put a card on the table. On the front, it had a picture of praying hands with the message, "Jesus Loves You." When you opened the card, it read, "But everybody else thinks you're an asshole."

It was a bold move, but it got everyone's attention and drove home a point with humor: Everybody feels loved by the people they represent, but what does the rest of the state think about you if you're selfish with your water?

I didn't have to give out the card that day. There was alignment on 90 percent of the issues raised. Subsequently, we had meetings to continue the discussion because they had been helpful to all participants. Leading with humor had a humanizing effect and paved the way to successful communication.

Why is it so important to learn these skills? Because we all need others to buy into our dreams. If you can learn to communicate with clarity and compassion, not only will others know *how* to better help you, they'll *want* to help you.

Chapter 7

Having the Courage to Take Action

𝓕OLLOWING THROUGH ON curiosity can help you develop a vision you want to pursue, but, as I've said, it's the *execution* that makes all the difference. Execution is what separates most people from their ultimate goal of success.

But first—what *is* success?

Is it available to everyone?

In my opinion, the answer is yes. Not only is success available to everyone, it's important that everyone finds it. My definition of success is similar to how I also define beauty: it's in the eye of the beholder. Therefore, I'm not talking about relative success, but individual success. For me, **success means accomplishing what you set out to do without deviating from your core values.**

If I'm content with life and enjoying the ride, *that's* success. My definition does not have a dollar sign attached to it. One of my former

> *Success means accomplishing what you set out to do without deviating from your core values.*

campmates and friends, the late Jack Parker (who had been the vice chairman of General Electric), wrote a book titled, *Have We Done Everything We Came Here to Do?* If I can answer that in the affirmative, then I'm being successful.

So how does the execution piece of the dream-building process happen? Through belief, strategy, and action. Let's take a closer look.

Hope Is Not a Good Business Plan

I hope your vision becomes a reality, and I'm sure you hope that as well. Everyone needs hope that good things await in the future. Unfortunately, while hope is essential to making progress, it's not enough to get your idea off the ground. Without a plan, your path to success can quickly become a path to frustration. You need a *strategy* to back up your *beliefs* and *tactics* to get the job done.

In our company, we decide which ideas we're going to pursue by first sitting and talking about our **beliefs**. What do we think is going to happen in the market, the economy, and political climate? Are we going to do anything about it or let a potential opportunity pass? Again, opportunity cost plays a role. We discuss those beliefs and decide which ones are worth doing something about. For those we decide to pursue, we develop a **strategy**, which serves as a master plan. Last, we develop incremental **tactics**, which are the *how* of the process. They are the specific steps we'll take to put our strategy into action.

For example, one of the beliefs of our company today is that workforce housing is becoming less affordable in California and in most of the rest of the United States, especially in coastal states. The cost to build or buy new housing is not a viable option for many people. There are a lot of cases out there where the existing stock of housing has not been taken care of well or could be upgraded to bring it up to today's standards. We believe that there is going to be an insatiable demand for affordable housing and that, if we can create a supply for that demand, there's a profit to be made. Our strategy is to acquire housing that we can then reposition by increasing its value. Our tactics include hiring people who do nothing but try to find undervalued property. We analyze the potential of those properties to determine whether or not the property is worth pursuing.

Throughout the process, we review our results and ask: *Are our efforts making a visible difference?* If they're not, it may be time to change tactics or revise the strategy. Just like a dream or a vision, strategy is only as good as the ability to execute it.

When Fear Strikes

Even when you have a good strategy based on a solid belief, it can be overwhelming for some people to move forward. To many, the sheer number of unknowns can be frightening, not to mention the risks that might need to be taken.

One of my favorite quotes about fear is the following, from Chris Johnson, author of the forthcoming *Faith and Execution*: "Faith and fear are polar opposites, but they share one characteristic . . . They both want you to believe something that hasn't happened yet."

Without a doubt, fear can be very real and difficult. While some people are naturally more comfortable with risk-taking, I believe anyone can develop tools for confronting their fears and for moving forward with confidence. Here are a few strategies I've used:

1. **Start small.** You don't have to try everything at once. Don't try to send the rocket to the moon on the first shot. Take bite-size actions that you *do* feel confident will succeed—those accomplishments will grow your courage. In time, as you continue to achieve, not only will your fear decrease, but you'll start to see yourself as successful.
2. **Visualize yourself succeeding.** When fear rises, go back to your vision and reflect. Remind yourself of what you're trying to create and why it is important to follow through. When people can't easily understand or visualize how something can work, they often become negative and fearful of trying it. When things aren't going right, visualize how you're going to get yourself out of the present situation and how the future can be brighter. Be more interested in the success of your dream than the roadblocks. Your vision of yourself and your dream can pull you up.
3. **Allow yourself to mess up.** If you're going to take action and risks, you're bound to experience failure. Not everything you set out to do will work. When something doesn't work, it doesn't help to think that you're a failure. There's a big difference between thinking *you* are a failure and that *your idea* failed. Winners see mistakes as temporary setbacks and treat them as learning experiences. If you fail, don't think of yourself as a loser. You made an incorrect decision, which we all do.

And we all have unfair and undeserved setbacks, too. There are certain things you learn only after doing it wrong. With that knowledge, you can certainly help the next person avoid making the same mistake. Learn from the wrong turns and keep going forward by focusing on managing the outcome.

HAVING THE COURAGE TO TAKE ACTION

As my friend Jim Morgan advises in his book *Applied Wisdom*, "The cost of perfect information is too high. Most people over-analyze decisions and under-manage the consequences. Do basic analysis, make a decision, and then pay attention to managing the consequences. Success is 10% strategy and 90% implementation."

4. **Be grateful.** Appreciate the freedom you have to try out ideas and the abundance of opportunities that exist. The more grateful you are, the less second-guessing you'll do. As you deal with fear, remind yourself that bad times in business are occasions a good learner would not miss. Mistakes and setbacks can be cause for gratitude. Why? Because achieving—through *overcoming* setbacks—creates confidence and happiness.
5. **Get feedback.** You can't do it alone, and you don't have to. Collaborate with others, and seek help as needed. If you ask five people about an idea, and they all give positive feedback, your fear will go down. If you ask five people, and three think you're crazy, then you'd be wise to adjust your tactics or strategy.

Making the Unmanageable Manageable

What if your progress is stalled because you just don't know where to start? How do you get your act together when you have a zillion problems running through your head and you don't know which to tackle first? The following is what works for me and the many others I have shared this exercise with over the years.

I've found that, if I make a list of my challenges, the unmanageable starts to become manageable. The act of writing helps me identify with more clarity the issues I face. This exercise not only helps me gain focus, but it also keeps me on track and reduces the "overwhelmed" feeling.

When I have too many ideas swimming through my mind, I go someplace quiet and private and start a free-write phase to transfer all challenges, opportunities, and concerns (regardless of their size, order, or importance) onto paper. It's very important to write down even the most trivial challenge so that when your list is complete, there are no unwritten challenges remaining in your mind. Transferring *all* your challenges onto paper is almost like turning them over to somebody else, even though you haven't, and it makes the challenges look more academic.

As you write, it's important not to limit or second-guess what deserves to be written down. You can expect to write down stuff that's hard to admit and you wouldn't want anybody to see, but no one ever needs to see your list. You can burn the list in the fireplace when you're done.

Next, I consolidate and group challenges into categories such as business, family, and community, and try to group issues that tie into each other. Then, I take each challenge and sum it up (condense it down) to as small as one sentence, if possible, for clarity purposes. The very difficult process of taking a complex human problem and putting it down very precisely really helps simplify the challenge.

With the issues clearly defined, I write out a brief (one sentence, if possible) solution to each problem. Even though I don't know *how* to obtain the solution, I know what would work for me. I identify an answer that would be an acceptable starting point.

Before taking action, I prioritize the problems in order of importance (because you can't work on everything at once). With that specificity, I can then go for help without rambling around.

At the end of this exercise, I've transferred the challenges that weighed me down to that piece of paper and leave with a manageable set of actions. Seeing solutions clearly outlined on paper provides a motivating sense of hope and control.

Establishing Priorities

With clearly defined action items, all that remains to be done is to manage the overall progress. How are you going to do that? How will you make sure that you distinguish, as Stephen Covey put it, the urgent from the important? You can get trapped in completing only urgent things and end your career having accomplished nothing important.

The fact is, the things you *measure* are the things that tend to *improve*. There's a popular saying: "People do what you *inspect*, not what you *expect*." Therefore, if you want to improve something, measure it.

I've found success with the ABC System of Prioritization, which I learned about at a YPO meeting and have used for decades since. Organize your goals by importance, and concentrate on the most important ones, with "A" being the most important to "C" being the least important. Simple tasks that take an hour or so a day can be accomplished easily, but if they're a "C," then checking them off your list is time taken away from executing the tasks that matter most (the A's). It's more difficult, but crucial, to discipline yourself to jump in and attack large, long-term goals that may take years to accomplish—but these are the very goals that will make a difference in your life.

Make sure you spend your time on the "A" priorities, even if they are large. Take regular bites out of your big goals. As it's been said: "The way to eat an elephant is one bite at a time." The main thing is to keep working at it even if it doesn't feel like you're making progress. Others, as well as yourself, can see your priorities through your actions. When you get discouraged, remind yourself that *you* set the ranking. Nobody else.

If you've identified the most important things in your life, make sure you're putting time toward improving and working on them! You owe it to yourself. Do what you promise yourself you're going to do. Breaking promises to yourself is demoralizing, depressing, and bad for your self-esteem. Keeping your word to yourself will give you the chance for positive self-talk, which is much more beneficial to your mental health.

I've found that when I keep plugging away at the goals that matter most, all of a sudden, one day, I'm there.

Digging In: Where's the Next Stoplight?
Anticipating Change and Taking Action
A Closer Look at Belief—Strategy—Tactics

Not long after I began selling houses in Stockton in my early twenties, my commitment to being a good observer of changes in the real estate market started to pay off. After a couple of years, I sold five houses in one day—all re-sales—in different parts of the city. I still feel a sense of accomplishment when I reflect back on the logistics of writing up the deals and getting five families to sign all in one day. It was complicated enough to do then, and you couldn't do it today because it's even more complicated, but I was dedicated to my trade. I worked hard, put in long hours, and kept an eye out for opportunities.

And I was always on the lookout for properties with untapped potential. Around this time, I saw a house for sale on a corner lot of a busy intersection for $100,000. It was priced too high for residential in that area and wasn't selling. That would be more than $800,000 today. Considering the size of the lot and its proximity to commercial development, I **believed** that it was only a matter of time before that corner would be re-zoned for commercial development.

Before approaching the owner, I did my homework. I talked with city staff to see what they were planning for the area. I wanted to see if my gut feeling that they'd be putting in a stoplight to support commercial development and mediate traffic was accurate. It was; they confirmed that they would be putting in a traffic light within the year. I knew that would change the value of that intersection.

My vision of that corner's potential took shape. The owner wanted to sell and couldn't find a buyer. I was confident I could solve his problem and capitalize on the parcel's potential.

I remember pulling into his driveway and seeing all the trees around his house looking as if they were trying to protect him from the commercial development that was coming. I told him that I didn't have enough money to buy his property but that, if he would give me time, I would put together leases. With those leases, I could go to the bank and borrow against the income stream from the leases to pull out enough money to pay him for his land *and* build a strip shopping center. It was a creative financial **strategy** that allowed me to build my first strip shopping center.

He agreed to a one-year option for 10 percent of his asking price. I didn't want to sell any of my cows to raise the capital, so I partnered with my close friend Dino Cortopassi. Together we were able to put up $10,000. I had been deferring consumption since I was fourteen, and, despite being only twenty-five at the time, I had the $5,000 to invest, which would be about $40,000 today.

I immediately began to take action on implementing my vision in incremental steps. Here are the **tactics** of how I deployed my strategy:

1. I learned how to get the parcel rezoned as well as what was required to build a strip shopping center. I had strong resources to tap into in both my father—who had built a successful shopping center in 1951 that had grown to about thirty stores by this time—and city staff.
2. I got permission from the City for the necessary curb cuts and from the neighboring property owner for openings between the parcels. We convinced him it was in his best interest to

HAVING THE COURAGE TO TAKE ACTION

give us egress—permission to enter his property—and to take down the fence between the two properties so it would look like one big commercial piece and patrons could easily move between the two. Getting his permission to take down the fence played a central role in getting a service station in my shopping center.

3. I tracked down leases. I worked to make it as easy as possible on those who were going to be tenants and convinced them that my shopping center fit their needs and was in their best interest. For Standard Oil, I had a traffic count done so I could show the representative why I thought this would be a good location. In time, I also got Taco Bell, Swanson's Dry Cleaners, and a local Mexican restaurant—Señor Campos—on board. With Standard Oil and Taco Bell on the lease, I knew damn well that the bank would lend me money. Likewise, the Swanson's Dry Cleaners was owned by a pretty high net-worth individual.

4. I kept communication lines open with the owner. I didn't wait until the one-year mark to see him. I checked in with him every month or two to tell him how I was doing. When I got close to a year, I said, "I'm kind of stuck here. These guys have sent the lease to headquarters, but I haven't got it back yet. I should get it anytime." He said, "Okay, I'll give you three more months, but I want another five grand." So, Dino and I came up with the money.

During those three months, I got the signatures we needed and secured the loan, and then we immediately paid off the landowner. I didn't waste any time tearing down the house and starting on the construction.

In just a little more than a year after we'd purchased the land, we had our very first strip shopping center underway, and, with our new financing, we were able to pull out our option money, recouping our $15,000. There have been several other times throughout my career where it wasn't my money that got a deal done. **The ability to execute is more valuable than money.** If you're creative, you can make money without using much of your own.

Think of how many other real estate developers drove by that corner every day and never approached the owner to make a deal. I don't want to give myself too much credit—the future of that intersection was *apparent*—yet no one else took action.

Take time to reflect on your idea, and ask yourself:

▸ Is it based on a firm belief?
▸ Have I considered my strategy for achieving it?
▸ Am I using solid tactics to deploy my strategy?

Chapter 8

Building Confidence and Trust Through Action

So how does a twenty-eight-year-old kid build a $75 million development? I mean, where did I get that kind of money? And once it was started, how did I get people to move there, especially in the face of competitors spreading rumors of the smells at *Stinkin' Village West* (much of the land was bounded on the east side by a sewer plant that was subsequently relocated).

Lincoln Village West was built on all the principles I've mentioned so far in this book—vision, creativity, curiosity, hard work, responsibility, and courage. Building it also took trust. I had to trust in myself, and I had to get others (bankers, investors, government officials, employees, and homeowners) to have faith in me. I had my work cut out for me!

With Lincoln Village West, I wasn't just building a master-planned community—I was building my reputation as a developer/builder.

When you constantly do quality, honest work, people will begin to trust you, and you can move your dream forward.

Building on My Father's Legacy

My father was a great example of having a vision and being a confident businessman. In the 1930s, he was a realtor in Stockton, and by the mid-1940s, he and business partner Roy Sims owned the largest real-estate and insurance-brokerage firm in Stockton and had developed Caldwell Village, a small neighborhood just south of the UOP campus.

In 1948, my father and Sims went to San Francisco to attend a California Real Estate Association meeting. Serendipitously, the Community Builders' Council of ULI was holding a meeting in the same hotel. ULI was still in its infancy as an organization compared to today, and the council, which addressed postwar suburban growth, had been formed only four years earlier.

Attending that meeting was a tipping point for my dad. He, along with Sims, returned inspired to bring a new type of community to Stockton—a village-like subdivision complete with homes, schools, parks, shopping centers, churches, and even a community swimming pool for residents.

Upon their return, they started looking for the best location to develop their planned community. They chose to option a 1600-acre parcel of farmland five miles north of Stockton's downtown. It was all under one ownership (property from the estate of Benjamin Holt, inventor of the Caterpillar tractor), and they chose it for several reasons, including its size and suitability for a future shopping center. They did their research! Ultimately, they did develop 850 acres (and

BUILDING CONFIDENCE AND TRUST THROUGH ACTION

I later developed the remaining 750 acres into what became Lincoln Village West).

My father's vision was met with skepticism from city officials, who saw his proposed development as too far from the current city limits and denied the request to annex the land. Undeterred, my father went forward and developed within the county. In order to finance his dream, he raised money from more than fifty investors and formed the corporation Lincoln Properties. Over the next seventeen years, they developed Lincoln Village—following in the tradition of the local school district, which was named after U.S. President Abraham Lincoln—into the dream they had imagined, and the community was a tremendous success.

My father saw a need and didn't give up on filling it. He eventually sold his share of Sims & Grupe to his four other partners (before I went to work for the company as a real estate salesman in 1962) and put all of his time into managing Lincoln Shopping Center, which continues to be a thriving commercial hub and landmark for the City of Stockton to this day.

And it's still part of our family. About fifteen years before my father passed away in 1995, I approached him about his estate plans and told him I didn't need to inherit anything. I was doing fine on my own, and his example and good name in the community were inheritance enough. Ultimately, he accepted my wish, and he and my mother left all their assets to my two sisters, including their interest in Lincoln Center.

A Dream Unfolds

Lincoln Village West didn't happen without some luck. My favorite definition of luck is **when opportunity meets preparedness**. At the time, I was busy selling homes and simultaneously managing the farm-exchange deal and the small strip shopping center I've mentioned. Always on the lookout for a new opportunity, my big break came when someone else couldn't make a go of the development he had started.

Village Homes—a talented and quality homebuilder—had bought forty-five lots from LILVAL (Live in Lincoln Village and Live!), just west of where Interstate 5 now runs. A spin-off corporation of Lincoln Properties, LILVAL purchased this parcel of land, prepared it for development, and sold lots to Village Homes for zero down, with the arrangement to pay LILVAL once the homes sold. So, when Village Homes ran into financial difficulty and couldn't pay the bank, the bank started foreclosure proceedings on the twelve built houses and thirty-three vacant lots, leaving LILVAL with nothing but an IOU from Village Homes.

My dad's challenge was to figure out how to collect the debt from Village Homes, which would not happen if the bank foreclosed. He suggested I go to work for LILVAL and strike a deal with the bank to stave off the foreclosure, get time to sell the completed houses, and sell the remaining lots to another builder. My dad was strongly opposed to me becoming a homebuilder because the builders he had worked with previously had gotten into financial difficulty. The bank agreed to go along with the proposal if I agreed to personally guarantee the loan. I said I would do that if I could control 51 percent of the stock in LILVAL. My father sold me his 24 percent interest and the board of LILVAL issued me enough shares so that I could have 51 percent control and gave me ten years to pay for it. My compensation as LILVAL's only employee would be $1,000/month plus 20 percent of all the profits I could earn.

I went to work and decided that I not only wanted to clean up and sell the twelve built homes, but I was confident that I could

BUILDING CONFIDENCE AND TRUST THROUGH ACTION

also build homes that would sell on the remaining thirty-three lots. I went to my uncle Walt Hachman, who was a general contractor but not a homebuilder, to get advice. He encouraged me to go forward and advised me on things I would need to learn if I wanted to be a homebuilder. Since I knew what I wanted to build, I needed someone with a contractor's license. I hired Jack Kern, an experienced licensed contractor who was recommended to me to fill the position.

I got a team together to finish out the development, which at that time was still part of Lincoln Village. I hired the previous home designer for Village Homes, Bernice Nickols, as well as the company's office manager, Marge Barnes, and building superintendent, Frank Passadore. Frank turned out to be a great construction executive, later became my partner, and is still with the company to this day.

We had a lot of work ahead of us. The completed homes had fallen into disarray, with weeds growing all around as they just sat there with the project going into default. We made them more presentable and priced them reasonably, so I wouldn't get stuck holding them. I sold the homes myself, as well as paid a commission to anybody else who would do it. Immediately, folks started moving in.

As we built out the Village Homes development, I was gaining confidence that I could be successful at building homes and make money doing it. I was succeeding at turning around a development set for failure, and it felt rewarding. Pretty soon, Warren Atherton, who married Benjamin Holt's daughter and was lawyer for the Holt heirs and father of the G.I. Bill of Rights, wanted to sell an additional 750 acres of the land for urban purposes because it was valued at five times what it was worth to farm. He was in a bit of a predicament, though, because the land he wanted to sell was below sea level. The area where Village Homes had been developing was just high enough and had enough clay in the soil that you could build houses on standard foundations. The further west you went, however, the land dropped below sea level and had a lot of peat dirt in it. That acreage—which many people called a peat bog—had been written off as undevelopable because the topsoil was too organic to build homes upon. As it stood, the city and county wouldn't allow it to be developed. No one else had tried to adapt that land for building houses because, at that point, you couldn't.

Where many had seen a problem, I saw a challenge that had to have a solution. With an idea in mind for turning the land's weakness into a one-of-a-kind opportunity, and with my father's help, we got the Holt family to sell the land to me for no down payment and subordinate their equity to bank and bond financing. It was easier then to get entitlements, prior to the California Environmental Quality Act (CEQA), which adds years to the process.

Overcoming Challenges

The very design and layout of Lincoln Village West was a response to the challenge that had held up its development. For us, a lake system was not only a future amenity that would help sell the master-planned community, but it was also a means to getting the necessary soil composition to build houses on that land.

Through my father's involvement with ULI, he introduced me to a talented land planner from Denver, Colorado, by the name of Robert O'Donnell. Bob came aboard and devised a plan to make the digging of a lake and building of levees *part* of the solution. While we couldn't build a foundation on peat dirt without it costing more than the entire value of the house, we could work *with* that dirt. Our engineering firm, Stockton's RW Siegfried and Associates (today known as Siegfried Engineering), provided an analysis that showed

BUILDING CONFIDENCE AND TRUST THROUGH ACTION

Breaching the levee to flood the marina at Lincoln Village West, 1968.

Lake and marina under construction at Lincoln Village West, looking east, 1967. The future locations of the lake, marina, and Interstate 5 are identified in the photo.

once you dug past two or three feet of peat dirt, you hit clay. And if you mix clay with peat dirt (compacting it with tractors) you can get conditions for a normal foundation.

Bob came up with a design that strategically placed the lake and marina, and repurposed the extra clay from the bottom of the lake and the excess peat dirt to build levees as a necessary flood-protection measure, and also used it to create soil compatible for building.

But executing the plan came with its own complications. For example, the perched water table was so close to the surface, it made it impossible to use heavy equipment for construction. Civil engineer James Yost, of Siegfried and Associates—who would go on to build eight lakes with us in Stockton—figured out how to work around the water table by building a trench alongside the lake that was four feet deeper than the water table. That allowed for the water table to be drained and to make way for construction. Interestingly enough, by the time we developed Brookside in the 1990s, just south of Lincoln Village West, we still had the same water-table problem. By then, we had learned that we could drain it just as successfully with well points. That just goes to show that even if you pioneer a solution, it's to your benefit to stay open to change.

Our solution brought unanticipated economic benefit. From digging up the lake, we had more dirt than we needed for the levees. Seeing that Interstate 5 was going to be built, I offered to give the dirt to the contractors who were building the freeway in exchange for them building part of the development (whereas, if I had sold the dirt, I would have had to pay taxes on it). I ended up getting parts of the development built for the value of the dirt I was providing—a win-win for both of us.

BUILDING CONFIDENCE AND TRUST THROUGH ACTION

Introducing a New Way of Life

There was solid competition in Stockton when we started Lincoln Village West. Brothers Max D. and Merrill L. Stone began Stone Bros. and Associates in 1948 and developed in North Stockton, including the Stonewood subdivisions and the 500,000-square-foot Sherwood mall (construction began in 1964), one mile south of my dad's Lincoln Center. West of Lincoln Village, Ed Westgate was developing Park Woods, and within his development, you could buy a lot that sat on a creek and had an oak tree for less than in Lincoln Village West.

But if we were going to do a lake community, we couldn't continue on with the same products that were being built in Stockton. I knew that just from my experience as a house salesman. I had been doing solid research for eighteen months when we broke ground on August 24, 1966. Two of those months had been spent visiting other lake communities throughout the state. I visited lakes that were each created for a different reason, learning a tremendous amount about marketing and the value they provided.

That helped me identify the value *I* was bringing—a revolutionary development, a community that brought a new way of living to the city of Stockton. A "dream" lifestyle for four thousand homes and apartments in a beautiful community that was safe, affordable, and improved the environment.

What did we introduce to Stockton through our accomplishments in Lincoln Village West?

▸ **Lakeside living!** There was no one else around with lake expertise. We offered life on a beautiful 57-acre lake with a 3-acre beach (sand having been brought in from Pebble Beach), a state-of-the-art clubhouse, the first waterfront restaurant in Stockton, and one of the largest covered slip marinas in the western U.S. at the time.

Lincoln Village West Marina, circa 1977.

- **Abundant amenities.** We offered extensive recreational facilities such as tennis courts and beach volleyball courts and devoted 25 percent of the area to open space. We put in cable television for our residents eight years before a commercial system was offered to other parts of the city. We also ran utilities underground—at our own expense—because I had seen that done in Southern California and knew it was more than the fad some claimed it to be. We also built a childcare center, as we would in future developments, to allow children of two-income families to spend their days playing with other neighborhood kids.
- **Innovative street designs.** A main collector street carried incoming traffic to quieter streets that fed into smaller neighborhoods

within the development. This approach not only reduced traffic but lowered crime, as there was really just one way in and one way out to the overall development.

- **New housing concepts.** We offered ten basic house plans. Eighty percent of the housing stock was customized, which was unique and differentiated us from our competitors. We were the only builder in Stockton that had professional designers on staff to work with the homeowners to customize homes. At our peak, we had *five* designers on staff, which was unique anywhere, let alone in a city the size of Stockton. Also, because of Lincoln Village West, the City of Stockton approved an ordinance to pass cluster housing, where dwellings were designed in a cluster of buildings in single, double, triple, and quadruple structure. The homes had separate foundations but joined roofs and a three-inch separation between each unit. By 1970, we were introducing this entirely new housing concept for the city, one that helped people who had been priced out of the market.
- **Mixed-income housing.** Speaking about price, I've always believed that police officers, firefighters, and schoolteachers should be able to live in the same place as wealthier business owners. So maybe their house isn't as big, and maybe their lot is smaller, but they can still live in that neighborhood. That was true of Lincoln Village West and has stayed true for every one of our master-planned communities that followed. Our approach drew attention from *California Builder* in 1968:

> One unusual feature of the development is the placing of variously priced homes across from or next to each other. This social mixing of different income classes is

abetted by architectural designs that stand comparisons, despite varying quality. In one block the prices ranged from $26,000 to $90,000. [In 2019, those houses sell from $300,000 to $1.2 million.]

All of these details took a lot of research, hard work, and patience. It took almost two years to run Lincoln Village West through the Local Agency Formation Commission, the city staff of planners, engineers and architects, police, fire, and traffic departments. This seemed like forever at the time. Today, the speed of that processing would be impossible. The planning commission and the city council all provided input on how to make Lincoln Village West an outstanding community for their city.

How did so many people buy into something that surely seemed impossible for someone so young? I think the story I had was so compelling and had such great potential for the city that people bought into it—from top government officials to young couples on the market for their first house. There were no other lake communities in Northern California other than Tiburon in the Bay Area, so Stockton now had a unique and rare development, unlike any other in the city.

Financing the Dream

To do all this cost a lot of money and, being young, I had to get *very* creative with the financing. None of the amenities I wanted could be financed through normal secured debt.

The bank would not lend me the money to build the lakes, bring the levees up to one-hundred-year-flood standards, and meet many of the off-site and underground-utility requirements. The City of

BUILDING CONFIDENCE AND TRUST THROUGH ACTION

Stockton was interested in helping, but only if the land was annexed and I built *within* the city limits.

My father had always developed in the county. Neither my father nor Warren Atherton (who represented the heirs that owned Benjamin Holt's land) liked doing business with the City of Stockton because they had old memories going back to 1948, when they wanted to start Lincoln Village and the City wouldn't annex that land. They wanted to continue developing in the county because that's how my dad had developed Holt's land up until that point. That said, neither one of them wanted to guarantee a loan for me, either. Just like my father wouldn't guarantee a loan when I was in college trying to expand my herd, he wouldn't when I was building my first development.

That was probably the first big disagreement that I had with my father. I had such big plans for the nearly one square mile that would become Lincoln Village West. But they were ideas that required capital I didn't have.

I had to be honest with him and Atherton; if they didn't guarantee the loan, I didn't have a way to develop the land without going to the City. Perhaps begrudgingly, they saw my point and told me to go ahead and negotiate with the City.

Stockton officials and staff were excited for the development to be within city limits because of the new concepts it would bring and how it would help the city's image. I was honest with them about the way finances stood. "If you want this," I told them, "can you help me figure out how to finance all this cutting-edge stuff?" The city manager, the city finance director, the head of planning, the engineering department, as well as the city council and mayor were eager to figure out a way to make such a pioneering development work. It took everybody.

They agreed to guarantee the bonds we sold to finance the digging of the lakes, the building of the levees, the underground utilities, and other required infrastructure. I was able to do *all* that work with *no* cash out by finding the right people to buy into my vision. When I look back on it, it was pretty amazing that a twenty-eight-year-old with minimal net worth or track record was able to pull that off.

Presenting the Dream to Others
It takes a talented team to execute a master-planned community and sell the dream. I first had to get my own team, investors, bankers, and city officials to buy into the vision. Later in my career, it was the team's job to sell the dream to the public, but when I started Lincoln Village West, my team consisted of only Jack, Frank, Marge, and myself. I didn't have a staff member to delegate that task to, so it was up to me.

We call people who buy in new planned communities "pioneers" because not everybody will do it. It takes a leap of faith, especially if you're buying from a young man who's never before built a master-planned community. Imagine, the development is unfinished, all of the landscaping isn't in, the schools aren't there, and everything is brand new. For some, it's too big of a risk.

My strategy was to set my sights on selling to key people in the community so as to boost the confidence of others to buy. I called these key people my "bell cows," a term that came from my ranching experience.

When cattle are sent up into the mountains for summer grazing, you put a bell around the lead cow's neck, and wherever that bell cow goes, the others follow. It also tells the cowboy where the cattle

BUILDING CONFIDENCE AND TRUST THROUGH ACTION

can be found when they're on an open range. I've found people act similarly, choosing people they trust as their own "bell cows," such as leaders in the community.

I went to my head banker and said, "You know, you've got to move out there. You're going to be lending me money to build these houses, and if you or somebody from the bank doesn't live there, it's going to be harder for me to sell. It would be a big boost for the community if you would buy one of the first homes." He agreed, and I next went to the superintendent of the schools with the same proposal. I invited a number of other leaders in the community, knowing that, if they "bought in," others would follow.

In the beginning, we used Sims & Grupe to sell the homes. As our operations grew, we hired our own salesmen, Tim Cashin and Tom Welch, who were terrific. By 1969 the "LILVAL Gang" numbered almost thirty.

Moving into the 1970s, the "LILVAL Gang" continued to grow to keep up with the development of the community. John Dinkel and Doug Unruh came aboard and became key to growing our operation. I met John when we both served on the Stockton Real Estate Board. He owned a brokerage firm in Stockton, and one day I approached him and said, "John, I think you could be better off with us than running your small brokerage." He joined our team in 1970 to head marketing, started Grupe Realtors in 1973, and would become the president of Grupe Sales Company and chief operating officer of Grupe Management Company. He stayed with the company until 1994.

Doug Unruh joined our company in 1973 (and stayed until retiring in 2002). A recruiter pointed me to Doug, who was in a management role in the land-development department of The Irvine Company in Southern California. Beginning with Lincoln Village West, Doug oversaw getting all the entitlements, working with the land planners, coming up with the master plan, putting in the infrastructure, putting in all the lots, and doing everything necessary before the houses were built for most of our master-planned communities.

As our team grew and Lincoln Village West was well underway, we had *a lot* of fun marketing. We enjoyed devising ways to help prospective buyers visualize how they could belong in the community.

We built the sales office on the edge of the lake, next to the three-acre beach and recreation center. On the weekend, we hired kids to sail around the lake. As the children of potential homebuyers observed other kids sailing and playing, you can bet that they'd go home and tell their parents, "I want to live there! That's where *all* the kids are going to be."

To help the parents fall in love with Lincoln Village West, we had a twelve-passenger pontoon boat built so they could not only see the promise of living on Lake Lincoln but experience what it was like to be out on the water. The parents could also see—from the ten-by-ten-foot topographical map mounted on the table that was located in the center of the sales office—where schools, shopping, the marina, and parks were going to be located. Subsequently, when the sales center was no longer needed, we took on the Herculean task to move the whole building a quarter of a mile west, where it became The Marina, Yacht, and Tennis Club.

A big part of Lincoln Village West's marketing success came from everyone's belief in the project. As John Dinkel recalled, "We had a lot of fun. We really enjoyed what we were doing. I think that's why everybody sold really well. You were proud of what you were doing. It was a very special place that you could sell and be very honest about it. Of course, I moved my family out there immediately." John wasn't the only one. I moved out there, and so did Frank, Doug, and other executives.

The Legacy of a Dream

In 1969, when I was thirty-two years old, LILVAL received the Award of Excellence from the Stockton City Planning Commission in recognition of the "skill and imagination displayed in the accomplishment of Lincoln Village West Subdivision design, which reflects the aspirations and dedicated efforts of the people of Stockton to continually beautify and strengthen the face and the character of the City of Stockton and thereby contribute to the betterment and well-being of its citizens." The City was so happy with the end result that they named a 20-acre park within the development after me five years later. I was surprised and honored, as I thought they only named parks after the deceased!

When I took over LILVAL, the stock was valued at $11 a share. When I liquefied the marina and some apartments that LILVAL

Aerial view of Lincoln Village West, 1980.

owned, I returned to the stockholders a $3,000-a-share dividend. Going from $11 to $3,000 endeared them to me. Not bad for a young kid, right?

The response from Lincoln Village West residents was just as warm. Only recently, I received a letter from one of the "pioneers" (Dr. Tod Anton, a retired school superintendent of Lincoln Unified School District), an original homeowner who moved to Lincoln Village West with his wife in 1972. In his letter of thanks, he shared what living in Lincoln Village West for forty-five years had meant to him and his wife:

> As we sit on our back deck in the evenings, we acknowledge how much we love our home and how happy we have been with our home as a center for life with children, grandchildren, and great-grandchildren.
>
> We are appreciative of your brilliance as a developer, thinking beyond profits, to build homes and communities that foster family life and community betterment. When we think about a retirement residence, my young wife of 86 balks and says she wants to stay in our wonderful home as long as possible, and I agree. We love our home.
>
> . . . I love the LILVAL decal on my Sunfish sailboat. I love walking (no longer running) in Grupe Park each day. Shopping at the Marina Center is good. Thank you, Fritz, for your great creations for better living.

This accolade is as big a reward to me as any other recognition I've received.

BUILDING CONFIDENCE AND TRUST THROUGH ACTION

The responsibilities I feel as a developer of master-planned communities are great. It's not just about the land plan or the buildings and their design; it's about creating a safe, sustainable, and beautiful community that will serve as the backdrop to thousands of people's lives over generations.

We loved our time living on Lake Lincoln and associating with the many other families with children the same age as ours. We especially enjoyed sharing a backyard and dock with Phillip and Anne Berolzheimer, of California Cedar Products and Duraflame, and their family. Our children enjoyed sharing a swing set as well as fishing in the lake together. Halloween was a big time of the year, with everybody out trick-or-treating and sharing hot chocolate and barbecued hot dogs. The annual Fourth of July sailboat races were held right in our backyard—those are memories and traditions you don't find in every master-planned community.

My children were unaware that I had built the neighborhood they lived in, but they have fond memories of growing up on Merrimac Court and can probably still list everybody who lived around us and the sense of community we shared in our cul-de-sac. Our children had lots of friends and loved running down to the swim club or going off on their bicycles and riding wherever they wanted to go. Even though it was not a gated community, we felt very safe.

The lake created value for the whole community, not just for the people who lived on it. That model of waterfront living and the effort that went into building a *sense* of community worked so well that, by 1982, my company had created six lake communities in Stockton, with the lakes totaling nearly 200 acres of water and adding twelve miles of lakefront living. Through these communities, people—thirty thousand plus—who wanted to live in Stockton for school and work could still enjoy living on a lake, just as I had loved as a child.

Chapter 9

Practicing Patience

*A*NYTHING THAT'S REALLY WORTH achieving will take time. Sometimes, it'll even take a lifetime. That's why I believe it's so important to distinguish *accomplishment* from *accomplishing*. Accomplishment, such as the winning of a race, gives good feelings, but those feelings don't last. The process is the key; it is the *accomplishing* that produces the lasting good feelings. And accomplishing isn't always about moving forward; sometimes it's about not losing ground.

> *Accomplishing isn't always about moving forward; sometimes it's about not losing ground.*

We've had many waits in our life together that took more than a decade, such as growing a cattle operation to the scale we had dreamed of. We found that our faith and love for life made the waits more than just bearable. We accepted that God's timing may be different (and better) than ours.

During the long waits and unexpected detours, we kept ourselves open to new opportunities and tried to enjoy the ride. Those waits were important times of learning and growth. As the Bible teaches, "And patience develops strength of character in us and helps us trust God more each time we use it until finally our hope and faith are strong and steady." (Romans 5:4 TLB)

I've learned that, while things might end up differently than I imagined, I'm not sure that I really want to know *everything* that will happen in my future. Almost always, in hindsight, the path we have taken, even with the detours and stops, seems like the one we should've been on all along.

Waiting Is Part of Life

Growing up on a farm, I was exposed at an early age to the complete cycle of life. From raising my cows to planting and harvesting alfalfa, I learned that there are some things in life you just can't rush. If you plant trees that aren't supposed to produce for five years, then that's just part of the plan.

Long waits—and the rewards they'd bring—didn't stop when I left the farm. I pursued Phyllis for months before she finally agreed to go out with me in college. She and my sister Luanne were roommates, and Luanne had warned Phyllis, "Don't ever go out with my brother. He's really wild." Phyllis stuck to that advice for most of that first semester, but my resolve won out eventually. Over time, and lucky for me, she saw my persistence as the genuine interest that it was and agreed to go out on a date!

In real estate development, exercising patience is a necessary and important part of the work. On certain projects, a decade might pass before the project is even started. And the total time until completion might be twenty to thirty years. For example, the Lincoln Village West Marina had to go through twelve local and state agencies for approval. The permit process alone took three years for the marina and ten years for the docks. Without dipping into deep reserves of patience, I couldn't have seen that project through—and I am very glad I did. In almost every case, the reward of waiting by far outweighs the alternative.

Getting Our Farm

I opened this book by recounting events that led up to a major tipping point for Phyllis and me—our decision to move to Stockton temporarily in 1962 so I could earn some money for us to buy our own farm. It was a difficult decision at the time, and it forever changed the course of our story.

After we moved, Phyllis and I never lost sight of our dream to live on a farm. In 1966, when Phyllis was pregnant with our youngest daughter, Michelle, she began a cross-stitch sampler that read, "I will build myself a farm." Nearly ten years later, it would finally hang in the large country kitchen at our very own Brookside Farm.

How we got there is truly a story of patience. We adopted an attitude of continuous preparation so that when we met with the right opportunities, we were ready to act on them. Some people say, "Oh, how lucky" without realizing the years of preparation. Our preparation happened through many of the points I've already made: by deferring consumption and living within our means, by weighing opportunity cost, and by working really hard. In short, we built the *achieving* of our dream into our everyday actions.

Our first home in Stockton was a modest rental. In time, our income allowed us to move to bigger homes, eventually building one of the first homes on the lake in Lincoln Village West. When we were finally ready to build our farm, we considered moving back to Bellota, but the forty-five-minute commute—combined with the long hours and weekends I was working—would have cut into our prized family dinners.

In 1975, opportunity came knocking when a broker approached me saying he had 500 acres up for sale immediately south of Lincoln Village West. My 542-acre development Quail Lakes had just won council approval the previous year, so I didn't need to be looking for the next development just yet. But, I saw the chance to purchase some land that I could someday develop in close proximity to Lincoln Village West and Interstate 5.

Although there was a risk, Phyllis and I figured if we could carry the cost while we waited, it would be worth it. I got a group of people together to put up some money along with us. We made an agreement that, when the time came to develop, I would buy the other investors out based on a predetermined formula. Then Phyllis and I carved out 50 acres for our home—Brookside Farm—with the remaining acreage going to crops, such as corn, wheat, tomatoes, and safflower. After thirteen years, we had our farm!

And it was idyllic. We accessed our home by driving down a long, half-mile lane we built that came over the levy and down into the property. It was bordered by a white-rail fence lined with trees and a view of green pastures, farm animals, and critters native to the area.

We built a beautiful two-story white wood farmhouse with a wrap-around porch. The design was based on one of our standard plans from Lincoln Village West, but we expanded it to better fit our needs. Phyllis designed several architectural features based on a lithograph of the original John Carsten Grupe home in Linden. Surrounding our home were a couple acres of lawn, a tennis court, a swimming pool, a pond, and a bridge to an island. It was our very own farmstead to enjoy horses, cows, and sheep. We built a barn and, after we had been there for a few years, a big indoor riding arena. We had all the best opportunities to live in the country but still be in the city.

Our home at Brookside Farm, 1975.

We intended to live there for five years as we developed the acreage around us. However, three years after we purchased the land, the *unforeseen, unforeseen* hit. The City of Stockton restricted building north of the Calaveras River in 1978 to force downtown development. It was a move that made it impossible for us to develop. We *thought* that we might be able to change the policy in a year and, at most, live there a couple of extra years, but that was not the case. It would be eight years until we could get a citywide vote to override the city council, allowing for the development of the Brookside community.

Fourteen years after we purchased the initial 500 acres, the pre-zoning for our 1,200-acre Brookside development was approved by the city council on April 17, 1989. We continued to live at Brookside Farm until 1995—twenty years total—and moved to the Lodi countryside once the community was well underway.

Although it was not exactly how we had planned it, the long wait to develop Brookside Farm into Brookside community was beneficial to us in many ways:

- The extra years gave us ample time to increase the acreage (buying out the eight other owners to accumulate the 1,200 acres total).
- The 1978 building moratorium forced my company out of Stockton. If it hadn't been for that, we may have just been content being Stockton builders and missed out on the experience and fun that came from building fifty communities in ten states.
- During our wait, we continued to educate ourselves and grow. Through my involvement with ULI and YPO, Phyllis and I traveled a tremendous amount, especially around Europe, and those experiences had a major influence on our design choices for Brookside and our future home Shady Oaks.
- In the meantime, we used Brookside Farm as a marketing tool. We held big functions showing what we thought the future would be. Through these events and fundraisers, we introduced the community to the beautiful space and its views.

People became very familiar with "Brookside" and built good associations with the name. When it came time to build, we had a long list of prospective homeowners.

Just like we never gave up on our farm, we didn't give up on the possibility of the Brookside community. We kept preparing so that, when the opportunity came, we would be successful.

We stayed *active* in making our dream a reality. We were patient and didn't let unexpected holdups get the best of us. We continued to make decisions in the interest of our dream. In short, we adopted an attitude of *expectation* (that someday, in God's time, we would build Brookside) and *gratitude* (for the gift that Brookside Farm was to our family). With this mindset, we didn't just make the most of our wait—we enjoyed it, and everything worked out better than if we had planned it.

Digging In: From Sharing to Selling the Dream
A Closer Look at Creating a Sense of Urgency and Marketing a Master-Planned Community

Not everyone has vision. That's just a part of life. Some of us can easily see potential, and others of us need a little more help.

As one of my former chief financial officers, Don Benioff, shared, "When Fritz and I would go out and look at a piece of dirt we were going to develop, he could see what it would look like if a community was sitting there. I just saw a piece of dirt."

In order for a dream to become a reality, people need to buy into it. How's *that* done?

Well, it's simple. If it's in their best interest, they'll do it. And if they feel it's urgent, they'll do it *now*.

Let's take a look at how that works.

Designing Our Product

It takes a lot to launch a master-planned community. Land planners, engineers, architects, investors, bankers, city officials—a long list of people (and at least twenty government agencies) have to buy into the vision and want to work with you before a single house goes up. It requires a lot of convincing over a five- to ten-year horizon. During that time, change is constant. To me, those waits have been another example of why the process of achieving is as important as the end goal of achievement. Ten years is a long time to wait for happiness, or to feel like you're achieving anything.

Case in point, the opening cost of our 1,200-acre Brookside community—not counting the land—was $90 million in 1988. When the community was finished, it had more than three thousand homes and one million square feet of office space. Now, how many people would want to take the risk of borrowing that much money?

Why were we so convinced we could do it? Our previous successes were encouraging, and we believed strongly in the product we had developed. We did a lot of research to understand the market, whom to appeal to, and what would draw people to the community. We

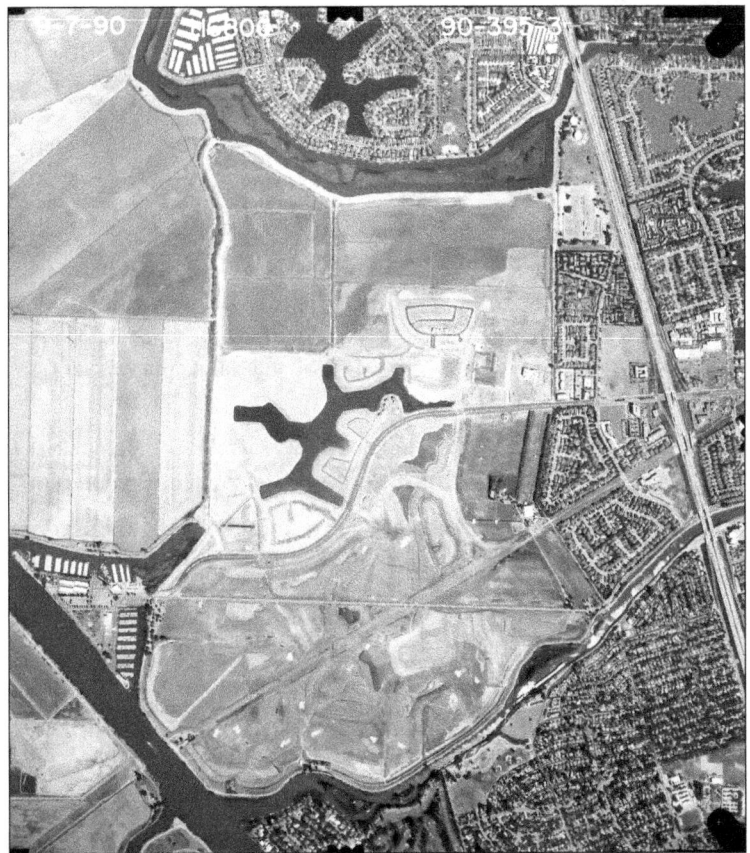

Aerial view of Brookside in the rough. Lincoln Village West at the top, Quail Lakes to the right of Interstate 5, and our barn (the white square) in the middle right of the aerial, 1990.

An aerial view of Brookside ten years later, 2000. Our 1974 development, Quail Lakes, is visible in the foreground. Lincoln Village West, Quail Lakes, and Brookside provided more than ten thousand single- and multi-family homes and two million square feet of office and commercial space for Stockton.

built specialized teams within the company and recruited experts, from builders and architects to engineers and marketers, to iron out plans for a successful execution.

All the while, we stayed open to input. Later, I'll talk about the role a ULI panel of nine land-development experts played in reviewing our plans, but we also created focus groups composed of community representatives to give us feedback.

It took teamwork. It required good management. It demanded patience.

But all those efforts paid off. The master-planned community of Brookside was *the* next big change in land use for Stockton. As a headline in *The Stockton Record* read in April 1990, "Grupe project changes face of Stockton." People were eager for something new, exciting, and not yet available in our region.

Brookside introduced Stockton to a completely new way of living. It was a challenge to change a flat, 1,200-acre parcel of land into a picturesque master-planned community. Unlike some communities, the design *didn't* start with the natural beauty of the land. We had to add a lot. We dug a lake and used the excavated dirt to build a hill, the highest point in the city of Stockton, on which we built the clubhouse which has 180-degree views, clear to Mount Diablo. We added 950 trees (some mature, specimen trees) and 15,000 shrubs. The community included 156 acres of parks and open areas and an adjacent 100-acre wildlife habitat. We also increased Stockton's lakeside living by creating a 45-acre man-made lake with 13,000 feet of shoreline. Everything was laid out with special attention to maximizing view corridors so that the beauty of these additions could be enjoyed unobstructed.

What really set apart Brookside was the golf course. We built an 18-hole Robert Trent Jones Jr. golf course and 750 golf-area homes. There hadn't been a quality golf course built in Stockton since the Stockton Golf and Country Club in the 1920s, so it was a big deal to have a big-name architect come and design an $18 million course.

The beauty of Brookside's homes and infrastructure defies what most expect of a master-planned community. Many refer to their house as a vacation home. Our team discussed every feature, from mailbox design and electrical box placement to the craftsmanship of the most utilitarian features such as the hand-forged stop signs.

Phyllis and I took a personal interest in the details. We spent three years of research and a hell of a lot of money on the more than six hundred lampposts of the "King Ferronite Standard Design No.

108," a design installed in Stockton's own downtown in the late 1920s. Not all developers spend that kind of time on the details, but it made a *visible* difference.

Despite all these new planning elements, we kept true to our tradition of offering workforce housing. We built homes targeting first-time homebuyers. That isn't the case in all master-planned communities. The development became a major draw for Bay Area commuters, as the average house price was 50 percent of Bay Area prices.

When we sold the last house in 2004, Brookside had brought 3,248 residential units and commercial space for 4,000 jobs to Stockton, hitting an impressive job and housing balance and providing some relief to the congestion of the travel to downtown.

But perhaps most importantly, our development had challenged the image many had of Stockton. It's hard to see Stockton as a place of high crime and economic instability when you're in Brookside. The community has continued to be used as a recruiting tool by hospitals and universities as they try to entice professionals to move to Stockton.

We had built the better mousetrap, if you will, but that wouldn't have mattered if we couldn't get others excited enough about the quality and promise of Brookside to buy in and to do so *now*.

Marketing and Selling the Product

We've always had a lot of fun marketing our developments. We started our marketing efforts at Brookside years before we had models homes available to tour or completed homes ready for purchase. As I mentioned earlier, I bought a 500-acre parcel just south of Lincoln Village West in 1975 with the intent to develop it as my company's next big project. We were blindsided when a no-growth initiative passed three years later, making it impossible to continue. It was not until 1986 that we could move forward with developing it. By then, I had grown it to 1,200 acres through negotiating with adjacent landholders.

During the wait, our reputation for being a reliable master-planned community developer and homebuilder with a track record of beautiful, quality communities fed excitement for the project's completion. Many of our former neighbors and friends from Lincoln Village West were eager to come join us at Brookside. "We followed you to Lincoln Village West," they'd say. "We want to follow you to Brookside! Get on with it and start building!"

To keep that excitement up and energize those not familiar with our name, we came up with a lot of creative and nontraditional marketing

My parents, Anne and Greenlaw Grupe, Sr., were one of the first residents of Brookside, *ca.* 1989.

ideas, and because of those efforts, almost four hundred homes sold before any advertisement was printed. It was an exciting time, and *many* felt a sense of adventure. In fact, one of the first lots that closed at Brookside was sold to my dad and mom. My mom was especially excited. As she said at the time, "We look forward to being among the first people to live in the community. It's as if we're following in the footsteps of our pioneer forefathers who came to California."

Here are eight tips to keep in mind when trying to sell a dream:

1. Know how to differentiate your product. We built our reputation by delivering more than we promised and handling complaints compassionately. Customers need to have faith that the manufacturer of the product will be around to address any issues that arise, and need to trust that *when* issues arise, they'll be handled. We made lifetime customers by having a home-warranty program that went beyond what was required (discussed in Chapter 15). Those who had bought from us before felt confident to say, "Buy a Grupe home. They're good for it." We got our name out into the community through our *The Blueprint* publication and by giving back to the community.

To build your reputation and brand, zero in on what *you're* really good at. I was at a YPO meeting at Gallo Winery with Ernest Gallo, who started the winery with his brother Julio right after prohibition. At the meeting, my friend, campmate, and fellow YPO forum member T. Gary Rogers of Dreyer's Grand Ice Cream, asked Ernest, "Why don't you get into other businesses? You're so successful with wine, why don't you start doing other things?" Ernest replied, "Why would I when I don't have 100 percent of the wine business?" That's an example of focus. Know and play to your strengths, and communicate that in your marketing. Again, make people happy. It's possible.

2. Know your customers. If you don't know who the customer is, or what they want, how can you have a marketing strategy? We've always spent a lot of time trying to get into the customer's head and heart (or, in the words of Steve Jobs, "Figure out what they're going to want before they do"). Qualifying the customer is a time-consuming endeavor but rewarding when you're trying to launch a new master-planned community. We put together focus groups, hired outside consultants to do market studies, and spent a lot of money on research to understand trends and preferences of the area at that time, as well as to identify voids our development could fill.

What should you look for in a customer? People who are open. People who will trust you. People who will ask questions. People who are willing. I talk about the principle of working with the willing (Matthew 10:14) in Chapter 20, but it applies here, too. It's certainly easier to sell something if the customer is passionate and *wants* to buy from you. As the old proverb goes: "You can lead a horse to water, but you can't make him drink."

3. Pay attention to the details. Creating a great space usually takes a lot of tweaks. To make sure I wasn't overlooking any details, I sought advice from a ULI panel of nine distinguished land-development experts, such as Peter Rummell (then president of Disney Development Company) and Charles Fraser (one of the largest developers of golf resorts in the U.S. at the time), to review our proposed Brookside plan. This was a five-day process, including tours by boat, helicopter, bus, and horse-drawn carriage, that resulted in suggestions that we then took back to the drawing board and incorporated into our plan.

I still remember so clearly what Fraser told me as we stood on the bare land: "Regarding your country club, Fritz, the best advice I can give you is that the first thing you should do is buy the chairs."

Doesn't that sound odd for someone's best advice? His point was that in projects such as a big master-planned community (a billion-dollar deal), money often runs out before all the details are covered. People end up in beautiful country clubs enjoying an exquisite view on terribly uncomfortable chairs. In other words, what can seem like minor details can have a major impact.

Phyllis, who'd been helping design the interiors of our model homes for twenty years, was instrumental in the design of the country club, the biggest and most complex project she had ever done for The Grupe Company. She insisted that Stockton didn't have a beautiful venue for weddings and special events. She dreamed of designing something that would have a great sense of arrival with beautiful views and an interior that could support any type of event. To achieve this, Phyllis collaborated with a professional designer to balance function and beauty, creating a space with a 180-degree view.

Phyllis and I also enjoyed selecting art for the development. We wanted Brookside to be pedestrian friendly, and saw the inclusion of art in public places as promoting that and encouraging people to get out of their cars. We also saw it as further accomplishing our goal for all Grupe properties—to create a space where people want to experience it, share it, and take a photo in it. When I explain to an architect or a planner what I want in a community, I say, "I know we're successful when people come here to get their picture taken."

For each of the sculptures, such as artist Lyle Johnson's ten-foot-high bronze of four dolphins, Phyllis and I worked with the artist on the design. Phyllis found the antique fireplace for the country club. I came across the inspiration for the stop signs. The lakes and fountains were another art form. Usually, it's hard to beat Mother Nature as far as landscape goes, so within each of our developments, we try to enhance the natural environment as we add trees, plants, and shrubbery. The architecture of the buildings is another art form. Humans feel comfortable in certain spaces and not others. Would you enjoy dinner with a significant other if sitting at the sole table in the middle of a ballroom built for two hundred? We want people to feel comfortable in the spaces we create, whether it's the magnitude and form of the buildings, or the distance between the homes and amenities.

4. **Create a sense of urgency.** The value of any commodity depends on its scarcity. Time, which was once abundant to me, is now becoming scarce and therefore has skyrocketed in value.

Beautiful Brookside Country Club, *ca.* 1990.

For a master-planned community, success depends on a large volume of sales. When you have an endless supply and a limited demand, how do you create urgency? That's marketing: figuring out how to create a sense of urgency when there is ample product available.

Why buy today when you could buy next year? To counteract that thinking, we had multiple product lines with a limited supply of each. We had small lots, large lots, lots on the levy overlooking the main channel of the Calaveras River, homes on the lakes, and homes on the golf course. There was something for everyone, but in limited supply, which inspired people to act before what they wanted was gone—or increased in price.

To further encourage swift action, when we started to release home sites for sale, we used a lottery system to determine who among our long list of VIPs—about 350 people who had expressed interest in buying at Brookside long before the groundbreaking—could choose their home site first. At each drawing, we released a limited number of homes, again creating a sense of urgency and excitement. This tactic was very successful; some people were offered $10,000 for their spot on the list. And this was in 1988 dollars and in Stockton!

5. Invite people to experience the dream. Getting people out to the site and using the development to benefit the community is good for business and publicity, but it also is one of the most rewarding aspects of the job. During our fifteen-year wait to start building, Brookside Farm had really become a community gathering place. We continued a tradition started at Lincoln Village West, using our home as a promotional tool. We hosted leadership luncheons and other small-scale events that familiarized many people with Brookside Farm.

PRACTICING PATIENCE

One way we shared our site was through partnering with schools in the area. We had elementary students visit the construction site as part of our Grupe Hard Hats Program, and we developed an outreach program, The Belgians Are Coming, that focused on our champion horses and stars of the Rose Parade. In the first eighteen months of that program, we reached six thousand children. Each assembly ended with children receiving "passes" to come to an upcoming grand opening and ride a trolley pulled by our Belgians. It was a part of marketing that people *loved* and getting to share such a one-of-a-kind asset with the community brought us great joy.

This promotional brochure from the 1990s captures the magnitude of our Belgian horse operation.

149

One strategy we used, every other year, to bring attention to the Brookside location was to sponsor and host The Country Fair (see Chapter 20) to raise money and awareness for the needs of our community with a focus on children and public education. The Country Fair brought in big-name country-western entertainers as well as a lot of exposure to the site. In fact, at the first fair *after* we started construction of the Brookside community, we rented a full-size Ferris wheel so guests could look out over the project. Each of these efforts got the name of Brookside out into the community and brought people to the site to experience it directly. By the time we were ready to sell, the name "Brookside" was very much a brand in its own right.

A Ferris wheel at The Country Fair gave guests a
panoramic view of the future Brookside development.

6. **Collaborate with community partners.** We didn't just get *expert* input when it came to the development of the land. We wanted stakeholders to feel that they were part of the process. For example, before we built the schools, we partnered with the school district. We actually flew school-district officials to schools outside of California so they could observe the most advanced thinking in public education at the time and bring back ideas to help inform plans for Brookside. We contributed $18.3 million for the three schools we built, about $10 million more than we were required. We took an unprecedented role in the development of the schools and hoped to set a model for the state of how a builder could be involved.

7. **Find your Bell Cows.** To build confidence in our product, we encouraged pillars of the community to move to Brookside, just as I had done with Lincoln Village West. In the 1960s, I had to find and approach the "bell cows" on my own, but our operations had significantly grown by the time we developed Brookside, and our executive team joined me in recruiting community leaders. The Country Fair not only helped raise awareness of the Brookside community as well as several million dollars for charity, but the corporate patrons of that event were many of our first homeowners.

8. **Keep it fun.** As one of my executives, Ann Quinn, observed looking back on the success of Brookside, "It was fun for families, and that's what sold. The houses were neat, but it was also the lifestyle and the environment and the neighborliness of it."

Whatever you're promoting, keep it fun, accessible, and enjoyable. We loved selling the lifestyle of Brookside. Our daughter Bonner organized Get to Know Your Neighbor parties to give people a taste of the community life Brookside offered. We also hired a gentleman to sail on the lake, a visual reminder to potential homebuyers of how they could spend their afternoons.

Summing Up:
Our marketing efforts resulted in people buying into the dream at a very low cost on our end. We estimated that our creative efforts saved the company nearly $500,000 (in 1990s dollars) in marketing expenses.

> *When you're trying to get people to buy into your vision, find ways to boost their trust in your ability, and give them a taste of what your dream has to offer.*

Quality and excitement speak for themselves. When you're trying to get people to buy into your vision, find ways to boost their trust in your ability, and give them a taste of what your dream has to offer.

Who doesn't want to believe in something great?

Chapter 10

Valuing Relationships

*S*UCCESS DOES NOT HAVE TO come at the expense of having time for relationships. On the contrary, I think success is best felt when relationships—from family and friends to colleagues and business associates—remain a priority.

Despite how busy my days became as I was building my career, I still made time for family and friends. I made it a priority to be home for family dinner. If I had more things to do that day than I could get done by dinnertime, I worked after dinner. Along the same lines, I've hosted the annual dove hunt for many of my friends for forty years without missing a year. I believe friendships are just that important to a fulfilling and meaningful life. In fact, a recent article in *The New York Times* showed that a network of close friends is as important to good health and longevity as exercise and diet!

The Blessing of Family

My longest and most important partnership is with my wife, Phyllis. I can't overemphasize the joy partnering with her has brought to my life. Phyllis has been the ultimate friend, confidante, colleague, and helpmate. She has been a stable force in my life, a compassionate sounding board, and a constant example through her firm faith. In addition to being a great mom and grandmother (and now great-grandmother), she has been the ultimate support system.

Phyllis was just twenty when we welcomed our oldest child, Mark, in 1961, about fifteen months into our marriage. Within six years we added three daughters: Sandy, Bonner, and Michelle.

Phyllis and I aligned our roles along what was traditional for the time. I took care of the financial needs of the family, and she took care of the children. She loved the adventure and fun of raising so many children so close in age, but there were difficult times, too. I think Phyllis often felt like a single mom, so to speak, as I was very busy turning Lincoln Village West into a reality.

But she helped make it a reality, too. Phyllis really added value to The Grupe Company by volunteering her talents to oversee the interior design of the model homes, which were up for awards many times. Together with Lana Passadore, their efforts helped visitors see the potential of our homes and feel what it would be like to *live* in them. She decorated spaces to reflect how people really lived and tapped into local culture, often decorating a room to look like it belonged to a student going to UOP, the local private college.

Seeing how roles have changed and the increased time that fathers now spend with their families, I have felt some regret for not spending more time with my children when they were so young. As they grew older, it became a little easier as we established family dinners, took vacations, and acquired our beloved cattle ranch in Mariposa as well as a home in Aptos on Monterey Bay, which gave us quality time with the kids away from Stockton.

Phyllis and I have always felt fortunate that our children share *many* of our interests. Mark was an avid hunter early on and raised a steer just like I had in my youth. Our children participated in 4-H raising sheep, as well as other school extracurriculars. Sandy and Michelle were cheerleaders in high school, while Bonner did a lot of modeling.

Growing up, horses were a huge part of our children's lives. Bonner still remembers riding her horse up March Lane to a 7-Eleven for a Slurpee or teaching her horse to step through the drive-through line at Wendy's. She ordered takeout horseback before she could even drive! Just like my sisters and me growing up on the Bellota ranch, the children had the liberty to take adventures on their horses.

The girls participated in Gymkhana—which is a horse sport that includes barrel racing and pole bending—and enjoyed going to the county fair to compete from the age of eight to eighteen. Bonner represented the State of California in 1984 at the American Quarter Horse Association World Championship in Tulsa, Oklahoma.

There was a lot of laughter and singing in our household. The children share our love of humor, and Mark has earned the recognition of being the funniest. He has also carried on the tradition of pulling pranks. Just like I had tormented Leo, Mark tested out his creativity on our housekeeper, Alice Yates. Poor Alice. Once, Mark tied a snake to the hood ornament of her car. She didn't realize it until she got on the freeway and the snake started flapping violently! She turned around, but by the time she got back to Brookside Farm, Mark was long gone. Thankfully, Alice could handle the pranks and stayed with our family until she passed away, which was after our children were married and off on their own.

Many of our children have exhibited an entrepreneurial spirit from a young age. Mark started a firewood business as a teenager. He bought chainsaws and spent summers in Mariposa at our 8,000-acre ranch alone with Kevin, who I'll introduce shortly, cutting firewood in temperatures of more than 100 degrees. We had a lot of family friends who needed wood, such as our friends from YPO in the Bay Area, and Mark operated a business making $125 a cord.

Sandy came up with her own business plan at the age of thirteen by asking us if she could start a summer camp, A Week on the Farm, at Brookside Farm. Sandy felt blessed being surrounded by horses and cattle and knew that most children in Stockton didn't have that opportunity. She designed a program for children ages three through six that included riding horses, art activities, a nature walk, and playing in the swimming pool. Phyllis was very hands-on with the program. She photographed the children and helped Sandy create a photo album for each child at the end of his or her experience.

It was through that program that Kevin Huber came into our life. Kevin is our son-in-law, but he has long since felt like a second son. As Phyllis likes to say, "Kevin came to dinner and stayed for forty years."

Kevin first met Phyllis at Al's Stables, where he worked and we boarded horses. He met the rest of the family when he showed up to help his twin sister, Kathleen, who was working with Sandy on her A Week on the Farm summer camp. After finishing his assignment, he came across Mark loading hay into the barn and offered to help. With that task completed, Mark asked Kevin, "Do you want to go hunt something?" and that was the start of their friendship.

Thanksgiving family photo with Kevin (center), about 1980.

Kevin soon became a regular at dinner. He was bouncing between the homes of his parents and siblings at the time, so when he heard me mention the need to hire a guard to live in the old duck club building—a metal Quonset hut on the edge of Brookside Farm—he offered to live in it if we didn't charge him rent. So Kevin came to live on our property as a junior in high school. In time, he moved to quarters behind our barn.

He quickly became one of the family. He was with us so much that when it came time to send out the annual Christmas card, we couldn't find a picture that he *wasn't* in. Eventually, it just felt more natural to introduce him as our son whenever we were asked about our children.

Kevin will tell you that in high school he became enamored with The Grupe Company and set a goal to become president one day. He graduated from UOP's Eberhardt School of Business and gained work experience outside of the company for two years prior to joining The Grupe Company in the fall of 1986.

Although we already considered him a son, I guess it became more formalized in 1986 when Kevin and Sandy married, having begun to date their senior year of college. Kevin became president of The Grupe Company at the age of thirty-seven in 2000 and in 2010 shifted his efforts to Grupe Commercial, becoming its president and CEO.

Each of our children has contributed to the family business in ways that reflect their own strengths and interests: Mark's love for the outdoors has been poured into our ranching operations and game efforts at Mariposa as well as our farming operation in Lodi. Sandy's education in child development from UC Davis helped elevate the educational standard of the childcare centers we built in our master-planned communities. Her strong faith inspired her to lead and develop Bible studies for women and teenage girls, and her love of gardening and education led her to spearhead the creation of Stockton's University Park World Peace Rose Garden in 2015. Bonner's talent for organizing and event planning equipped her to run our biennial charity event, The Country Fair (an event that grew to thousands in attendance and raised close to $5 million for public education programs) and organize our equestrian Combined Driving Events. She and her children also currently show prize Hereford cattle. Michelle's sparkly personality has played a valuable role in team building at The Grupe Company since 2010, and she has followed in the footsteps of Phyllis with her design work.

Our family—which at present includes twenty grandchildren and three great-grandchildren—brings us immense joy. To enjoy their company, see them happy, and to watch the good things they're striving to do is a wonderful thing and the ultimate satisfaction. Each of our children has blessed our family in their own unique way and brought joy beyond measure to our family as a whole. We are most proud that they have each become caring adults and good citizens for our community. Phyllis and I are grateful for them every single day.

Grandchildren and great-grandchildren in front of our home at Christmas, 2015.

Friendship

When it comes to relationships, studies suggest that friendship may be what matters most to a person's well-being. Why? Friends help us adjust to change, bring continuity in an ever-changing world, and validate who we are. The fun we associate with friendship—shared experiences, inside jokes, traditions, conversations—provides fulfillment in the moment and lays the groundwork for future well-being.

Yet, many people go through life with numerous acquaintances and not one good friend to whom they can really talk.

I have been *lucky* to have a network of friends with whom I can shoot the breeze, talk business, or wax philosophical. I've learned a lot from my male comrades and cherish those friendships, many of which have stretched forty to sixty years. Even better, our families became very close friends and share many memories of traveling together or supporting one another.

You never get so successful that you don't need friends. Having a network of people who genuinely care for my well-being and ultimate success has been a tremendous reservoir of strength. Friendship involves listening, sharing, reserving judgment, and forgiving. Like marriage, it is not a 50/50 venture, but a 100/100. Phyllis taught me that. As she says, "Who wants to work with someone who will give you only 50 percent?" Or, what happens when your partner is a zero, and you need to be a whole hundred? People get sick—there are all kinds of examples of when one person has nothing to give and the other has to carry the full load.

I have a lot in common with my good friends. If you don't have similar values, to me, that's a non-starter. Certain things are essential, such as being trustworthy, loyal, appreciative of each other's strengths, and forgiving of each other's shortcomings.

Since 1978, I've enjoyed bringing together friends to an annual dove hunt at our Mariposa ranch every first of September. It's a multiple-day event, and over time, as my friends and I have aged, it's become less about hunting and more about breaking bread, checking in, and enjoying each other's company. I have fond memories of sitting around in the hot tub while drinking a bit of brandy and listening to my friends recite poetry by Robert Service or Bruce Kiskaddon.

Annual Dove Hunt at our G Ranch in Mariposa with me, Frank Passadore, and George Brown, 1995.

> *If you want joy and support in your life, make time for your friends. They are without a doubt one of life's greatest treasures.*

If you want joy and support in your life, make time for your friends. They are without a doubt one of life's greatest treasures.

Business Relationships Are Still Relationships

I choose to conduct business with people who share similar values. Working with people who I respect (and who respect me) and value relationships has made a difference in the joy I derive from business.

When I first got into the real estate development business, relationship banking was more common than it is today. Even the largest national and international banks practiced it by giving regional representatives a lot of power to make decisions. They acted as partners who had the enterprise's best interests in mind.

The first great relationship banker I met was Ed Hemphill. It was 1962, and I was in Willows, California, pheasant hunting with one of my fraternity brothers. We went to the Blue Gum Café for dinner, as all the hunters and local ranchers did on the opening day of hunting season. I began to tell my friend about my plans to become a builder, and, as I started to talk about financing, my friend offered to introduce me to Ed, the manager of the local Bank of America branch, who was also at the Blue Gum Café that night.

Ed had been out hunting all day as well, and we hit it off right away. It just so happened that he was about to be transferred to Stockton to be the manager of Bank of America's main branch for all of San Joaquin County. After listening to my plans, he told me, "When you're ready, come and see me." A few months later I did, and he took good care of me for twenty years until he retired.

I had a lot of respect for Ed's banking style, which was built on integrity and loyalty. For example, he once overrode his boss on my behalf. I brought to his attention a discrepancy between what we had agreed upon as our line of credit and loan fee for the coming year and what the head of real estate for the Bank of America headquarters in San Francisco had written up. Recalling the meeting the same as I had, he stuck by me, told me not to worry, and fixed it.

When Ed retired, I told one of my mentors, Robert Nahas, a major developer in the Bay Area and Lake Tahoe, that I didn't like the new direction Bank of America was taking with its branches. Bob was on the board of directors of Wells Fargo and offered to introduce me to the president at the time, Carl Reichardt. We met and respected

VALUING RELATIONSHIPS

each other's approach to business. After that meeting, we fortunately switched much of our business to Wells Fargo.

Our relationship was put to the test when the savings-and-loan crisis hit (which I talk about in a later Digging In). I owed Wells Fargo more than $100 million, and I went to Carl to explain how the federal government was not going to honor the take-out loans both he and I relied on. "I'll help you through this," he reassured me, "but I do want all of my loans paid off." I agreed. I got the time I needed, and he got the money due to the bank. I appreciated the faith and trust Carl put in me. Even then he didn't treat me like I was just a commodity.

One of the best relationship bankers I've ever known is Doug Eberhardt, a community banker who became the president of the Bank of Stockton. Doug and I met when Phyllis and I moved to Stockton in 1962. Doug and his wife, Margie, became close friends of ours, and Doug and I hunted and fished together for forty years. We had been friends for about ten years when I started to bank with Doug. I wanted to give him business, and his attentiveness, trustworthiness, and understanding of our business won me over.

Doug stuck with his customers through some real dips in the market. I was always impressed by how Doug knew his customers on an individual level and tried to help them ride out any storm. Because he understood the total business of his borrowers, he could move faster and make quicker decisions than larger banks.

At our company, we place a lot of value on relationships as well. It's always been my hope that nobody feels short-changed or disrespected.

Our efforts to build relationships with all who join the Grupe team have brought their own reward. Longevity and loyalty are commonplace and have been a blessing for all of us. One of my favorite photographs is of our extraordinary team members standing in front of one of our signature communities, taken for the cover of *Builder Digest of Northern California*. The picture reminds me of how committed so many of our associates have been. Some have relocated to other cities to help implement our dream. Many have stayed with the company for decades. A few have shown the utmost loyalty by going to work for other people when the economy was down and then returning to us when it picked back up again.

Standing with company executives in front of Lincoln Village West, 1995. Left to right: Doug Unruh, Frank Passadore, Mike Clark, me, Patricia Carmichael, Don Benioff, and Nelson Bahler.

My daughter Bonner was a full-time Grupe employee at the time of that *Builder Digest* cover. In the accompanying interview, she shared that she didn't see much difference between my role as father and CEO. "Not that he runs his family as a company," she clarified, "as much as he runs his company as a family, drawing out individual strengths and assisting associates to be the very best they can be."

It made me proud to know that she thought so. It's exactly what I try to do!

The Beauty of Trust in Relationships

I have heard people say, "Do not do financial deals with your friends because if anything goes wrong, it could ruin your friendship." For me, it's been the opposite. Who can you trust more than a good friend? It's easy to be loved when things are going great, but who's going to have your back when things go south?

My longest friendship is with Dino Cortopassi, who I met at UC Davis in 1955. That's more than sixty years ago. In fact, when Phyllis and I returned to Bellota as newlyweds, it was Dino's wife, Joan, who first called on Phyllis. Joan drove up with two little kids in tow and got out of the car to introduce herself. It was a very warm, memorable outreach to Phyllis, who didn't know anybody in the area, and it was the start of a beautiful friendship. As Dino and I plotted and planned our various business dealings, Joan and Phyllis worked together canning tomatoes and peppers, chasing kids, and keeping our households functioning.

Dino and I did our first business together in 1964—the small strip shopping center I've already mentioned. We have done many more investments together over the years because we trust each other's judgment. Once we were at a party, and I told him about this ranch I was buying in Oregon. It was very remote, with three miles of headwater of the Williamson River going through it, and it needed a lot of work, as the existing owner was overgrazing the land, ran the cattle on the stream, and left all the deadfall strewn on the ground after selling the timber. But it had real potential to be beautiful and a great trout stream if managed properly.

Spending time at Big Bow Ranch in Oregon in the late 1980s with Jim Auble, Mark Grupe, and Dino Cortopassi.

After hearing me describe it, Dino said, "I'm in."

"I'm not looking for a partner," I told him.

"Fritz, we always partner in fun deals," he said. "I'm in."

"Okay," I said. "Go look at it to make sure, because it's going to take a lot of money."

"I don't need to look," he replied. "I understand your vision, and I trust your judgment. I'm in for half."

And that was it.

We hired a company to restore the stream and spent many wonderful summers up there fly-fishing. We brought in a modular home and built a big deck overlooking the stream and 300-acre meadow. It was gorgeous.

The house had a good-sized kitchen/great room. On the wall, at the end of the dining-room table, we had a flip chart to write down our great ideas, which seemed to flow more freely after a little wine. As is typical with my good friends, Dino started referring to me with a lot of descriptive adjectives many people would find unflattering. So I wrote them on the flip chart and said, "What do you think about all those adjectives?"

He lovingly said as he was cooking dinner, "Fritz, you know those are terms of endearment. Besides, I am an Italian. I cook. You are a German. You're supposed to clean up the mess us Italians make."

The same thing happened when Dino asked me if I wanted to buy out his brother, who was a partner in his farming operation in the Stockton Delta and, a few years later, asked me to buy a large 4,000-acre ranch for him to develop in the Central Valley (Berenda) of California. I reviewed his ideas, gave my input, and said, "Okay, I'm in." Did things go as he had planned? No. See his very-well-written book, *Getting Ahead: A Family's Journey from Italian Serfdom to American Success* (2014), to learn how that story ends.

There were other major land deals in Stockton, plus smaller deals and decisions we have partnered on over fifty years. There were problems, even major ones, but overall we trusted each other's judgment, and there have been more wins than losses. He always comes to opening day at our ranch for dove season, and I always go to his annual salami-making day. Both of us still cook for the gang (our hunting group of twenty-five) and share sixty years of memories.

That is the constant.

Whatever a man sows, that he will also reap (Galatians 6:7 RSV) My 80th birthday celebration reminded me why it is so important to put relationships before work and other pursuits. That night we celebrated our tight-knit community of family and friends that has developed over the years. As my children delivered sentimental toasts and my grandchildren donned white cowboy hats, I marveled at our family, which, as my campmate UC Berkeley Professor Emeritus of Political Science Ken Jowitt puts it, is of "biblical size."

As I drove my championship team of four Bay horses onto the community of Brookside's golf course to greet family and friends at the beginning of the party, I was reminded of how thankful I was for having prioritized health and personal interests. It was a true family affair, with Phyllis at my side, Sandy and Michelle riding at the back of the carriage formally attired as grooms, while Mark filmed the event. Bonner had channeled her efforts into decorating the reception hall, and her son Dervin sounded the coaching horn for our arrival. It reminded me of the many times we had worked so well as a team before and of the good fortune Phyllis and I have when it comes to family.

Are you investing in the relationships around you—relationships that will last much longer than any business deal?

Chapter 11

Prioritizing Relationships

*S*OMETIMES MAKING TIME for relationships is easier said than done. You may need to settle for being less than perfect in some areas so you have time for what's most important. There are certain priorities that don't leave room for failure, while others allow for some wiggle room. If you put the same degree of importance on going out hunting or fishing with buddies as raising your family, you're going to have a problem.

Deciding to have a family was a tipping point for me, and a commitment I don't take lightly. Here are ten actions Phyllis and I have taken to safeguard our relationship with each other, and with our children and friends:

1. Connect
There's no substitute for the parent who is present. Being home at night for dinner with the kids whenever possible was a top priority for me, no matter how busy my workday.

Our dinners usually lasted an hour, and we each learned a lot by listening to each other. This was at a time when, according to an article published in 1976, the average American family talked with each other only twenty minutes *per week*. The family dinners gave Phyllis and me the opportunity to check in with the kids and provided us all with practice in learning *how* to talk with one another and how to listen. It was a safe, judgement-free time where the kids could troubleshoot scenarios and learn how to navigate difficult ethical situations.

Even before Smartphones, Phyllis and I had to be proactive about limiting outside distractions. We didn't have a TV at the ranch for years, until the kids wanted to watch Phyllis drive her Belgian horses in the Tournament of the Roses Parade one year. During this time, *The Nielsen Television Report* stated that average TV usage was a little more than six hours *per day*.

Today, *nobody* comes to our table with a cell phone. They wouldn't think about it! We don't even have to say, "Put it away," because they know we're there to connect and enjoy one another.

Connecting with those we love can be simple. Actions both big and small count. Some days, it's Phyllis writing a thank-you card to one of our children. Other days, it's having everyone over for a family BBQ. We are blessed to live in an age where it can be so easy to connect with those we love.

2. Build Relationships on Trust and Respect

We gave our children a lot of freedom, and that is something they've expressed appreciation for as adults. We turned them out to nature often and let them tap into their own creativity. We enjoyed watching them discover the world around them. As Sandy put it, "Mom would let us do all this crazy stuff until she learned how dangerous it was, and then she would take it away." Phyllis removed the trampoline when the children discovered the fun in bouncing each other off, resulting in Sandy dislocating her jaw. But the trampoline was soon forgotten as it was replaced by bright-red three-wheeled motorcycles. Eventually, those got taken away, too, as the number of crashes and injuries mounted. As Sandy put it, "As she removed the present danger, we were onto the next."

In addition to feeling our trust, we wanted our children to feel our respect for them. There are many things you can't change—family being one of them. The key is to learn how to manage difficult situations with respect. We all make mistakes, and we all say things that irritate other people. None of us are exempt from that. But don't break the trust and respect. As Michelle recalled about growing up, "I never felt like Mom and Dad got mad at me. There were lessons here and there, but they were always just super supportive."

When I went off to college, my dad told me, "If you get into trouble, I want you to call me and tell me about it." Phyllis and I have always wanted our children and grandchildren to feel that same invitation. What they choose to share with us is never used against them or thrown back in their face. We don't have *I told you so* moments. If every time your kid comes to you, you hit him on the head with a tennis racket, he's probably not going to come back very often. We always focused on helping our children move forward. As our children and grandchildren have learned, when they confide in us about a mistake they've made, we respond with love and encouragement. We'll say, "Okay, that's behind you. What did you learn?" Just because they made a mistake doesn't mean they're a bad person.

Using understanding over shame taught our kids that you *can* move on successfully from mistakes. Choosing compassion has paid big dividends as they became adults and started experiencing different kinds of stresses in their lives but knew they could always trust and talk to us.

3. Look to Learn from One Another
I think it's really good when a family learns each other's needs as well as their wants. Raising the kids, I always enjoyed walking down the beach with each of them individually, listening to their observations and concerns for the future. I always learned a lot when I was able to spend time alone with them.

I've also looked for opportunities to pass on what *I've* learned in life. Just recently I spent three hours with one of my grandsons and two of the key men who run our farming operation. I wanted my grandson to see firsthand my thought process for planting some new walnut orchards. When we were all done, my grandson said, "Boy, that was a great morning, Papa. That was really good. I learned so much, and now I have to go try and understand everything I learned." To have a grandson so enthusiastic about spending three hours with his grandfather and feeling that he learned a lot—that's the kind of joy that makes me feel so good.

4. Create Opportunities to Work as a Team
Our kids learned teamwork at our G̲ Ranch in Mariposa. Phyllis and I worked with the kids feeding cattle, riding horseback, and touring around in the topless Jeep to check on the livestock and other ranch operations. Even feeding the cows was a team effort. Somebody had to load the hay, somebody had to drive the truck, while someone else had to be on the back throwing the hay off.

In the spring, our annual roundups to brand calves born earlier in the year put our teamwork to the test. When you're branding the calves, someone has to rope the calf, others pin the 150- to 250-pound calf to the ground, and others vaccinate, castrate, and brand—all within two minutes! To accomplish this, our kids learned to work as a team with the ranch crew. We have kept this tradition going with our grandchildren and great-grandchildren—and enjoy watching them learning teamwork through it, too.

5. Seek Adventures Together

When our children were young, in spite of the demanding schedule we had, Phyllis and I made sure to keep in touch with nature. We would trailer our horses to the mountains, park, get the horses out, saddle them, and go horse backpacking, taking off for a couple of days and living off the fish we would catch and what we could carry in our saddle bags. As the children got older, we took the family camping in the High Sierra for five days at a time with, again, only what we could carry by horseback. Time alone as a family was what brought us great joy.

High-mountain camping with the kids about 1985.

As our travel increased through our participation in ULI and YPO, we enjoyed sharing the discovery of new cities, countries, and cultures with them. As our children grew closer to becoming adults, we continued to make time for family adventures. One year when our two high-schoolers and three college-aged children were out of school for the summer, we had the opportunity to spend two weeks in the charming and magnificently vast state of Alaska. From fishing to viewing wildlife to listening to Phyllis read books while I drove as we covered one thousand miles, it was a wonderful trip. Though our adventures lasted only days or weeks, the memories from those trips continue to bring us together and allow us to share laughs as we look back on them.

6. Serve One Another (and others)
Phyllis has played an incredible, supportive role to our children and me. From leading the children's choir and teaching Sunday school, to donating time in the children's classrooms and designing and making cheerleader outfits and helping with 4-H, Phyllis sought out opportunities to help our children.

In looking back on his high school experience, Kevin recalls that I came to more of his football games than his own dad. As I've mentioned, my father never came to *any* of my football games even though I was captain, and I wanted to set a different example for my children. I wanted to work with each of them to help them succeed in whatever *they* wanted to do.

We also encouraged our children to serve and support others in the community at whatever capacity they could. When we held The Country Fair at Brookside Farm, each of our children had a role and

PRIORITIZING RELATIONSHIPS

made significant contributions to our ability to carry out such a massive event. For example, at only sixteen, Bonner—who, as I've mentioned, eventually took over running The Country Fair—supervised some three hundred volunteers and did a marvelous job.

By working on large volunteer projects together, we hoped to instill in our children an early confidence in their talents and the desire to share those talents for the greater good. We wanted them to feel firsthand the popular adage, "It's amazing what you can accomplish if you don't care who gets the credit."

7. Take Chances Together (and laugh when things don't work out)
Sometimes our love of adventure allowed my children to see me screw up. During the summer of 1983, I purchased a sixteen-foot catamaran (a small sailing boat with two air-filled pontoons connected by a big trampoline). Before taking the catamaran around Monterey Bay, I made sure our family took lessons in ocean sailing and bought the proper equipment, including life jackets and wetsuits, which, I was told, would protect us from hypothermia in the event we capsized and couldn't upright the boat.

My first cruise on the catamaran from Santa Cruz to Aptos around Capitola Point with our daughter Bonner and her friend was a grand voyage. The breeze was brisk, and the catamaran hummed across the ocean waves. We sailed into the shore for a perfect landing and dragged the boat up onto the sand by the house. The rest of the family cheered and photographed this momentous occasion.

The next day, I returned to the ocean for another adventure, this time with our daughter Michelle and her friend, Susie, who were both strong swimmers. We donned our wetsuits and life jackets and

175

set out for the voyage. Our boat skimmed across the waves, reaching speeds of more than 15 knots. We sailed more than a mile out, and with the swells, we couldn't even see people on the shore. By our third trip out, we were really flying. Then, crisis: we hit a huge swell and did what is called a pitch pole dive. The boat flipped over, nose first. And although we had been trained in how to right the boat, our combined strength couldn't make up for the fact that the pontoons were taking on water!

My heart sank as I remembered the final instructions of the salesman. "When you get home and leave your boat overnight on the beach, be sure to remove the plugs from the pontoons, otherwise someone might maliciously remove the plugs. But, be sure to put the plugs in before you sail again," he warned, "or your pontoons will fill with water and you'll be unable to upright the boat."

That was exactly what had happened. I had removed the plugs, but in our excitement to sail I had forgotten to replace them before we embarked on our voyage. I was honest with the girls about my mistake and that we would have to make a difficult choice. We could try to make the swim to shore or stay with our mostly submerged boat—not knowing if help was coming or not.

We hoped Phyllis, who told us she would watch us with her binoculars, had called for help (which she had), but the rescuers were slow to respond. We waited an hour and then made the decision to swim ashore. We said a prayer, and staying close to one another and very grateful for our wetsuits and life jackets, we set off on our long swim back.

About two hundred yards from the shore, help finally arrived. When they got to Michelle, she objected to being "rescued" because she'd come so far. "Let me swim!" she said. But, they prevailed and pulled her to shore on a life preserver. Soon after, the Coast Guard showed up and towed the catamaran to shore. I never forgot the plugs again!

Although frightening at the time, the story has become one of my daughters' favorites to tell. It was a great learning experience, and it brought us closer together.

8. Make and Keep Traditions

In 1957, my father started the "Annual Poverty Hill's Duck Conference," his way of referring to the opening day of hunting season. He had a very dry sense of humor, and when he created the Poverty Hill's Duck Club, he assumed the position of executive director and told all of the members that they were also part of his executive committee, which, among other things, did *not* give them a right to vote. He would send out reminders for membership dues on official letterhead, and, when the ducks were low in count, he'd remind everyone that a beautiful blue sky and good fellowship were still to be enjoyed by attending.

I have enjoyed carrying on that wonderful tradition of hunting and camaraderie at our ranch in Mariposa, along with the spring roundups. Despite the challenges and distractions that life might throw our way, those are events that, as one of my closest friends, Jim Klingbeil, says, "We don't cancel."

Our children credit our Mariposa ranch weekends with helping them keep on the straight and narrow as teenagers. They did their best to complete their homework and steer clear of any discipline issues that would result in us saying, "Okay, you can't go to Mariposa." As Sandy put it when thinking back to those memories, "I wanted to be with them. They were happy and fun. And, it was more interesting, probably, than what my other friends were doing."

9. *Live* Your Priorities

When others see that you're committed to your priorities and that you act on them, it builds trust. As I've mentioned, Phyllis and I attend church because we believe in *showing* our children that commitment to faith is one of our core values.

Phyllis has personally demonstrated what it means for community service to be a priority in life. Her decades-long dedication to improving public education and her founding role in the Community Partnership for Families of San Joaquin (CPFSJ)—which has helped thousands of individuals and families break the cycle of generational poverty and prepared children of those families for success in school—have left an indelible impression.

10. Love Unconditionally

Everything you possess is temporary, so appreciate it. Cherish the relationships you have, and put in the work to keep them healthy. The longer they last, the more you will realize the blessing they are to your life.

Dino reflected on what our sixty years of friendship means to him:

> You can count on this person to love you notwithstanding your defects—which is really, to me, the definition of real love. You know, sixty years of that, and you still want to be friends, and you still want to see each other. That means that you accept each other's imperfections along with the positive things. And you say, "I love this package, and I'm not trying to change you." That's what sixty years is.

Taking the time to foster relationships is one of the surest ways to remember *why* relationships are worth the time and effort, and so central to our happiness and well-being.

Digging In: When a Dream Comes to Fruition
Creating Shady Oaks

Ranches have been a tipping point in my life. From growing up on my parents' ranch in Bellota and returning there with my new bride, to raising our kids between the G Ranch, Brookside Farm, and Shady Oaks—each has shaped the course of my life.

When Brookside was developed to the point that it was too citified for us country folks (neighbors were complaining that the chickens would crow and the cows would moo), we knew it was time to move on.

That was 1988, and at the time we were in escrow to buy a 1,300-acre farm in Lodi. We were aware of 20 acres, covered by 250-year-old majestic oaks, on the center of the farm's eastern property line. It was owned by three different owners, but we believed that 20-acre grove (surrounded by the other 1,300 acres we were buying) could be a terrific home site and completely secure our eastern boundary if we could pull the three parcels together. One of the parcels—a two-and-a-half-acre site with a nice home—was listed for sale, so we bought it and started negotiations with the two remaining landowners, closing on them within a few years.

There was a lot of work to be done. Despite abandoned chicken coops, a falling-down barn, and weeds and thistles that grew almost head high, we saw the potential. Majestic oaks ranging from young trees to matriarchs and patriarchs of 250 years towered above the dirt and dust. What history they could tell if their leaves could talk!

In 1992, we began our plans for the property, which we decided to call "Shady Oaks." By then, we had done a significant amount of travel due to our involvement in ULI and YPO. Phyllis had kept a comprehensive scrapbook of different transferable concepts in architecture and design that we had seen and loved. We were deeply influenced by beautiful European gardens and homes and the sense of history our travels exposed us to. Phyllis began interviewing architects with these influences in mind.

Each came back with either a contemporary house or, what we would call, a "contemporary castle," with plaster falling off to expose the underlying brick. To us, the designs looked too contrived.

Phyllis got frustrated, so I suggested she talk with Robert Arrigoni, who had designed homes for The Grupe Company. Every architect doesn't fit every person, but I had a feeling it would be useful if they just talked.

As we sat at our dining-room table with Bob, Phyllis thumbed through her scrapbook of ideas, describing what she envisioned and how we wanted this home to pay homage to the oaks. We didn't want a big two-story house that would compete with them. We wanted it to look like the home could have been built a hundred years ago, and, if you didn't have a car or anything in front of it, you wouldn't know any better. He listened and in about five minutes sketched the exact front of our house onto a piece of tissue paper. It's never changed.

But that was just the beginning! Creating Shady Oaks was an adventure. All the wood in the house is recycled. In our quest to find what we wanted, we went up to Oregon and looked at some beams taken out of old timber mills and made from heartwood milled 150 years ago. We went to Rocky Mount, North Carolina, to select the wood for the cabinetry, all old heart pinewood. We settled on floors of reclaimed virgin Douglas Fir milled in the nineteenth century and previously used to build warehouses in Chicago.

We designed the cabinetry as well as the casting on the fireplaces. The ironwork was done by a young man who had been a horseshoer.

Hand-carved wood doors, custom ironwork-adorned doors and gates—there are personal touches throughout.

Pulling all of these pieces together took talent. Our contractor, Steve Saccone, provided direction to the people painting tiles and the fellow who arranged the logs (from Montana) to create my favorite room—my office. It's designed to look like you're inside a log cabin, complete with mountings on the wall that reflect my love for hunting and art pieces that reflect my appreciation for history. The fireplace in the room is framed with river rocks selected by our grandchildren from the river that runs through our Mariposa ranch.

We found a wonderful landscape architect from the Bay Area with an even more wonderful name—Jonathan Plant. Isn't that just the best name for a landscape architect? As a team, we transformed Shady Oaks from a dump into a beautiful park and garden. Jonathan designed the garden so that there is always something in bloom.

And of course, we had to have a lake! A five-acre lake was designed to fit outside the drip line of the precious oaks.

It's a beautiful place, but it's not without work. We are blessed and thankful for those who helped bring our vision to life and who continue to help maintain the property. Everyone has taken so much pride in what they do. That's something Phyllis and I will always remember; those who helped us build out our dream wanted it to be perfect, too.

We enjoy living so close to our orchards and vineyards. For about fifteen years, we ran our purebred cattle operation here and had a sale barn where we held auctions. Shady Oaks also became one of the finest driving venues in the world for the sport of combined driving, which I tell you more about in Part Two. For more than twenty years, hundreds of our equestrian friends enjoyed competing through endless roads winding through orchards and vineyards perfect for drivers, horses, and carriages alike.

Today, the barn is relatively quiet. Phyllis's and my days of competing are a fabulous memory. I competed until I was eighty-one. To compete at my level required three days of training per week. So, after twenty years, I decided to drive just for pleasure. We're now turning land that had once been used for driving to agricultural purposes.

Shady Oaks is the center of our family, with both Sandy and Mark living on the property with their families, as well as some adult grandchildren and three great-grandchildren. I enjoy working with Mark on farming projects in our apples, walnuts, cherries, olives, and vineyards, and my home office (and dining-room table) is often a hub of farming and corporate activity.

The details of Shady Oaks remind me of the wonderful journey I've shared with Phyllis and our children. To have such proximity to our family, animals, and orchards—all that Phyllis and I dreamed of so long ago—is the ultimate reward.

And it's nowhere near over! I hope I never see my newest orchard or community at its peak. As long as I am of sound mind and body, why not start the next one?

Solid Foundation

As you go after your dream, bear in mind that true success means achieving while staying true to your core values. It means making time for your faith, spouse and family, friends, occupation, the community, and personal interests. A solid foundation not only brings joy, but it also offers protection

> *As you go after your dream, bear in mind that true success means achieving while staying true to your core values.*

when the winds of fortune turn, and the harsh, unexpected realities of life strike. The stronger your foundation and the more optimistic your outlook, the more resilient you'll be.

Let's take a closer look now at how I have weathered setbacks.

Photos

Home & Family

One of our favorite photos from Phyllis's 70th birthday party, 2010.

Poppies in the spring at our home at Shady Oaks (built 1993–1995).

Driving my champion team of beautiful Dutch Warmbloods into Brookside Country Club for my 80th birthday party. Daughters Michelle and Sandy as grooms and Phyllis at my side, 2017.

Surrounded by grandkids and great-grandkids at my 80th birthday party at Brookside Country Club, 2017. All wore white hats to identify as grandkids. The great-grandkids, Clara & Evelia, wore pink. Baby Zeya took a nap.

Grupe Developments

The Grupe Company's first redevelopment in downtown Stockton, 1980. We restored and brought up to code the historic Bank of America building and established the headquarters of the Grupe Commercial division and The Grupe Company boardroom on the top floor.

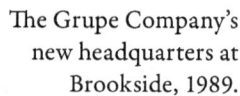

The Grupe Company's new headquarters at Brookside, 1989.

A view of waterfront living and offices at Quail Lakes.

The Country Fair

"King of the Cowboys" Roy Rogers and Dale Evans were the headliners at our first-ever Country Fair.

Our family with 1989 Country Fair headliner Reba McEntire.

Left to right: (back row) Mark, Bonner, Kevin, Michelle, and me; (front row) Sandy, Meredith, Reba, and Phyllis.

A bird's-eye view of The Country Fair at Brookside Farm, 1984, the year Kenny Rogers headlined and two thousand attended.

Mariposa Roundup

Storytelling at the Mariposa Roundup, 1980. Moving clockwise from me (in white): brother-in-law Wil Smith, Doug Eberhardt (president of Bank of Stockton), Ed Stanley (International President of YPO), and cousin Tim Hachman.

Kids on horseback at the Mariposa Roundup. The bus in the background shuttled families up to the day's festivities.

The power behind the scenes at the Mariposa Roundup and The Grupe Company. Margie Barnes (my first assistant) and her successor, Ann Quinn.

G Centennial & Family Branding

Celebrating the G Centennial with our children in Mariposa, 2017. Left to right: Bonner, Sandy, Mark, Phyllis, me, and Michelle.

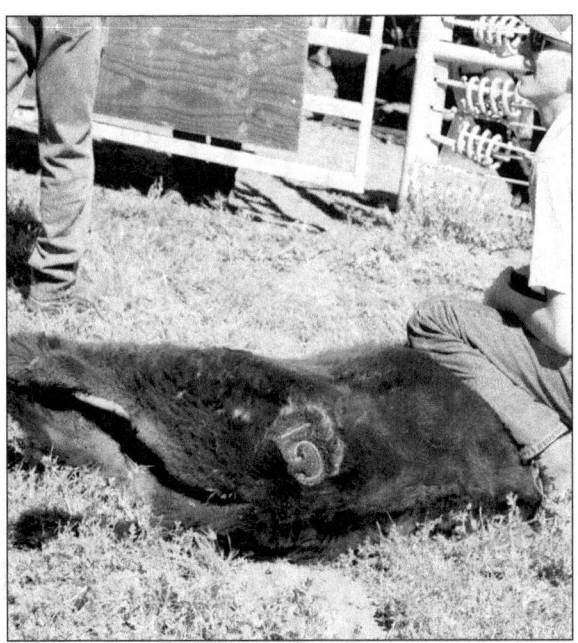

Fresh G brand with grandson Dervin Murphy pinning calf, 2017.

Hunting

With Dino, my friend and partner in Brack Track Ranch, 1981.

A note from Dino on the photo: The end of a successful first year and the contemplation of many more!

With grandson Fritz Huber at Greenhead Duck Club, located in the Butte Sink in Northern California, 2001.

With son, Mark, at Greenhead, 2014.

With grandson Davis Grupe at Greenhead, 2016.

Bohemian Campmates, Spouses & Friends

Joining campmate John O'Connor and his wife,
Supreme Court Justice Sandra Day O'Connor, at campmate
Bo Callaway's "Callaway Gardens" in Georgia, circa 1995.

We brought Firestone (Phyllis's champion Belgian draft horse)
to the opening of campmate Robert Mondavi's Opus One Winery.
Pictured here with Robert and his wife, Margrit, 1991.

Sitting with Pelican campmates at the Bohemian Grove, famed WWII pilot Jimmy Doolittle (center) and Dana Leavitt of Transamerica Corporation, 1987.

Ed and Cathy Rasmuson host us, along with the Browns, Voits and Eberhardts, for fishing in Alaska. Pictured here in front of the float plane at their Golden Horn Lodge.

California Leaders

First lady of California Maria Shriver Schwarzenegger visits us to promote literacy in San Joaquin County. Her security is caught off guard when I take her for an impromptu trip around Shady Oaks farm in my carriage.

Ronald Reagan, campaigning for second term as Governor of California visits our home in Lincoln Village West on his way to victory, 1972.

Excursions with Friends

In Nepal looking for rhinos and leopards with the Klingbeils and Cortopassis, 1985.

High Sierra Camps in Yosemite (fifty-seven-mile hike in five days), 1997.

Left to right: Jim and Sally Klingbeil, Jackie and Jiggs Davis, Patti Garamendi, and Phyllis.

Foreground: John Garamendi and me.

Visiting Bill and Debbie Harlan at their Napa Valley home and vineyard. Left to right: Bill Harlan, Sally Klingbeil, Deborah Harlan, me, Phyllis, and Jim Klingbeil, 2012.

Combined Driving

Driving my team of Dutch Warmbloods through the water obstacle, winning the Shady Oaks Triple Crown, 2016.

On my way to winning the 2005 U.S. Championship with Magnum and Ravell storming the water hazard at the Black Prong Combined Driving Event.

Winning the U.S. Singles Championship with Umico in 2009.

World Championship

Phyllis and I representing the U.S.A. on the U.S. Equestrian Team in Salzburg, Austria, 2005.

Navigating the marathon with coach Koos de Ronde at the 2005 World Games in Salzburg, Austria.

Draft Horse Days

One of four appearances in the Tournament of Roses Parade.
Driving the parade's Grand Marshal, Bob Newhart, in 1991.

Phyllis and her pair of Belgian draft horses carry the
Pasadena Tournament of Roses Association's president, 1991.

Part Two

Being Resilient

*I*N PART ONE, we looked at building a foundation on solid principles and values that have helped me, and others, move toward our goals.

In my life I've found joy and satisfaction by focusing on achieving, not achievement—but what about when neither of those seems to be happening? What about when things go wrong?

My now-deceased friend, Claude Ballard, past president of ULI and head of real estate for Goldman Sachs, said to me on a quail hunt at our ranch below Yosemite, "When the shit hits the fan, it's not distributed equally!" How true.

I've been dealt some pretty bad hands. I didn't know you could get that many bad cards at once, but I did. One thing we can always count on is that change is coming—and it won't always dovetail with our plan or vision. Sometimes, it'll even threaten to derail us completely.

The question isn't whether there will be change, but how we choose to handle it. Placing blame and playing the victim is a sure path to failure. On the other hand, accepting responsibility for the problem is the surest path to finding solutions.

Being resilient is as much about knowing when and how to adapt as it is knowing when to pull the pin and quit. It's important to understand your limits. I like the story of the six-year-old who asks her mom, "When Daddy comes home late, why does he seem tired and grumpy?" Mom answers, "Well, your daddy has a big job that takes him a lot of time, and he has a lot of work to do." So the six-year-old replies, "Why don't they put him in a slower class?"

Knowing your limits and sticking to them is especially important when it comes to your values and life balance. Surrounding myself with people who share the same values and whose advice I trust has kept me on track and given me a strong network to tap into during setbacks.

Now, having made it to the other side of many setbacks, I see how they were opportunities to learn and gain confidence. You can't stop setbacks from happening, but you can control how you respond and how quickly you bounce back.

Chapter 12

Accepting Consequences

*W*HEN PHYLLIS AND I WERE dating, we visited one of my fraternity brothers at his parents' home. His father was the chief financial officer for American industrialist Henry Kaiser, and they had a lovely home in the Bay Area. We were in the backyard, and the setting and mood were right, so I swept Phyllis off her feet and declared, "I'm going to carry you across this lily pond."

Well, it was dark, and what I *thought* was a lily pond was actually the cover on a swimming pool. I had never known anyone with a swimming pool, let alone knew they even made covers for them. You can imagine what happened after I took two giant, gallant steps—we broke right through and were submerged in water. We didn't have a proper change of clothes—this was at a necktie party—so we had no choice but to return to the other guests, sheepish and dripping wet. Phyllis's soaked wool dress immediately began to shrink, and our friend was visibly annoyed. The worst part was facing his parents the next morning. I offered to pay for the cover, and while they were understanding and generous, at the time it was humiliating.

Now, this is just an embarrassing story that we've enjoyed sharing over the years, but it illustrates a simple truth: Life is full of surprises. Inexperience, misjudgment, the nature of life—there are many reasons *why* things happen. But I've learned that, rather than dwelling on *why* it's much more productive to focus on *what now*.

The Power of Accepting Bad News

The Bible says that life won't be easy, so why are so many people surprised when they're tested and things don't go according to plan? Why is it so easy to forget that God loves us and that there *is* a purpose? Challenges, setbacks, and accidents are educational opportunities that, when viewed with the right attitude, can strengthen us and carry us to even greater heights.

I've had a lot of physical injuries. Some people might even say I'm accident-prone. The injuries really aren't that remarkable in and of themselves until you add up all ten or fifteen.

Some were the result of naiveté, such as severing two fingers (which were thankfully saved) as a toddler when I picked up a sharp piece of glass in my grandparents' backyard. Others were the result of misjudgment, like when I drove my motorcycle through a gate I couldn't see in the dark. Quite a few weren't really my fault at all, such as being hit in the face with a baseball bat in grammar school, being in a car accident caused by a drunk driver, getting run over by a tractor trailer (which broke my collarbone), or having my horse throw me into a barbed-wire fence. A number were a byproduct of having an active, sports-driven lifestyle, such as breaking my nose in football, my knee and shoulder during skiing accidents, and eight

ACCEPTING CONSEQUENCES

ribs (and collapsing a lung) when I was thrown from my carriage and hit a telephone pole while competing in France in preparation for the Equestrian World Games. With every injury, I kept the attitude that I had been lucky. Each accident *could* have always been far worse, and many could have been fatal.

As I learned with each physical injury, recovery comes down to your will, attitude, and how you go about handling it. As Phyllis once shared when reflecting on a serious carriage driving accident she endured, "If you're going to do something competitively, you have the essential ingredients for an accident to happen. I don't think any of our accidents have ever developed into a fear. Some were judgment calls or lack of experience; others were just things that have happened that were totally out of everybody's control."

If you can learn to *mentally* weather a setback, that's half the battle of adapting and adjusting your plan. For example, when Stockton passed a moratorium on building north of the Calaveras River in 1978, where the land we'd been planning to develop was located, that decision by the city council stopped our development business in Stockton dead in its tracks.

Now, I could have said, "This regulation has control of my future," or "The City *caused* me to have to quit business." But instead, I chose to have the attitude, "If they don't want me in Stockton, somebody else wants me because I'm good at what I do. I'll just go to another city and do my thing."

So I did just that. I went to Sacramento. I went to Bakersfield. I went to Modesto. I got the hell out of town. The sun doesn't rise and set only on Stockton.

If I would've said, "I'm the victim," like some builders did, think of all the opportunities I would have missed, such as enjoying Brookside

Farm for as long as we did. When we started building out of state—a result of that moratorium—I had only been to Stateline, Nevada, a couple of times growing up and once to Hawaii, having won the incentive trip I described. Talk about a new adventure! My skill set as a businessman improved greatly because we were forced out of town—so how can I not be grateful?

Turning Weaknesses into Strengths
To be resilient means learning how to work with the hand that's dealt, which includes what we see as our own personal weaknesses. Viewed with the right attitude, sometimes it's our challenges that set us apart and allow us to reach greater heights.

As I've already mentioned, dyslexia has been a struggle for me since the early days of elementary school. It's certainly not helpful when you're trying to read and do math. But none of that stopped me from getting pretty good with numbers or, generally, from going after the things I wanted. I pushed myself to figure out a way to work around that handicap and turned it into a positive in my life.

As it happens, I might not be the only businessperson who's done that. Dr. Julie Logan, a professor of entrepreneurship at the Cass School of Business, City University, London, has found that 35 percent of the entrepreneurs she surveyed in the United States were dyslexic and shared several traits: a clear vision for their business, a confident and persistent attitude, a proclivity to ask for help and delegate, and strong (as well as charismatic) oral communication skills. Her research is also starting to show that dyslexic entrepreneurs give a lot of credence to intuition.

I had known my friend Chuck Schwab, another Northern California YPO'er, for more than five years before I found out that he was dyslexic. Just look at what he has accomplished. He is one of the most visionary entrepreneurs of our time. And talk about tenacity and being able to be a comeback king—he is *it*.

Consider what you identify as your weaknesses and whether you can turn them into strengths. Find them, refine them, and use them to your advantage.

Preparation Pays Off

The more you go for it, the greater the odds that things will go wrong. But that's better than the alternative—not going for it and missing out on a lot of great opportunities. It's better to aim high and miss than to aim low and hit.

I enjoy and thrive on risk, but I don't like to take *undue* risks. I believe in being prepared. As the Bible teaches, "For which of you, desiring to build a tower, does not first sit down and count the cost, whether he has enough to complete it?" (Luke 14:28 RSV) When we started developing Lincoln Village West in 1966, we were a company of only four working out of a one-room office. And we were *young*. I was twenty-eight, and my second-in-command, Frank Passadore, was twenty-six. There was a lot we didn't know, but we approached each challenge with the attitude, *Hell, yeah, we can figure it out*. At those ages, we hadn't failed much yet.

Even in 1969 with Lincoln Village West well underway, just twenty-seven of us comprised the "LILVAL Gang." Halfway through building Lincoln Village West, we formed The Grupe Company. Our first project was Quail Lakes, a 542-acre development just south of my father's Lincoln Village, which got city council approval in 1974. Ten years later, we had grown to five hundred employees and $350 million in revenue, with projects in nineteen cities and eight states.

As the company expanded, we tasted success but also felt growing pains. As you can imagine, for each of those nineteen cities, we were dealing with unique and differing city staffs, planning commissions, city councils, codes, economies, and weather. There was a lot to keep track of, a lot to learn, and endless opportunities for setbacks.

The bigger we grew, the more there was at stake, and I knew it. In the back of my mind, there was always the constant warning from my father: "You know, Fritz, you're going to be like the other big builders. You're going to get bigger and bigger and bigger until you take too much risk, and then you're going to go broke."

With my father at the Quail Lakes groundbreaking, 1974.

It didn't take me long to see that, as my responsibility expanded, it required new skills to manage everything efficiently and keep control of operations. As Robert Powell, who developed some of the most beautiful communities in all of Sacramento, said to me around that time, "One of these days you've got to decide whether you want to be the biggest builder or the richest. And, they're usually different." At his death, Bob left $125 million to UOP (and wasn't even an alumnus), so he had learned how to do well in a cyclical and tricky business, in a single city—Sacramento.

I *knew* the development business was risky. That's why I took a number of precautions to put me in the strongest position possible:

1. I started diversifying by having multiple streams of income so if everything went to hell in development and construction, I'd still be able to live off the cash flow of the income properties I had built, as well as my farming operation. My goal was always to build enough assets so that I could live off of something other than real estate development.
2. I increased the net worth of my company by leaving most of the profits in so that the company's net worth grew to be high enough that banks would accept the company (not me personally) as the guarantor of the loan because of its assets.
3. I made sure that the company had a lot of liquidity.

Solid measures, right?

But no matter how much you plan for setbacks, they can still get you.

You Can't Win Them All

We all taste failure. What I've learned from interacting with people at the pinnacle of success is that they are still human. They go home and struggle with the same problems as everybody else. Even research-based decisions don't pan out sometimes for a variety of reasons. But viewed in the right perspective, failure is a sign that you're reaching for more. As Norm Augustine, my Bohemian Grove campmate and former CEO of Lockheed Martin, and his coauthor Kenneth Adelman said in their book *Shakespeare in Charge: The Bard's Guide to Leading and Succeeding on the Business Stage* (1999), "Those who don't fall short every once in a while are not stretching, either themselves or their teams, to go beyond ordinary activities into extraordinary challenges and successes."

Here are a few examples of projects that did not work despite being based on sound research we had available at the time:

In the early 1990s, we developed thirty-six luxury homes in Topanga Canyon in Los Angeles County before pulling the pin and changing direction. As I reflected on that project with my executives, many of us couldn't help but laugh in disbelief over the endless stream of challenges and setbacks we faced from all directions. As Nelson Bahler, our general counsel who has worked with the company for forty years, recalled, "*Everything* went wrong in that project, starting from the decision to buy it."

It was a long entitlement process to begin with, but we finally received city council approval. We decided to close on the purchase of the land even though the public still had thirty days to appeal that decision. We took the risk, assuming no one was going to appeal. Of course, someone appealed. It took two years until a resolution was reached. By then the market had changed, affecting our projections for the development.

And that was just the beginning. An uncommonly wet winter led to flooding, and the pressure of the soil collapsed parts of the retaining wall, which was made out of clay. Since the project was up in the canyons along a ridgeline, the homes were right under that crib wall, and we had to come up with about $5 million more than our budget to repair it.

That subdivision would still be affected by several additional delays: the 1993 Malibu firestorm (which didn't impact the buildings but delayed construction), the 1994 Northridge earthquake, the discovery of Native American remains, and—to top it all off—residents of the development suing the County in 1996—and later us—for failing to enforce regulations, which boiled down to our not installing fire sprinklers in the homes, a decision we made because the fire department produced a letter stating we didn't need to install them. A story like this could talk a lot of people out of going into the development business altogether. We stayed in the business but got out of that canyon!

Or, sometimes you'll discover that, even when you're at the leading edge of innovation, you're at the bleeding edge when it comes to profits. In 2009 with Green Home Solutions, we got into the business of making homes more energy efficient. When I first started building homes in the late 1960s, the building code only required two inches of ceiling insulation because energy was so cheap and wall insulation was optional. Most people didn't even install insulation because their utility costs were so low—$10 per month. Unlike today, the utility companies were trying to get consumers to use *more* electricity rather than conserve.

Green Home Solutions was—and is—a solid and timely concept, but we just weren't able to grow it to a big-enough scale to justify the effort. It took us three years just to get in the black. There's a whole bunch of reasons why Green Home Solutions didn't do better. The public financing for the homeowners we were counting on didn't come through, and the market wasn't ready to pay for the improvements. Everyone talks about being green, but they aren't always ready to write the check. We also weren't always the lowest-cost producer because we guaranteed our work at the highest ethical standards and wouldn't promise things that shouldn't be promised, like some others in the industry. While we've helped a lot of people save substantially on their energy bill, and done probably $10 million worth of retrofits, we have not been able to figure out how to make a profit in this industry, but neither have our major competitors who have operated at a much larger scale. So, unable to make a reasonable profit, we pulled the pin in 2017 after considering opportunity cost.

Even going back as far as 1982, I had to accept that sometimes major decisions don't pan out. After The Grupe Company bought a Sacramento real estate company, Olympic Realtors, we lost half of the four hundred agents within the first year. The problem was a culture difference. We treated our agents like employees and gave them all the benefits of an employee, such as healthcare. So when we acquired Olympic Realtors, we changed their commission structure to reflect ours, which had worked well for our Stockton employees. But the Sacramento agents just didn't value it, so they quit. At first, we were surprised. We wondered, *What's wrong with these people?* In time, we ended up changing over to higher commissions with fewer benefits as we realized our agents preferred it that way.

I haven't escaped trial and error in farming, either. I entered the olive oil business in 2002 by planting a 270-acre orchard based on the research and advice I had at the time. As it turned out, the olives in this particular microclimate didn't work as well as expected, and we had invested $10,000 an acre—that's $2.7 million, not counting the land it takes to plant it. And it would be another five years before we would be able to determine our production capabilities.

These olives—and the investment—were supposed to last for fifty years, but after about seven years, I had an opportunity-cost decision to make. I could keep a crop that made a small profit or go for a crop that had three times the potential. Production had been 80 percent of what I had expected, and so I chose to pull out 170 acres of olive trees. I left 100 acres under the power lines in case I was wrong. Then I started all over again—this time with walnuts, which look like they will make three times the profit of olives—knowing it would be another seven years before I'd learn if I was right and see any profit from the new plantings. Why not, right? I'm only eighty-one years old.

Owning up to failure isn't easy. As U.S. President John F. Kennedy said on April 21, 1961, during a news conference, and as most CEOs would attest, "There's an old saying that victory has a hundred fathers and defeat is an orphan."

Failure is part of playing the game—a necessary and unavoidable part. It's probably no coincidence that the leaders in home-run hits are on another important list—those who have struck out the most. You can't hit a home run if you don't swing!

When failure occurs, be grateful you had the chance to try, and *keep going*. Remember, the big picture is worth it!

You Can't Plan for Everything

Sometimes, things will go wrong that have nothing to do with choices or decisions you've made. When you're in a cyclical industry like real estate or farming, you can expect that some periods will be leaner than others and that you will lose money some years.

Consider the impact of the weather for farmers. You know it's going to rain, but you just don't know when. Boy, don't I wish I could know if it'll rain on my cherries next May! Statistically, it won't—*except* when it does.

One of the best ways to mediate risk is to try to anticipate it. Augustine and Adelman suggest companies compile a "worry list" that identifies the top events that could most easily put their business in danger and anticipates consequences, the cost of prevention, and the likelihood of occurrence. But what happens when you get hit with issues that never even made it on that list?

Most of the big setbacks I've had weren't caused by to-be-expected cycles of the market or identifiable consequences to decisions I made. They resulted from the *unforeseen, unforeseen*—events I had no way to anticipate. For example, I did not foresee the savings-and-loan industry disappearing overnight in the late 1980s. I could not foresee a housing bubble in 2006 lasting as long as it did and breaking many of the large banks and Wall Street firms in the United States. Those events cost me a lot of money, but I can't blame only myself. I could say I should have never taken those kinds of risks, but if you only act out of fear, then you're never going to try anything.

It didn't take long into my career to learn that things happen in life that you cannot anticipate—but you still need to take responsibility for them. While developing Lincoln Village West, I had the opportunity to assist with the development of the Bear Valley Ski Resort, situated in Alpine County between Lake Tahoe and Yosemite. The family I bought my purebred horned Herefords from had owned property in Bear Valley since 1952. In 1963, their son acquired acreage north of the family property with the vision to develop a complex for winter sports.

ACCEPTING CONSEQUENCES

I had been buying cattle from the family since 1951, and they asked if I'd be interested in building the first condos up there as well as the day lodge. At that time, few had building experience in the Sierras, let alone flatland guys like us. But we jumped at the chance because we saw a demand and thought it sounded like fun. I thought we'd just go up there and bang them out in the summer. Well, I was wrong.

We soon realized what it meant to build in the Sierras—building roofs to accommodate snow loads and melting issues, and the effect of blizzards on construction timetables. Frank Passadore, who had become the head of construction for the company by this point, and I had a lot to learn about what to expect while building in the snow. For example, we started to notice in weekly reports that labor was going over quite a bit, in terms of budget and schedule, as productivity had really slowed. So, we made the long drive up to give our crew a pep talk.

Once we got there and opened the car door, we were overwhelmed by the freezing temperature (it was about three degrees above zero) and strong winds. We immediately realized why production had slowed and reduced our rehearsed pep talk to just one sentence: "Keep her going, boys!"

Around the same time, my cousin, Bud Klein—a great businessman and an incredible athlete with two stadiums named after him and his family, at UOP and Stanford, respectively—got a contract to buy the deeded portion of the land that is now Kirkwood Meadow Ski Resort. We invested as a partner with Bud to be the developer of Kirkwood and to build the first condos there, too. This was before Carson Pass was open in the winter, so we'd go as far as we could by car and then take skimobiles the rest of the way. We took on a lot of debt to build the condos as well as the chair lifts, but we expected to draw people from the Valley and Bay Area to help recoup our costs. Everything was looking promising.

Then, in the year we opened Kirkwood, there was an unprecedented gas shortage caused by the Organization of the Petroleum Exporting Countries (OPEC) embargo on oil. We got hammered because people couldn't get gas to come to our ski resort. How in the hell do you plan for that?

The unforeseen is knowing you're going to have a bad snow year. The *unforeseen, unforeseen* is an oil embargo. It's the *unforeseen, unforeseen* that can kill you. If we would have had 100 percent of our capital tied up in there, the project would have been toast.

In 1986, the *unforeseen, unforeseen* pulled the rug out from under me when the Tax Reform Act of 1986 broke the savings-and-loan industry, which financed 50 percent of the housing industry of America. I was left with a $500 million unfunded loan commitment and ten thousand housing units under construction, and a lender that was taken over by a federal-government entity who refused to finish funding their committed loans. At the time, I was listed as one of the housing giants of the United States, and I prided myself on my integrity and the quality of my work. But now, despite our preparations and research, the *unforeseen, unforeseen* had hit and was threatening to destroy everything we had built.

We could have thought of ourselves as victims (I mean, who would expect such a big institution to fold or the government to leave us high and dry?), but thinking that way or focusing on the unfairness wouldn't get us anywhere. I didn't let myself think, "They control my life." Although they certainly controlled a big part of it (all my loans), I could make sure that they didn't control me or my confidence.

I knew right away that I would work my way out of it (and I explain in the next Digging In exactly how I did that), but I also knew it would take a long time. When I thought about what would happen *after* I recovered, the thought of restarting was daunting. *By the time I get through this*, I wondered, *am I going to have the guts to restart? Is anybody going to believe in me? Was my father right—did I get too big?*

All of those fears were legitimate. Sometimes the scariest part of the journey isn't the initial steps, but when it's time to reset.

The Courage to Start Again

The way we view success and failure changes as we grow and gain experience. For some who have experienced success, the definition of what constitutes failure can broaden.

I have a grandson who, after making a great professional achievement at the age of twenty-five, felt a sense of discomfort and fear. He made a sale that brought in $850,000 profit—the biggest sale in his company's history. Of course, it got a lot of attention. Despite the recognition and substantial commission, he shared with me his mixed emotions. While he was proud of his accomplishment, he asked me if it was normal to feel uncomfortable with all of the recognition. I told him it was totally normal and that I had felt that way before myself. He was probably worried that everybody would now expect him to keep making sales of that scale. He acknowledged that he was afraid of being labeled a one-trick pony.

Fearing that we fall short of other people's expectations can be as paralyzing as fearing that we can't do something at all. But it's important to work through those fears. It takes guts to restart—whether after success *or* failure. That's why you keep going one step at a time and congratulate yourself on every small achievement.

ENJOY THE RIDE

Tips for Keeping a Positive Outlook
In the next chapter, we'll take a look at the *actions* I took when things didn't go as planned and I needed to adapt, but often the first step I took was to get my head and heart in the right place. The following tips have helped me keep my attitude optimistic:

1. **Be Thankful for the Day.** Research shows that, if you work at being grateful, you will develop a more content perspective on life. I remember listening to Gerald L. Coffee, U.S. Naval Captain, who was a Vietnam War POW for seven years and spent much of his time in solitary confinement; he was happy to see a blade of grass. His faith in God and the ability to communicate with other human beings was all that kept him alive and sane. His story reminded me that having the freedom and resolve to work through difficulties is a blessing in and of itself.
2. **Keep Things in Perspective.** When things went wrong, I grew up hearing my mother say, "In a hundred years, will it make a difference?" The magnitude of a problem is determined by your perspective of the problem. If you're enjoying the journey of *achieving*, it will be easier to keep mistakes in perspective, and they won't feel so all-consuming. As I learned with every injury and accident growing up, things could *always* be worse.

> *The magnitude of a problem is determined by your perspective of the problem.*

220

ACCEPTING CONSEQUENCES

3. **Take Responsibility for Solving the Issue.** When you fall in the lion pit, don't blame the lion. Life is not fair, never has been, and never will be. How are you going to deal with the unfairness? If you blame others for your position, you transfer power and control of your life to them. Why would you want somebody to control your life?
4. **Stay Solution Focused.** Don't dwell on what went wrong—focus on how to move forward. Within the sport of combined driving, there is a competition known as obstacle/cones driving. In it, the driver and horse(s) navigate through cones that have a tennis ball resting on top. Knock off a ball or fail to keep pace with the allotted time, and you're penalized. After a less-than-stellar performance, which resulted in my dropping from first to fourth place in the overall three-day event, Phyllis gave me some tremendously useful advice for when I would next compete: "Stay between the cones and go faster."
5. **Look to Learn.** There's a saying often used in sports: "Sometimes you win; other times you learn." If you can think of problems as learning experiences versus something that should never have happened, that can make a huge difference. Founding Father Benjamin Franklin gave such good advice on the power of remaining optimistic and confident in the face of failure that I had the following quote made into a plaque so I could share it with my executives: "I didn't fail the test. I just found 100 ways to do it wrong."
6. **Talk About It.** As American singer Lena Horne said, "It's not the load that wears you down. It's the way you carry it." If you are willing to open up to other people about your problems,

you'll receive support, guidance, and a confidence boost to help you get through the rough spots. Getting what you're feeling off your chest is good. Having close, trusted friends has been of immeasurable value to me. By sharing my burdens with them, I didn't feel like the Lone Ranger when all hell was breaking loose. My friend Jim Klingbeil has been that person for me. We've had a similar ride, and I talk about how that friendship has been a source of stability for more than forty years in Chapter 17.

7. **Keep Your Word.** Honesty should be part and parcel of everything you do. Your ethics and values are what *shouldn't* change during setbacks. We all have different temptations and bait. Expect it! Be prepared to handle it. And be honest with yourself and others about your mistakes. When times have gotten really bad—such as during the savings-and-loan crisis and the Great Recession—we didn't walk away from our loans. Financially, I might have been better off walking, but it's not the way we do business.

8. **Forgive Others and Yourself.** Remember to consciously forgive people who hurt you even if no apology is offered. The first thing both U.S. President Ronald Reagan and the Pope did after being shot in 1981 was to forgive their attackers. They each knew that harboring a grudge would prevent them from healing. Grudges eat away at your soul and are more harmful than the person who hurt you. It's important to move past those heartbreaks. Be genuine in your forgiveness. As I once read: "Saying you forgive but still harboring a grudge is like drinking poison and waiting for the other person to die."

Forgiving does not mean forgetting or trusting. It means to move on and live in peace.

Accepting responsibility is different than berating yourself for your mistakes. It's okay to be frustrated and upset with yourself, but don't punish yourself by throwing in the towel on your dream. A lot of people don't like to admit when they've made a mistake because they think there is a sense of failure attached to it. I don't look at it that way. Don't attach being a personal failure to failing at a task. You have to separate the two. As my son, Mark, says, "Mistakes do not define who you are or what you can end up being."

9. **Get Back in the Game.** When things aren't going as planned, get proximate, and get to work. If you're hoping that your problems will go away—isn't that wishful thinking? If they're not going to go away, what good does it do to defer or procrastinate working on them? **Hope is not a strategy.** If you ignore what you know you need to do, it's going to nag at you forever until you solve it. You might as well get on with it. Learn from the past, keep reminding yourself of the future you want, and pour your efforts into the present.

> *Hope is not a strategy.*

And be ready to adapt.

Digging In: Dealing with the *Unforeseen,*
Unforeseen with Integrity and Confidence
Rebounding from the Savings-and-Loan Crisis

It wasn't easy being a homebuilder in the early 1980s. Under the Carter administration, interest rates had climbed to 21 percent. In that climate, we couldn't successfully sell homes.

So we adapted.

We came up with a business model that worked extremely well until the Tax Reform Act of 1986, when, as my then-manager of commercial syndications Niem Dang put it, "the party ended."

We had started an investment-condo program by 1982 and built high-quality apartments across the country. We entitled the units and built to condo standards so that they were financed as condos and appraised as condos for tax purposes—with just the paperwork to convert remaining—and then had our management company rent them out as apartments during a holding period of several years. The idea was to rent them out as apartments for cash flow and then sell them as condominiums at a later date. For the investors, this program economically benefitted them as it dwarfed their initial investment over time because of the tax deductions they could take.

Our team was crucial to the success of this program. When we started building condos for rent, that's when we *really* started expanding. In addition to Niem's key role of doing cost-benefit analysis and projections (by hand in those days), our general counsel, Christopher A. Greene, and chief financial officer, Don Benioff, were essential to the success of our operations. Can you imagine financing this stuff all over America? Or, making sure that everything complied legally?

ACCEPTING CONSEQUENCES

Chris was a partner in the Stockton law firm of Neumiller & Beardslee and joined our team in 1979. Don was the head of real estate finance at Union Bank and joined our team in 1984. I had asked the head of real estate at our two major lenders, Bank of America and Wells Fargo, independently, "Of all the bankers you know, who's the best out there?" Both answered, "Don Benioff." He was well educated, honest, and a much-respected banker who had worked his way up in the industry. After I went to Don and invited him to join our company, it took him a few months to decide whether to come on board. But he did, and he commuted the hour from Walnut Creek for twenty-four years.

Our investment condos were remarkably successful. We built ten thousand units across the country. No one built as many investment condominiums in the United States as we did. Rents were greater than calculated, and units rented sooner than projected.

Our permanent take-out lender for this venture was American Savings and Loan, the thrift unit of Financial Corporation of America, headquartered in Stockton. The president was J. Foster Fluetsch, a visionary, proven CEO. I already had a standing relationship with them as they had been financing our homebuilding operation prior to that, and they had money they were eager to invest. American Savings and Loan financed our investment-condominium program ($500 million in 1982) as well as El Capitan Development Co. ($100 million), a corporate investment and development company we formed with them in 1982 to buy distressed real estate.

American Savings and Loan was the second largest savings and loan in the country, and we were their largest borrower. So when the U.S. Congress passed the Tax Reform Act of 1986—which broke the savings-and-loan industry—to say we were impacted is a gross understatement. It was the most devastating banking collapse since the Great Depression. Our lender was taken over by the Federal Government Resolution Trust Corporation (RTC). The RTC refused to honor my $500 million loan commitment, leaving me without funding and ten thousand housing units still under construction. On top of that, our business model for the investment condos was no longer viable. The Act disallowed the very tax deductions that had made our program marketable.

To put it in perspective, for three years—starting in 1987—I was losing $10,000 an hour, $80,000 a day, $400,000 a week, and $20 million a year. Adjusted to today's money, those figures would be more than double. It was a life-changing moment, to say the least. Some might even use the word "devastating." Everything I had created within The Grupe Company was suddenly on the line.

A crisis of that magnitude can really cause you to question all your choices and actions leading up to that moment. It certainly got me thinking about how I had arrived in that situation. I had been in land development for about twenty-five years and made many breakthroughs in the field, but that hadn't shielded me from such a massive hit.

Despite all of this, I kept things in perspective. I was convinced I hadn't failed. In fact, I felt more confident than ever that all my efforts and endeavors leading up to that point had been worthwhile. Since no one else in the United States was building investment condos to the same magnitude as us, great land parcels zoned for condominiums were available. The condo-for-rent communities we built in the Bay Area like Foster City and San Ramon (also in San Diego overlooking the ocean) cost $50,000 per condo and are now worth $400,000 to $500,000. So, it was a good idea!

ACCEPTING CONSEQUENCES

been syndicated. We were able to restructure the financing so as to keep that community. When the savings-and-loan industry went under, the price of real estate dropped by 25 to 30 percent almost overnight. I had assets worth $500 million that all of a sudden were worth $300 million. Despite the drop, I had so much equity in the assets that their value was the same as the value of the loans. Considering that every other savings and loan was folding, there weren't a lot of places to go to find new lenders. As Mark Fischer, president of The Grupe Company, put it, "It wasn't like we were an anomaly, and we could just go to the next bus stop and get what we needed. There was nowhere to go." So my team did an immense amount of work to negotiate cash-flow mortgages. I got buyers to take over the properties, pay off the lenders, and leave our investors in place. Even though they were second to the new capital coming in, over time, they got their equities back. It was *a lot* of negotiation, and it took a long time, but at least their investment was not wiped out.

- We sold our *very* successful self-storage business, Mister Space—twelve large, completed, cash-flowing projects throughout Northern California—to Surguard, which was a public company, and, at the time of the sale, I joined their board. This sale allowed us to pay off a lot of our lenders.
- We refinanced and restructured the loans with Wells Fargo and Citicorp so we could pay the loans back over time. On the whole, we found people were willing to work with us because they knew our people were honorable. Bank of America's approach, however, was to "take no prisoners," and they were merciless. They demanded we pay back the loans when due *despite* our lender going broke (it was our lender who was in default, not

us) and my long-standing relationship with the bank. They treated us like a commodity. That was the start of the change in banking attitude from relationship banking to commodity banking, as I described earlier.
- ▸ One of the assets we sold was our very successful Executive Living Program, headed by Kevin Huber. In 1985 we got into the hospitality business of furnishing our apartments and renting them out on a weekly and monthly basis to corporations that needed temporary housing for their employees. By 1985 we had suites in Foster City, San Ramon, Sacramento, and Stockton, with our sights set on establishing suites in every city where we were already managing rental properties. We had more than one thousand units in that program and sold the entire business and all of our contracts—not the apartments—to Marriott in 1999 for about $9 million, which went toward paying off Bank of America, Wells Fargo, and Citicorp.
- ▸ The Franchise Tax Board also came after us, saying we owed back penalties. We worked out an amortization schedule with them.

Incredibly, we climbed out of a very deep hole without stiffing anyone. Healing and recovery were not too far off. A few years later, when we were ready, we re-entered the self-storage business saying, "Well, let's gear up and start doing it again." Likewise, by 1990, we were well underway developing what many consider to be the pinnacle of all our master-planned communities, Brookside, despite having to find a new equity partner and source of financial backing when American Savings and Loan went under.

We found an excellent equity partner in Copley Real Estate Advisors—headed by Joseph O'Connor, a very successful, proven leader—which committed capital in excess of $50 million to the development of Brookside. Copley, which managed funds for New England Mutual Life Insurance, AT&T, and The Rockefeller Foundation (to name a few), was known for judgment, decisiveness, professionalism, and honesty. Copley chose partners following a formula I have also found great success with: "They look at the people first and foremost; then they look at the market, the deal; last but not least, they look at the numbers." And as it happened, though home sales were in decline at the time, Brookside did phenomenally well.

As real estate sales slowed in the 1990s, Copley began to wind down all their real estate interests. Unlike Bank of America, they gave us plenty of notice to find somebody to buy them out.

What did we learn from this setback and rebounding from it?

- Pick your partners carefully. There are some people who will stick with you and work with you to find a solution to a problem. There are others who don't care and treat you like a commodity. I've been blessed to work with a number of partners who share the same values as I do, and I've been able to do a lot of business on a handshake.
- We were better off for accepting the consequences, as unfair as they were, and focusing on making it through.
- Reputation matters. Our reputation for being honest and ethical carried us through. The majority of our lenders were willing to work with us because they knew that our word was our bond.
- While I forgave, I didn't forget the actions of Bank of America. I never did business with them again after repaying the loan, although their management has changed, and I respect their new people. I believe greatly in having respect for the people

I work with and deal with, and once that respect and trust is broken, it's not just a minor thing.
- Choosing the higher ground was worth it. Despite the financial hit, stress, and work it required, paying back everyone in full *in spite of* the difficulty was the right decision—and one I have never regretted.

Chapter 13

Embracing Change

A PERSON'S ABILITY TO execute is only as good as their ability to adapt. The same holds true for companies.

Change is inevitable and necessary. In my eighty-one years, I've learned that nothing we do is the same as the way we used to do it. You can't continue to grow apples exactly the same way over time, just like you can't continue to develop a master-planned community in exactly the same way. The first computer we bought from IBM filled an entire room; now your cell phone's got more capability.

While you can't change the wind, as the old saying goes, you can adjust the sails.

My company has had to adapt several times when the *unforeseen, unforeseen* hit. When faced with the 1978 building moratorium as a developer in Stockton, we began our first out-of-state venture the following year—a planned community in Boise, Idaho. When interest rates hit 21 percent under the Carter administration, we started the investment-condominium program. We've survived because we're comfortable with change.

I'm sure you've seen extremely bright individuals who, for whatever reason, fail because they can't cope with change. If you can roll with the punches, you'll emerge stronger because setbacks are a great opportunity to learn and, oftentimes, to improve your product.

As I said earlier, **the magnitude of a problem is determined by your perspective of the problem.** Obstacles *can* be overcome once you identify the problem and create a new course of direction.

The Possibilities of Change

For some, change is refreshing. It's a challenge and can be educational. For others, it's frightening—a risk with the potential to cause harm. Those who think they will be hurt by change oppose it. Those who stand to benefit still hesitate, because success is not certain.

I look forward to a new challenge. I find it exciting and educational. My comfort with change has been frustrating for some of my executives. In 1981, I hired Ann Quinn—a Phi Beta Kappa from Stanford and the executive assistant to the superintendent of a local school district—as my personal assistant. I had gotten to know Ann when our company built and donated a school store for Lincoln High School, and I thought she would be a great fit as our company expanded into multiple states. She was extremely bright, reliable, hardworking, and great at interacting in the community on my behalf. She was so talented that the school district later rehired her as the chief executive of operations for Lincoln High, the first non-credentialed person in the nation to hold such a position.

Although it *was* a great fit, Ann initially found the number of times I changed my mind frustrating. With every change, she'd have to rearrange appointments or reschedule what she had already lined up (cars, hotels, airplanes). As someone who took her duties seriously and strived to meet all expectations, she was concerned that my approach was affecting her ability to do her job.

She finally approached me about it and said, "Fritz, I could do so much more if you just wouldn't keep changing your mind." I reassured Ann that I had hired her so I *could* change my mind.

That particular tendency of mine hasn't dimmed with experience or age. As my current assistant, Jewl Muela, says, "Every time we do something, there's at least eight changes, and I tell Fritz that, until we've gotten to eight changes, I figure that he's probably not through yet." She's exaggerating, of course. Sometimes I change my plans only seven times!

I stand by that proclivity. To do well in business, you've got to be flexible. How can you ignore new information? Being open to change can make all the difference in spotting deals and making them work successfully.

You've also got to be willing to change your mind when you're the one who's behind the curve. I will admit that I was slow to hire women as real estate agents. I'm sure that anybody who knows me would be surprised by that. Early on, I felt like women were just getting into the industry and brought less experience than I wanted on my team.

In fact, when I formed Grupe Realtors in 1973, I had three conditions. First, I didn't want to do it just to get my name out there. It had to make a profit. Second, I didn't want to hire anyone who wouldn't live up to my ethical standards. Third, I didn't want to hire women. Even my aunt—who turned out to be one of the best real estate agents in Stockton—said, "Fritz, I want to go to work for you."

And I said, "Ah, I don't want to deal with women." I was, regrettably, slow to change. It took me four years.

Oddly enough, I didn't have that attitude in other key aspects of the company. For example, my first architect was a woman by the name of Bernice Nickols, and, from the start, Phyllis and Lana Passadore designed the interiors of our model homes.

I was also used to women being the ones to keep financial records. Where I was raised, a lot of wives like my schoolteacher, Elsie Armanino, did the bookkeeping while their husbands worked in the field. My accounting department reflected that familiarity. When I first started as a homebuilder, Margie Barnes did my bookkeeping just as she had for Village Homes (the company whose lots I took over). And one of my key executives for the investment-condo program was Niem Dang. Born in Vietnam, Niem emigrated to the United States to attend college, earning an MBA degree from Pace University in New York and starting as a CPA for Price Waterhouse. She joined our company in 1979 in her twenties as a financial analyst but quickly advanced to vice president of Grupe Financial Company in 1984. In 2015, she retired from The Grupe Company as a senior vice president of real estate finance.

But women, as realtors, were unfamiliar to me. My dad had owned a real estate brokerage firm, and he had never hired a female real estate agent and advised against it. Seeing my dad as successful, I listened when he gave advice.

The success of women in real estate sales challenged and ultimately debunked my assumptions. Although I didn't realize it at the time, women were not only in the industry, but many could, in fact, bring quite a bit of experience, having been in the field for decades. In fact, as I was developing my second master-planned community in the late 1970s, almost half of real estate brokers were women.

Today 80 percent of our agents are women, a percentage that is higher than the national average. They are a vital part of our success, and I am *really* glad I changed my mind!

You have to let others change as well. I've always found it unfortunate that, in our political system, when one politician changes his or her mind, others are quick to say, "Well, they used to say this, and now they're saying that—when will they change next?" They're labeled a "flip-flopper" and construed as a liability, but if *I* didn't flip-flop, I'd be dead!

When new information comes along, how can you *not* adapt in response? You can't see everything at once, and new information is always coming along. You'd be foolish not to adjust your views and actions based on what you learn.

At our company, we have all been wrong enough times to know that we don't always have the right answer, especially the first time. Therefore it doesn't bother us to admit, *Oh, well—that didn't work. Let's change course here.*

Learning to Handle the Emotions of Change

When change occurs—or is on the horizon—it can be very emotional and stressful. During times of change or setback, what you *don't* do can be as important as what you *do*.

Remember my first big deal, where I helped three individuals get what they wanted by exchanging what they had (a peach orchard, a walnut orchard, and 200 acres of bare land)?

Well, the night before the deal closed, the buyer of the walnut orchard called and woke me up. "I'm not going to do the deal," he said. This was after several months of figuring out all the exchanges and doing the legal work that was required. All that remained was for him to sign papers.

I was twenty-five and one night away from making $30,000 at a time when annual salaries were $7,000—you can imagine how that statement made me feel! Think that might upset you?

"What went wrong?" I asked.

He told me the current owner of the walnut orchard had removed one of the tool chests out of his shop.

Now, this guy ran a *big* operation. There was stuff all over the place. One tool chest was missing in the middle of all the other tools? I mean, that would have been almost unnoticeable compared to all the tools that were in there. It was minor—but it set him off.

"How do you know it's not relocated?" I asked.

"No, he took it. He's that kind of a guy. I'm not going through with this."

He went on and on. At one point I offered to buy him a new toolkit as a peace offering.

"That's not it," he said. "It's the principle of the thing. I'm not going to do it."

With that, he hung up before I could get another word in. I went back to bed thinking, *Am I going to lose the biggest deal thus far in my career?*

The next morning I called the title company and told them there may be a problem and that this gentleman may not show up. To my surprise, they said, "He just came in, signed the papers, and left." I couldn't believe it!

That was a day of celebration for me, but the lead-up had been nerve-wracking, to say the least, and cause for a sleepless night.

There were a couple of ways that I could have handled my emotions when I found myself with a significant, last-minute challenge that *could* have ruined everything:

- I could have blown up and responded with anger. "You're being stupid. What are you doing? This is crazy!"
- I could have panicked and gotten others involved to share the burden of the stress, such as calling my friend Dino, who was part of the exchange.
- I could have called the accused and coaxed him to get involved and make amends if necessary.

But I didn't do any of those. It was obvious that *for the moment* he had made up his mind and that he was very emotional. It was late at night, an upsetting issue, and I saw no way of positively impacting the situation, so I chose to give it some time.

I still don't know if he was furious, drunk, or just trying to ring my chimes. I don't know if he ever remembered placing the call. He never brought it up again.

I learned early on how important and necessary it is to handle emotional and unreasonable people. When things get too overwhelming, it helps to take a step back and take a breath. In some instances, time is the best cure.

That said, stressful situations can be stepped away from for only so long. Sometimes, your only choice is to work through times of great pressure or worry. The good news is that, as simple as it might seem, the act of just showing up *significantly* improves your success rate.

In the 1980s, I turned to Harvard scholar Anthony G. Athos's research as I navigated the growing pains of an expanding company. According to Athos, 60 percent of us will succeed just by showing up. If you get there on time, your chances increase to 70 percent. If you show up on time and "dressed to play," you have a 90 percent chance of success.

Likewise, it helps to remember past accomplishments, especially during trials. When times have gotten lean at our company, I like to remind myself and others of all we've accomplished together. We touch a lot of lives positively through our various operations. Our farms and ranches annually produce meat, cherries, walnuts, olive oil, apples, and wine. Our master-planned and apartment communities have provided homes and a unique lifestyle for more than a hundred thousand residents. Thousands of people buy resale homes from us, shop in our commercial centers, lease office space in our business parks, or occupy the space in our self-storage units. Remembering these past successes and how they enable me to still have a successful business can be motivating and inspiring.

In addition, I stay close to what matters most: my faith, family, and friends. Those cornerstones always provide perspective, relief, and motivation to show up and do my best with the hand I've been dealt.

How I Embrace Change

Adapting to change takes a lot of work, and it is a choice. So the question is: Do I want to use the resources necessary to fix this problem (i.e., opportunity cost)? To help with my decision, I take the following steps:

- ▸ **study the obstacle or challenge in light of the mission**
    - ▪ Why is it a problem? And whose problem is it? What can realistically be done to solve it? I've found that if I turn my

focus to what I *can* control in times of change (versus what is not working), solutions come much more easily.

- **identify strengths that remain**
  - It's tempting to be so distracted by the problem at hand that you forget about the mission and the things that still work. I don't let myself fall into the despair trap or allow myself to become a victim. I lean on my strengths and address the weaknesses.

- **find a solution or new direction**
  - Based on the new circumstances or information, what do I now believe? As discussed before, beliefs are the basis of strategy (master plan) and tactics (action items). Exploring how to work *with* the obstacle sometimes reveals that the challenge is part of the solution. If ever there's a time for curiosity and creativity—that is, to see the opportunities perhaps others have not seen or been able to execute—it's when we must work our way through challenges to find a solution or agree on a new direction. If any member of the team doesn't buy into the new direction, no matter how smart and hardworking they might be, the team is better off without them. Successful turnarounds are tough enough—you can't have internal fighting. Each member of the team needs to be comfortable with the changes ahead and confident about going after them.

- **establish clear and measurable goals**
  - As a team, we re-examine our strategies and tactics to make sure they support our current beliefs so we can set a new

course. Part of the process is setting a deadline and following through. It doesn't help to get caught up in indecision or analysis paralysis. As I noted earlier, perfection can be the enemy of progress.

Whenever there is change, there's some level of chaos going on; somebody is going to lose from it, and somebody is going to gain. Survival comes down to the ability to embrace change. A well-known quote (often attributed to naturalist Charles Darwin) puts it this way, "It is not the strongest or the most intelligent who survive, but the most adaptable."

A Case Study of Shifting Strategy

After the 1960 Winter Olympics in Squaw Valley, California, William A. Newsom, Sr.—whose grandson Gavin is the current governor of California—was awarded a concession to operate the base of Squaw Valley. Newsom was a longtime political leader in California and well connected in the Democratic Party, having close ties with the Brown, Getty, and Pelosi families. He had managed Edmund "Pat" Brown's two campaigns for San Francisco district attorney, served as treasurer in President Harry Truman's Northern California campaign in 1948, and held an appointment during Governor Pat Brown's administration (1959 to 1967).

Around 1973, Newsom had the opportunity to exchange his control at Squaw Valley (which the State of California wanted to regain), for state-owned land in Stockton. Not wanting to develop the 542 acres himself, he interviewed Stockton developers Alex Spanos and the Stone brothers (of Stone Bros. and Associates), who would have perhaps been the logical choice as they brought substantial experience and could have paid him in cash. And then there was me, still in the beginning of my career at thirty-five years old and up to my neck in Lincoln Village West with no money to put into a new deal. You can imagine how I must have felt to have such a public figure select me to develop the land.

Why did he pick me? Well, because I was creating something in Lincoln Village West that intrigued him. Money up front was not the deciding factor. We came up with a deal that I would pay him back when I could build the homes, as well as give him 25 percent of the shopping centers to be built. And it worked out great. The Newsom family and Gordon Getty remained in a Limited Partnership with us until 1996 when the life of the partnership expired. At that time, the family requested we buy them out (which we did).

We didn't anticipate much of a learning curve when we started the development, which would come to be known as Quail Lakes. It was really an extension of the concepts we were using at Lincoln Village West, which was still underway and making us extremely proud and profitable. We used the same team that made Lincoln Village West a success, and the city was familiar with us by that point, so everybody had an attitude of, "Play it again, Sam."

Still, we spent eighteen months working with the best land planners, landscape architects, building architects, and engineers in the country to come up with something that would really show off Stockton. We designed a lake community that included 2,800 homes, two man-made lakes, two parks, and a 56-acre commercial-office development. Once again, we built our strategy around families being our market base and wanted to offer everything from workforce housing to the most expensive housing in Stockton.

In December of 1974, about five months after winning city council approval for our project, we hit a speed bump when the Stockton

Unified School District unveiled a desegregation plan that involved crosstown busing. The plan was developed to comply with court-ordered desegregation, a ruling that was in response to a class-action suit filed by California Rural Legal Assistance in 1972. The October 1974 ruling would be put into full effect in September of 1977, busing six thousand youngsters across town to their first day of school. You talk about a surprise—there's a big one. I did not foresee that there would ever be busing in Stockton.

When that happened, we had to regroup because we knew that a substantial percentage of our planned customers—families with school-age children scheduled to go to a local school who would now be bused across town—would no longer buy. Location, safety, and neighborhood schools are the features buyers care about most. Some people are willing to try new concepts on their children, but most won't take that risk. Some parents just don't want to bus their children across town far from home and family care.

We could not fight the school-busing issue. In order to succeed, we had to accept the consequence and change our direction.

We had to look at it from a perspective of *how do we make this work?* We still had a hell of a development; busing didn't alter our commitment to quality, innovation, beauty, or integrity. We still had *a lot* to offer to the right customer. We just needed a new approach.

How did we adapt? We decided to design a whole new strategy around a new market base. We changed our product mix and house designs to appeal to empty nesters and families whose children went to private schools. We encouraged some private schools to give the public schools competition—which they did. We aligned our team to the new strategy; we were able to stay strong, adapt to circumstances far outside of our control, and successfully sell the homes within the development.

Changing Direction
Lincoln Village West and Quail Lakes were just the beginning for us when it came to master-planned communities. The Grupe Company built its reputation by building state-of-the-art, lifestyle-changing master-planned communities. We became known as "The Lake Builders." Our larger communities range in size from 1,500 to 4,000 homes each and often include a shopping center or an office park. These projects required the investment of hundreds of millions of dollars over five to ten years before becoming profitable. Often, projects took up to twenty years to complete. When down cycles hit—which is inevitable over such a long period of time—it requires a strategy to stay in for the total buildout to maximize profits.

We found success in our strategy by building our own market (3,000 homes and office space) and owning the only zoned shopping center land. We still own those centers, but we had to have tenacity and the ability to hang in there. This strategy worked for us from 1965 until the mid-1990s, when the regulatory environment changed, adding so much time and cost that it was no longer a good business model for a private company of our size, especially when compared to other opportunities where we could excel with our speed and nimbleness and be in and out in a few years.

But it's hard to change direction on a model that has been working for thirty years. That's where we're headed next—to the invaluable business skill of knowing when it's time to walk away.

Chapter 14

Making Difficult Decisions: When It's Time to Pull the Pin

NOT EVERYTHING CAN BE FIXED—or is *worth* fixing, once opportunity cost is considered. There may come a time when you'll feel you've worked very hard—perhaps harder than you've ever worked—but you're stuck, frustrated, or moving forward too slowly. What then? Well, it may be that your enterprise has run its course, and it's time to start pouring your efforts elsewhere.

I can't overemphasize how difficult it is for those of us who are tenacious to stop what we're doing and change direction, but when you stick it out too long on an idea, project, or person to the *detriment* of your overall goal, tenacity can become a weakness.

> *Making difficult decisions that have significant negative financial or human impact is what I call "pulling the pin."*

Making difficult decisions that have significant negative financial or human impact is what I call "pulling the pin." The fact is, sometimes there is no "good" or "easy" decision. You have to make the tough call.

Patience and Tenacity Are Different

It takes patience, as a developer, to build a two-hundred-unit apartment complex. From the start, you know it's going to take a long time to fill each of those units with tenants. You plan for it. An investment like that is actually called *patient capital* because, while the investment won't turn a quick profit, the expected return is worth the wait.

To build a master-planned community over the course of ten years or more—that takes *tenacity* because the end product isn't exact. By the time the community makes it through the review process and receives council approval, ten years may have passed, and the market may have turned. So, building a master-planned community requires much more than patience. It demands persistence, determination, and holding on even when the future is uncertain. It truly is, as Phyllis says, "courage in action."

Tenacity is a "must" in life as well as business. Here's a current example for our company.

In November 2008, we received unanimous city council approval for the 1,900-acre master-planned community now called The Peninsula, located on Shima Tract at the very west terminus of Hammer Lane in Stockton. This exciting development is set to include twice as many homes as Brookside, as well as office space, retail, three lakes, a marina, religious facilities, schools, a vineyard with its own winery for residents to grow and produce their own wine, and a lot of open space for recreation.

It took us *years* to get everything entitled, and, by the time we did, the market had turned. We were in the Great Recession. With the housing bubble having collapsed, there was just no way to start despite receiving the green light to do so.

At that time, we were involved in entitling four other master-planned communities, each one with a minimum investment of $5 million (for the Shima Tract, we had $15 million invested). All of this on optioned land. Despite all our work and the initial investment to entitle the land on those four other communities, we pulled the pin and walked away from the investments. Were we right? Well, it's been a decade, and none of those projects have been revived since. That market still has not come back enough.

But we've been tenacious about the Shima Tract and have kept it going because we felt it was different for two reasons: the potential of its location and our great relationship with the landowner (with whom we've done business for forty years).

You have to know your limits.

Tenacity's Grip

The line between giving your best effort and hanging on longer than you should can be very fine. I've noticed my closest friends, those who take commitment very seriously, struggle with this just like I do. But all of us have learned it's good to be able to admit the mistake and just move on.

Jim Klingbeil (chairman and CEO of a national real estate company) shared with me a moment of enlightenment he had while attending a management training course. On the first day, participants were asked to write down one thing they did that helped them make the most money. Jim wrote, "tenacity." Two days later, participants were asked to write down the trait that probably lost them the most money. To this, Jim wrote, "I'm no quitter."

The very perseverance that gets you to where you are can be a hindrance that stops you from getting to the next level. If you keep going deeper in the hole, it's time to consider whether you should stop digging.

In 2001, we pulled the pin after *eighteen years* of effort. We had partnered in 1983 to bring an unprecedented 5,000-acre master-planned community to the city of Tracy in the California Central Valley. Before closing on the land, we hired a company approved by the State to conduct a study to see if there were any endangered species, in particular, kit fox. After a one-year study, they could not find any kit fox on the entire property that bordered Lawrence Livermore National Laboratory (which had thousands and thousands of acres set aside for kit fox). Upon completing the study, we closed on the land and bought it, but other permitting issues set our development date behind.

By the time we were ready, the State came back and said, "Your permit has expired. You need to study the kit fox again." So we did. *Still* no kit fox. But, because kit fox had been sighted to the north and south of our property, the Department of Fish and Wildlife required we leave a corridor so the kit fox could go back and forth. That easement for the kit fox was 3,500 acres, or, 70 percent of the land. By the time we got through all of *that,* the market had changed. It was no longer the right time to start. On top of that, in 2000, voters passed a slow-growth ballot measure that limited the average number of houses that could be built in Tracy to six hundred per year, distributed amongst several builders. Such a restriction put the project on standstill.

By around then, we had been tenacious enough. The next year, we decided we were going to give up and sell it. We got as much of our money as we could and sold it to another developer. They worked on it for another ten years or more, couldn't get it approved, and *they* sold it to another developer.

In hindsight, it always feels like you waited too long. While we lost money (and not to mention time), as I watched other developers struggle with the same project, I became more confident in our choice and especially grateful we didn't hold on for another ten years.

Deciding to Pull the Pin
I've tried more than forty businesses and pulled the pin on a good number of them. Looking back, I'm glad I tried each of those businesses, as many helped us combine stages of production, such as getting into the lumber and cabinetry business; we gained experience that helped us better understand the industry overall. But you can only do so many things well, so it's good to constantly reevaluate how the ventures you've undertaken affect your overall performance.

For a time, I tried to be all things to all people. It's tempting, especially as a young entrepreneur who sees a market and wants to do and try everything. But opportunity cost dictates that it's not a good business strategy.

When I'm deciding whether to stay in or not, I ask myself four key questions:

1. Is the opportunity cost too great? Is the project causing me to lose too many other opportunities (in terms of capital and time) in return for my efforts?

2. Has the need for the product line run out? Am I making buggy whips when there's nobody driving horses?
3. Are other people doing it more efficiently and economically than I am or willing to work for less?
4. Is it no longer enjoyable? Am I no longer having fun?

The last is especially important to me. If you're not passionate about what you're doing, I think it's best to get out. Let's take a look at each of these more closely.

Is the opportunity cost too great?
I have most often pulled the pin when the opportunity cost—the value of the opportunities I was passing up—was too high.

- In the 1970s, I thought it would be a good idea to get into the lumber business so I could buy the lumber for my houses and apartments wholesale. It was my attempt at vertical integration. We were buying from a lumber company that was undercapitalized. We thought we would buy them out, improve their management, and add more capital. That way, not only could they supply us better and cheaper lumber, but we could also sell to other builders. We tried it for four or five years, but it turned out we weren't any better at managing the business and couldn't make any significant profit. Rather than spending more energy and time (since I was doing many other things that *were* profitable), it was better to just accept that it hadn't worked out. We pulled the pin and sold it.
- For a number of years we owned Hawkeye Security Service, a video surveillance company for commercial properties with more

than fifty security officers, and it worked well as we began our Brookside development. In time, however, it no longer fit our mold. It was too small, and the profit margin wasn't big enough. Our team agreed that we had bigger fish to fry. We separated the business and sold the monitoring service to Bay Alarm and the security half to a retired police officer from the Stockton Police Department who had been running the business for us. When that business ran its course for The Grupe Company, it didn't mean it had run its course for the new owner. He has made a living at it ever since and is still in business today. For him, it's been good. But for us, it was taking time and resources away from bigger projects.

▸ In Chapter 12, I wrote about building in the Sierras from 1968 to 1973, first at Bear Valley Ski Resort and later with my cousin Bud Klein (Kirkwood Ski Resort). At the time, I was young, and the whole idea sounded pretty romantic even though I wasn't a great skier. Traveling by snowcat, flying by helicopter to the top of the mountains at Kirkwood to try to figure out where to put the ski runs—it was a hell of a lot of fun, and I learned a lot, too. Would it be enjoyable for me at eighty-one? No. Was it fun at thirty-two? You bet!

I eventually pulled the pin because the risk was too high, and the effort just wasn't worth it. If I could make $100 an hour in the Sierras or $1,000 an hour in the Bay Area, why would I settle for $100? But it was a hard project to pull the pin on because my heart had taken over, and I didn't want to let my cousin down. I finally pulled out after about ten years, which proved to be the economically smart thing to do. Looking back, though, I have no regrets. I thought it would be fun, and it was.

- In the 1980s, we were in the oil and gas business for a few years. We reopened oil and gas wells in Oklahoma that had been capped off when prices were low, and it wasn't worth the cost to keep them open. It was speculated that the price of oil and gas would go up, and I saw a venture that could be very profitable. We invested some capital to open up these new wells and started pumping. It worked for two or three years while the price of oil and gas was going up, but as soon as prices dropped back down and the oil wells were no longer profitable, we quit. It was not my expertise and was meant to be only a temporary, side venture.

Has the need for the product line run out?
In 2006, we were building five hundred homes per year, which took a lot of people. After the 2008 financial crisis, there was no demand for new homes. I mean *zero*. And that was our product! What do you do when you're a homebuilder and nobody wants to buy your homes or lots? What happens when your company product no longer is wanted, period? Later, I'll talk about how we survived by reinventing our business. But that was the dilemma we faced: adapt or face the possibility of withering on the vine. We adapted.

Am I competitive?
In 1967, when we were building a lot of custom homes in Lincoln Village West, we started Grupe Cabinet & Door Company. It was an independent company that produced high-quality cabinetwork for use in our various projects and to sell to other contractors. We started with three employees in 1967, and, in the 1970s, sales volume increased six times. By the early 1980s, we had about twenty-eight

employees in a 26,000-square-foot shop. We were a total union shop, so when non-union competition came to town, it just killed us on labor. They started producing cheaper than we could. The industry was improving on the whole, getting bigger and better and more efficient. We couldn't compete, so we quit the business.

Is it still enjoyable?
You might find over time that the business you got into is not what you imagined it to be. I thought buying houseboats and renting them out would be both interesting and profitable, bringing something new to add to our marina business, which was the largest in the Delta. But talk about hands-on management. You have some clean-cut kid who comes along looking like he's just got out of church, and the next thing you know, you rent him a houseboat—and it's party city!

I did that for probably ten years until I realized it wasn't a good fit for what I look to get out of a business. It got to be such a pain that we sold the boats to another company. My prerequisite for most anything is that it has to be fun. If I'm not enjoying a business, I pull the pin.

Each of these experiences served a purpose, and I have no regrets about any of them. For many, they ran successfully for a course of time. For all of them, I learned transferable lessons and skills that I could apply to the next venture. And each time I pulled the pin, it saved me from taking a financial hit and made me available for better opportunities.

The Importance of Timing
Very few people have the ability to pull the pin precisely on time. It might be that you pull the pin prematurely. Unfortunately, that's a lesson you learn the hard way.

In the late 1980s, my company built an apartment complex at the entry into Blackhawk in San Ramon, California—a project which cost $12 million and had about $9 million worth of debt. We were feeding that project a couple hundred thousand a year during rent-up (the phase where we are filling the apartments with tenants and covering the interest payments on our loan in the meantime). Then, our investor got into trouble and wanted out. He pulled the pin, so we couldn't stay in and left the venture. Fifteen months later, that asset sold for $24 million—double the value. We could have made $12 million! Sometimes, financial capability can force your hand or, alternatively, allow you to hang on longer than what might be in your best interest.

During the Great Recession, two of our key executives wanted to pull the pin and close our brokerage firm, Grupe Real Estate, an independent financial arm of The Grupe Company, because it was losing money, and they felt that we couldn't afford to hold onto it and did not know how to fix the problem. I wasn't ready to let go. I guess you could say I took Plato's approach: "A good decision is based on knowledge and not on numbers." I started my career in that business and was confident we could turn it around.

My perspective was that brokerage companies go through cycles, and although these were *really* tough times, someday people were going to need an agent to sell their home again. Although it was frustrating in the meantime, the industry was not going away.

It was a tough spot to be in and a hard decision to make, but I decided *not* to pull the pin. It was a time to be tenacious and to focus on adding agents because others couldn't hang on and wait until the economy turned around. A close friend and YPO forum member, Paul Foster (president of the poultry company Foster Farms from 1969 to

MAKING DIFFICULT DECISIONS

1977), once told me that from time to time cyclical businesses must test the depth of capital to see who will survive, and that's *exactly* what happened in the case of Grupe Real Estate. It was a good test of capital. At that time, if you didn't have the financial capability to wait, you went under. Fortunately, because I'd practiced deferred consumption, I could hang on.

While we waited, we picked up a lot of agents as our competitors caved. How did we use the agents in a brokerage firm we had considered shutting down? We changed our market base. Our brokers switched from having *homeowners* as clients to the *lenders* who were picking up the foreclosed properties that had fallen into default. Remember, every time there's a trade, there's somebody on either side of it. If somebody loses a house, somebody gains a house. The houses didn't disappear. The owners just changed.

In 2017, about seven years after those discussions about whether or not to pull the pin, I received a call from my partner Jerry Abbott, who runs Grupe Real Estate, letting me know that he had just sent in the final check for the repayment of approximately $1 million the company had advanced the firm to make sure it survived. But more has been gained than a million dollars in the timeframe we toughed it out. In addition to getting all of our losses back, the number of agents we have has almost doubled, and we're the number-one office in the county. Grupe Real Estate is now very valuable.

I was confident we could make it work; that's why I took the risk. Your decision to pull the pin essentially must come down to your perspective and what you're confident in doing. The more you can focus on the big picture—the master plan of your dream—the easier time you'll have as you decide when to pull the pin.

The Emotions of Pulling the Pin

Deciding when it's time to hold on versus let go can be *really* difficult, especially when the change affects others. You may have to pull the pin on people who are performing well and rely on you for their income. You might have to pull the pin on a project you and others have poured money and time into without ever seeing any return for those efforts. But cutting away what's *not* working is about more than what you prune—it's about what you keep. Maybe you let go of three people, for example, but that decision means twenty *others* get to keep their job, and the three people who move on might reposition into a better situation for themselves.

I was still pretty young in my business career when I chose to let go of a long-time employee. We were expanding at a rapid pace, and to keep up required a lot of adaptability, but she wasn't comfortable with change. I finally brought her in and explained we could no longer keep her in her current position. It just wasn't working. We couldn't have her holding up the progress of the entire company. I went on to tell her of the arrangements we had made, such as six months of severance pay and how we could transition her into another position *within* the company that aligned with her comfort zone. She cried. I felt terrible.

A few days later she came back with a list of fears—What's to become of me? What about this? What about that? She didn't remember that we had gone through every one of those items.

I learned then that whenever you're the bearer of bad tidings, it's to everyone's benefit not to deliver all the news at once. Let the hard part sink in first. There's definitely an art to delivering bad news, and it requires a lot of respect, compassion, and fairness. Not only can it be done, but sometimes it *has* to be done.

MAKING DIFFICULT DECISIONS

Even now, I still hate pulling the pin when people are involved. There is nothing worse than employees fearing for their job—you can see it on their faces and feel it in conversations. But in a business that's cyclical, it's essential to make sure you are not overleveraged, whether that's capital or employees.

Sometimes we get emotionally attached to projects, too, and that makes it more difficult to let go. We don't want to give up on the potential we see. I'm no stranger to that. In my case, Phyllis and I own a golf course in the Gold Country town of Angels Camp, of Mark Twain note. To continue to own a golf course after you have completed the sale of all the lots and homes in the development makes little economic sense. I know that because we have built several golf communities with great success, in part because we sold the courses upon completion of the developments. So now I am in the hospitality business and probably a little too hands-on for an eighty-one-year-old. How do I justify this ownership? Best discussed over a glass of wine. However, hope springs eternal. We now have new leadership, and things are looking up.

Letting Go to Allow for New Opportunities

When we closed down the cabinet shop I mentioned earlier, we were left with a vacant building. The self-storage industry was early in its development then, and we were interested in giving it a shot. We decided to use that facility as our entry into the business.

At the time, people thought of self-storage as a temporary land hold. You'd put up these really cheap buildings, and then, in ten or twenty years, as the value of the land increased, you'd tear down the storage facilities and build something else. That was the original approach: cheap, temporary, and passable quality. But when we got into the business, we found out that people were willing to pay more for higher quality storage.

We started Mister Space and prized ourselves on making facilities that were safe, friendly, clean, and attractive. We built about twelve projects throughout Northern California and sold them only when we needed cash to survive the savings-and-loan crisis. We later returned to the self-storage business and, with our partners, built fourteen more projects and stayed in it until a couple of years ago, when we exchanged all but one of our projects into a public REIT. On the whole, our self-storage business was one of the most successful enterprises we've had. It was an opportunity that came because we *had* pulled the pin and, as a consequence, were left with a vacant warehouse. Talk about necessity being the mother of invention!

Coming to Terms with the Unknown
Part of the difficulty in pulling the pin is the unknown—you won't know right away whether or not you made the right choice. And maybe there's not always going to be a right choice, just a choice between rotten and rottener. As Austrian-born management educator Dr. Peter Drucker explained, "A decision is a judgment. It is a choice between alternatives. It is rarely a choice between right and wrong. It is at best a choice between 'almost right' and 'probably wrong'—but much more often a choice between two courses of action neither of which is provably more nearly right than the other."

Even if you choose *not* to decide, you've still made a decision. As I reminded the graduating class of 2016, when I received an honorary doctorate from California State University, Stanislaus, "All choices lead to outcomes." That includes the choice to do nothing because you're overcome with fear.

MAKING DIFFICULT DECISIONS

What do I do when I need to make a hard decision?

- **Set a deadline.** Postponing a decision comes at a cost. For me, there's usually an interest meter running and staff working on a losing project. I often calculate the cost of waiting to decide versus the consequence of making a bad decision.
- **Lean on research.** To work within the deadline I've set, part of that means accepting that I have to make a decision with the information I have at the time.
- **Turn to the best.** When my company was expanding in the 1980s as I started developing and building master-planned communities, apartments, and single-family home projects outside the state of California, I formed an advisory board that met quarterly because I needed to get advice from experts who could help me navigate this newfound growth. The advisory board was a hell of a blend: a celebrated professor from the Stanford Graduate School of Business (Jack McDonald); an economist and head of the graduate school of Real Estate at UC Berkeley (Ken Rosen); the president of several of Transamerica's companies (Dana G. Leavitt); the managing partner of Ken Leventhal (Stan Ross) which was the largest real estate accounting firm at the time and is now Ernst & Young; and one of the largest apartment builders in the United States (Jim Klingbeil). They were qualified, experienced, and top of their respective fields. I needed input from *each* of those perspectives to build a successful program.
- **Be honest about any indecisiveness.** Am I knowingly deferring dealing with the problem? What do I need to resolve to move forward? If I'm hoping my uncertainty will go away, is that

wishful thinking? Remember, no decision *is* a decision. As humorist Will Rogers said, "Even if you're on the right track, you'll get run over if you just sit there." If the problem isn't going anywhere, what good does it do to keep putting it off?

- **Listen to intuition.** Years of experience will pay off; I try to trust in them, and I listen to my gut.
- **Focus on the reward of taking action.** Joy comes from solving a problem, not ignoring it.

Digging In: When Surviving Is Success
Withstanding the Great Recession

In 2004, I stepped down as CEO of The Grupe Company at a time when it was doing very well and the housing market was strong. In fact, between 2000 and 2006, median home prices nearly quadrupled in Stockton. At the time, I was sixty-seven and wanting to become further involved in the equestrian sport of combined driving.

What had begun as a recreational pursuit only four years prior turned into a passionate focal point for a new period of my life. Phyllis and I were spending more time in Florida and Europe to train and compete at the national level, and, eventually, in 2005, I became the U.S. champion and competed on the U.S. Equestrian Team at the World Driving Championship for Pairs in Austria. Our love for the sport and evolving goals resulted in travel about six months out of the year—and a schedule incompatible with running the company's operations. It was time to make a change.

After I turned over the CEO role to my son-in-law Kevin Huber, the company continued to do very well and remained involved in some very interesting, one-of-a-kind projects, such as University Park (a 102-acre, one-million-square-foot medical, office, and education redevelopment project in midtown Stockton, which I'll revisit in Chapter 19). Housing was booming, with Stockton especially drawing buyers from the Bay Area, and the price of new homes continued to soar. In the spring of 2005, the median price of a new home in San Joaquin County jumped 35.7 percent over the course of a single year.

But whenever things start to look too good to be true, it usually turns out that they are. The nation's economy was on a collision course for financial disaster.

The Housing Bubble Bursts

During the 2000s, investors hungry for higher returns began to pour their money into the U.S. housing market through risky mortgage-backed securities (which bundled thousands of mortgages and sold shares to investors). Although not fundamentally sound, mortgage-backed securities received approval from credit agencies, which led to an increased demand.

To create more mortgage-backed securities, banks made loans (known as subprime mortgages) to people who previously would not have qualified. Some institutions used predatory lending practices, such as offering adjustable-rate mortgages that quickly outpaced the borrower's ability to pay. With people taking out loans they couldn't afford (sometimes willfully, with no intent to repay the loan) and banks making loans they *knew* couldn't be paid back, the mortgage-backed securities became more unsafe. Still, as the Financial Crisis Inquiry Commission (FCIC), established as part of the Fraud Enforcement and Recovery Act (2009), concluded, "financial institutions loaded up on them." For example, Lehman Brothers had real estate securities and holdings of $111 billion, four times its total equity.

As the Federal Reserve raised interest rates to combat inflation, people began to default on their mortgages. Banks foreclosed on houses and, as more and more foreclosed homes came on the market, housing plummeted in value. This was a major blow, as many financial institutions were overleveraged and working with too little capital. Some institutions, such as Lehman Brothers and Washington Mutual, declared bankruptcy, while others were forced into mergers.

From Wall Street to Main Street, people were doing things to excess as they took advantage of the escalating value of homes and threw caution to the wind. Thirty years of deregulation played its own role in precipitating the problem, as valuable safeguards had been removed.

Ignorance, intentional neglect, greed, and corruption at the consumer, investor, lender, banker, policy-maker, and public-official level collapsed the financial system. The stock market crashed on September 29, 2008, and the United States entered the Great Recession.

In 2011, the FCIC produced a report attempting to answer *"How did it come to pass that in 2008 our nation was forced to choose between two stark and painful alternatives*—either risk the total collapse of our financial system and economy or inject trillions of taxpayer dollars into the financial system and an array of companies, as millions of Americans still lost their jobs, their savings, and their homes?"

The answer to that question resulted in a mammoth report of some five-hundred-plus pages. A full analysis of the financial crisis is beyond the scope of this book, but the *root* of the problem, per the commission's findings, rests in personal responsibility. The commission also determined the financial crisis could have been avoided:

> The crisis was the result of human action and inaction, not of Mother Nature or computer models gone haywire. The captains of finance and the public stewards of our financial system ignored warnings and failed to question, understand, and manage evolving risks within a system essential to the well-being of the American public. Theirs was a big miss, not a stumble. While the business cycle

cannot be repealed, a crisis of this magnitude need not have occurred. To paraphrase Shakespeare, the fault lies not in the stars, but in us.

An $80 Million Hit

At The Grupe Company, we've always prided ourselves on our readiness to respond to our industry's cyclical nature. I knew the housing bubble wasn't sustainable. I just didn't know the magnitude of the financial crisis that would result, which eliminated much of Wall Street, crushed major banks, and wiped out nearly $11 trillion in household wealth.

We were not immune. As the value of real estate went down, we used about $20 million of our cash reserves to keep current with our lender and cover our pledges to fund different projects. We could have held onto some of our cash if we'd stiffed our partners and lenders and filed bankruptcy on some of our projects. But, as with the savings-and-loan crisis, we wanted to save our partners' capital and repay our loans in full.

We lost another $60 million in value of real estate we owned. We were in much the same predicament as the homeowner—we just owned *a lot* of real estate that dropped in value. Land that was worth $200,000 an acre became worth $20,000. We had a lot of communities and developments at different phases, which we had to stop. All the money and effort we had poured into those projects was just gone. The good news was, since we were not overleveraged, we did not have to sell any of our income-producing assets.

The *unforeseen, unforeseen* had hit, and it hit hard. It wasn't just us. It was a nationwide restructuring of real estate and the capital market. We were one of the players, but anybody who had any significant

MAKING DIFFICULT DECISIONS

amount of land in development or a lot of debt (such as the banks that were highly leveraged) was in trouble.

As the crisis unfolded, our company was in need of new ideas because our historic business of land development and homebuilding was no longer viable. Just to illustrate, construction permits fell 73 percent in Stockton from 2004 to 2007. There was zero demand for any new product or work for the people who built them. How could we survive without our traditional, core business? A drop-off in sales or profit is one thing, but six years with no demand for your product—that's a disaster!

While none of us had been through anything *exactly* like the financial crisis of 2008, I had been through the savings-and-loan crisis of the late 1980s and weathered the whims of the market for more than forty years. In 2010, Kevin asked me to come back to help our team reinvent the company. He had done a great job of cutting overhead and getting out of projects that no longer worked and wanted to concentrate his efforts on Grupe Commercial Company, which had opportunities to grow University Park (less than 50 percent complete at the time) as well as manage our shopping centers and office buildings. Our fourteen self-storage projects were all under separate management.

Withstanding the Downturn

Before I discuss how we survived the financial crisis and Great Recession, I'd be remiss if I didn't mention the importance of having the *financial capability to wait*—a byproduct of deferred consumption and living within your means. My ability to weather the storm personally allowed me to pour money into the company as well as reinvest in new ideas.

In business, especially real estate, the ability to suffer a downturn is one of the keys to weathering a setback. We were in a better position than a lot of other developers. While I wasn't prepared for a *Great Recession*, I had prepared for a recession by staying committed to goals I set at the very start of my career. I had equity because I had always deferred consumption. For example, I never spent more than that year's income when purchasing a home. And I had multiple sources of income: the development and building business (my primary job), owning income-producing properties, and farming.

Once the housing boom went bust, I was thankful I had diversified my options. The rent I collected from my income-producing properties (shopping centers, office buildings, apartments, and self-storage) and income from farming were enough to maintain our standard of living and reinvest in new ideas for The Grupe Company. My farming business did very well at that time with 1,500 acres of permanent crops (apples, cherries, walnuts, olives, and wine grapes). Additionally, our cattle business prospered during this time.

In short, because I had diversified, I did not have to depend on building homes to live, and I had plenty of equity so that I could invest in opportunities for rebuilding our real estate development company. Cash in the bank, alone, would not have been enough to withstand the Great Recession. What saved me was the other cash flow coming in, demonstrating again that **cash flow is more important than cash in the bank**.

The First Challenge—Surviving

So how did we survive?

Once we could see it coming, we did triage. We decided what to keep and what to sell. We created workouts with various partnerships and stabilized costs. We had enough cash in the bank and net worth to buy our way out of some contracts and walked away from land we had optioned (losing our big entitlement investment, as I described earlier). And to survive, we had to reduce overhead costs. As sales slowed, we wound down home construction by the end of 2007 and wouldn't begin again for another six years. We went from building five hundred homes a year to zero. In that climate, we had to go through the painful experience of laying off a significant number of good people. We let go of 80 percent of our employees focused on homebuilding, which was about three quarters of our entire company. It was devastating and the hardest consequence to accept. I value my relationships with my staff. We bring good people on board, so it's very difficult, for everyone, when they have to go.

Next, we looked at how to complete what we had underway in a market that was in a downward spiral. We adapted by offering a solution to new homeowners concerned with the rising cost of energy by creating energy-independent homes, an idea launched by Mark Fischer, who first worked with our company in 1984 as an auditor for Ken Leventhal. Mark joined our team in 1989 as a construction superintendent, earned a graduate degree from the University of Southern California, and eventually worked his way up to become president of The Grupe Company in 2010. As he explained to *The Sacramento Bee* back in 2006, "We thought it was the right thing to do. Every day, you pick up the newspaper, and what do you see? Oil prices are up. Gas prices are up. Energy prices are up in general. We thought it would be a great time to try and provide a solution to that, because it's really on people's minds like it's never been on their minds before."

It was Mark's idea to build Carsten Crossings as a totally energy-efficient community in Rocklin (about twenty miles northeast of

Sacramento, California). Known in the industry as "zero energy," these solar homes generated as much energy as they used. We were one of two projects that really paved the way for the zero-energy trend in the United States. Some of the energy-saving amenities included rooftop solar tiles, smart vent systems to pull in cool air at night so air conditioning units could kick in later the following day, higher-quality insulation, and tankless water heaters that would heat only on demand.

We did not pass along the extra cost of those energy-saving features to the consumer, but the extra $18,000 it cost our company per house was well worth it because of how quickly we sold the homes. As Mark said in 2009, "We outsold everyone 2 to 1. We were clearly the absorption leader." That innovation helped us to sell homes when nobody else could, to finish building out a number of lots, and to pay off the bank.

We did all of those things in order to survive where others faced bankruptcy because they didn't have the cash or liquidity to survive—and surviving was a big story, because many didn't. Surviving was success.

Down to 25 percent of our employees, and with no demand for the business we had historically been in, we had to figure out a way to generate income. What do you do when there's *no* demand for what you do?

That became our next challenge.

The Second Challenge—Reinventing the Company

Before we rebuilt the company, I knew we had to rebuild the confidence of the employees who remained. You can imagine how exhausting it would have been for the executives on the front line during a time of such uncertainty. For a while there, despite everyone's best efforts, things only continued to get worse. If you're crossing a swamp, it's hard to keep your eyes on its beauty while dodging the alligators. So once I stepped back in as CEO, my goal was to give them confidence that we could figure out how to weather the storm.

I still remember the first day I returned to the office. So much had been done to reduce costs that, when I entered, it felt abandoned. Lights had been turned off. There was no receptionist at the entry. The plants were dead. The doors to *many* vacant offices were closed. As I passed empty cubicle after empty cubicle, each served as a reminder of the far-reaching effect of the financial crisis. I couldn't help but feel that many had lost hope.

I wanted to help my team remember their strengths. One of our company's biggest assets has always been the people. You'd have to look far to find a team with more camaraderie, respect for each other, and loyalty to their company. There had always been a great atmosphere at The Grupe Company, and we were determined that, together, we could all pull through.

We got the lights back on, took down some of the cubicles to make the space more open, and closed off parts we didn't need, making it less apparent that many rooms remained unoccupied. Phyllis and our daughter Michelle redesigned the reception area and entry and made it very welcoming, open, and bright. Michelle and Mark Fischer started "the gong committee" to re-energize our team during a period we knew would be tough. The committee took charge of uplifting morale by congregating everyone to celebrate achievements big and small with the strike of the gong in our corporate office's central gathering place, which we named "Township Square."

We then moved on to figuring out a way to beat the downturn by adapting to fit the new needs the chaos presented. We broadened our energy-conservation efforts to retrofits, starting Green Home Solutions in 2009. While we couldn't build new houses, our company knew how to do a lot more than that. In our forty-five-year history, we had reinvented ourselves many times to withstand setbacks.

We engaged all the tips and principles I've outlined for creating solutions and embracing change to study the challenge, identify our strengths, and find the opportunity that this chaos and change had created. We didn't have to look far.

Stockton had the highest foreclosure rate in the nation in 2007 and remained one of the top-ten cities through 2012. With the rise of foreclosures and so many houses on the market, prices came crashing down by 70 percent. We could buy houses for *half* of what it would cost to build them and, despite everything, there *was* a demand for housing if it was cheap enough. We had the chance to buy at the bottom, and if you can structure your company and your investments so you can suffer through and buy at the bottom, you can make a successful turnaround. **One of the best real estate tips I can give is that you make your profit when you buy, not when you sell.** The way to make money in real estate is having the ability to avoid selling in a bad market because you need the cash or you can't afford to keep the project. If you buy the asset right, you'll make money on it. If you buy it wrong, there's not much you can do.

We met with a variety of banks and investors and got the necessary capital to start buying houses at auction through trustee sales, where the bank (or mortgage company or pension fund) had repossessed the home. We would fix these up and either resell them at a profit, or, in many cases, lease them out and just collect the rent. That was part of our solution (and by December of 2013 we had flipped three hundred homes), but we also wanted to develop a program that targeted the many people who had *chosen* to walk away from their mortgages (and consequently were foreclosed upon) as the fair market value of their home became *less* than the balance of their mortgage, known as an "underwater" mortgage.

By the fall of 2009, about one-third of California mortgage-holders had underwater mortgages. Seeing their home now as a bad investment, a large number of people chose to stop making payments and *let* their homes go into foreclosure. The penalty for that choice was that they couldn't get a new loan for another three years, but many saw it as the best economic choice in their situation.

We began to see an opportunity—one that would help the people who had chosen to be foreclosed upon as a strategic, financial decision get *back* into a house while still allowing us to turn a profit. In March 2010, we rolled out Fresh Start, our rent-to-own business, which was one of those programs that turned out a little better than we thought.

Our New Direction: Giving People a Fresh Start

During a time when people—even those who had *not* lived to excess—were bearing the brunt of financial disaster rooted in a lot of greed, deception, and corruption, our commitment to high quality and ethical standards, as well as our genuine concern for the consumer, not only still mattered but mattered *more*.

We adjusted our market base to attract individuals who had chosen to go into default on their previous home mortgage because they did not want to make payments toward a loan that was more than their house was even worth.

Those who had been foreclosed out of their home but had a stable job history and good credit *except* for strategically defaulting on their mortgage (so they didn't have credit-card debt or other debt that made them a high-risk borrower) could work with agents in our company to find a new home. We purchased the home of their choice, made any necessary repairs, and upgraded the house's energy efficiency. The prospective homebuyer signed a lease with an option to buy between the second and fifth year of the deal and made a $5,000 deposit that would go toward their down payment if they closed on the project. In the meantime, we rented the home to them at $500 a month *more* than the fair market rent. That, too, went toward the down payment. Adding that $6,000 a year to the $5,000 deposit resulted in participants having $23,000 to go toward the down payment in three years, so it was a "forced savings" on their account.

Through that program, we bought more than three hundred homes. About 85 to 90 percent of participants closed as projected, and for many, it allowed them to rebuild their lives. As *The Record,* Stockton's local newspaper, reported one participant saying at the time, "There is a huge sense of relief. I am happy, and this is truly a fresh start. I'm on track to owning this new property in three years. I've got all the essentials, and I like this neighborhood better."

So how did we make a buck?

We got the rent, *and* we charged them 10 percent per year increase in value that *we* would get. So at the end of three years, a $200,000 house had increased to having a $260,000 value. We'd paid only $200,000 for it; they paid us $260,000 for it. *But,* the house appreciated to more than $300,000 as prices came back.

And we went all in, executing triumphantly (not just somehow). As Michael Kristoff, a Grupe executive, recalled, "It was amazing. When everybody else is retreating and the banks are fearful everything was going to blow up, Fritz is putting the chips on the table. From *my* perspective, being in Stockton for only a year, I'm thinking, *Okay, this is gutsy. See what happens.* Sure enough, everybody's house is back up to a normal price, and our portfolio is doing well."

While we profited, participants did, too, as they benefited from the built-in down payment (the deposit and rent payments) and the equity in the house. So they made money, we made money, and everybody was really happy.

From 2011 to 2015, we purchased more than a thousand homes either to fix up, resell, rent, or use in the rent-to-own program. I've always believed one of the great American dreams is the opportunity to own your own home. It's a chance at having a piece of the pie. It was incredibly rewarding to find a way to help people get back on the path that led to home ownership at such a desperate time.

In 2014, with our recovery shored up, I reevaluated my role again, reconsidered my priorities, and decided to step down from daily operations as president of the company. I am still excited about the future of our companies and business. Change is here, but that is good. My role continues to change, and that is good as well. I've enjoyed the transition to coach and chairman. I still have plenty of ideas to offer, and I love being a sounding board for the talented team leading the company.

Our ability to adapt has been proven by our new leadership team, headed by President Mark Fischer, Chief Operating Officer Jeremy White, and General Counsel Nelson Bahler, along with our seasoned executives. We now have more new projects on the board than we have had in over a decade.

I am proud of the creativity, adaptability, and tenacity we tapped into that got us back on track.

Chapter 15

Leaning on Your Values

*O*VER THE YEARS, people have asked me if it's hard to keep ethical standards *and* do well in business. Especially during times of rebuilding, when there's so much on the line, how do you hold on tight to your beliefs but still find a way to stay flexible, adapt, and navigate sometimes-murky waters?

Honestly, I think it's *easier* to stick to your values. They provide the sturdy framework upon which to build your life.

While gaining the skills and confidence to adapt or pull the pin are key to overcoming setbacks, your core values—the very essence of who you are—will help you remain confident, motivated, and optimistic until you're back on solid footing.

Strategies should change according to shifting conditions—not values.

> *Strategies should change according to shifting conditions—not values.*

There's No Such Thing as Situational Ethics

One of the most crucial lessons I can share is this: If you base your life's decisions on high ethical standards—such as upholding honesty, integrity, and compassion—then everything else will fall into place.

As I shared in Chapter 2, my parents and religious upbringing were central to the development of my moral compass, but as I got out into the world, real-life experiences tested and strengthened my resolve to stick to what I knew to be right. For example, when I first started as a real estate salesman in Stockton in the early 1960s, many developers' or homeowner associations' covenants, conditions, and restrictions (known as CC&Rs) upheld racial segregation. I was stunned when I observed this prejudice firsthand.

I had just convinced a United States Army captain to purchase a home and had proudly walked into the office with hopes of completing the paperwork. As my sales manager reviewed everything, he asked, "What nationality is he?"

I replied that he was from Hawaii but that I wasn't sure of his exact heritage.

"You can't sell to Asians there," he informed me.

"But he's a captain in the army," I stated in disbelief, trying to understand the nature of his objection.

"It doesn't matter. He can make an offer, but you've got to tell him that the neighborhood's restrictive deed covenant says that he can't be an owner of that property."

I returned to the captain with this unfair news but promised, "I'll fight this thing, man. If you want to buy the house, I'm all in for you." And boy, his response just killed me.

"Fritz, I don't want to go where I'm not wanted."

That wasn't the last time in my career that discrimination reared its ugly head. About a decade later, an African American professor wanted to buy a home in one of our lake communities in a different city that had a long history of prejudice toward African Americans. In that climate, some would have been nervous making the sale, speculating how it might impact the bottom line. At this point in my career, it was *my* money at risk, after all. But my core values mattered more than the opinions of others. We sold the professor the house and warmly welcomed him to the community.

Always remember that you've got to do what *you* know to be right.

Faith—The Keystone of My Core Values

In the mid-1980s, while chairing the YPO university held in Vienna, my close friend Peter Ueberroth (who was *Time* magazine's Man of the Year for his organization of the 1984 Summer Olympics in Los Angeles, California) asked me to introduce one of the main speakers, Lord Donald Soper, and "stick with him" for four days. What a privilege!

Soper was one of the most influential Methodist leaders of the twentieth century. Known for his energy and wit, he was sometimes affectionately called "Soapbox Soper" due to his popular style of preaching in Hyde Park.

That day, several YPO'ers asked him questions. Two have stuck with me.

First: "Do you have to believe in Jesus Christ being the Son of God in order to go to heaven?"

"I don't believe so," Soper responded, and then quoted scripture about second chances. He then added, "One of the holiest men I have ever met was not a Christian. I cannot believe that he doesn't have a chance to go to heaven."

Perhaps encouraged by that response, another attendee got a little more specific: "Can a businessman go to heaven?"

True to his reputation, Soper answered, "Yes—but by a circuitous route."

I appreciated both Lord Soper's humor and open-mindedness. What you do in the workplace is no substitute for who you are in the broader scheme of life. We all need guidelines to live by and aspire to. For me, Christianity is the keystone of my core values. For others, it may be something else. Many faiths share the same, basic ethical teachings when it comes to defining what constitutes a principled, moral life. Personally, I believe that the birth, life, and death of Jesus Christ is the most monumental event in history and reshaped our world forever.

All of my adult life, especially during trials and setbacks, my faith has been a source of comfort because of the caring, consistent, and available nature of God. I believe God is there all the time. You don't necessarily have to go into your closet to pray to be with God. Not only did He give His only begotten Son for each of us, but His love for each of us is constant. He invites us to cast our cares upon Him and promises to strengthen and settle us.

Our commitment to the Christian faith has given our children a roadmap for making decisions. As our eldest daughter, Sandy, shared: "As I got older, I think my parents' guiding principle of faith became more and more important in my life, and the more grounded I got in my faith, the more comfortable I got in my life. It's a value now that I cherish very deeply and have been committed to with my husband

and in raising our kids. I think that value has been critical to decisions that I've made in my life."

Knowing *who* you are and *why* you do what you do makes it *easier* to know what is right.

Staying Honest in the Business World

Within our company, and our lives in general, we don't cheat. We don't lie. We don't steal. We make mistakes because we're human, but we own up to them. We choose to do what's *right* even when it makes things more difficult, or expensive, for us.

Wouldn't you find it advantageous going to work for a company where you know their moral standing? Wouldn't you feel more comfortable dealing with someone who is playing by the same rule book? On the other hand, how much risk would you take with a guy who'll be quick to file bankruptcy and stiff you at the first sign of trouble?

I take my commitments *very* seriously. So seriously that I once told Jim Klingbeil I wasn't willing to personally guarantee bank notes.

"Why?" he asked.

"Because I don't want to be obligated if something really went wrong," I explained.

"You'll pay back anything you owe anyway, Fritz," he chuckled. "Might as well sign it."

After I made my way through the savings-and-loan crisis having repaid everyone I owed in full—to the tune of $350 million—he said, "See?"

I remember telling our former Chief Financial Officer Don Benioff (who was extremely honest and moral and one of the best financial people I've ever known) that I did not personally guarantee loans.

He came from a banking background and, as a lender, would never make loans *without* the borrower giving a personal guarantee. I told him that wasn't how I operated but would instead sign the guarantee on behalf of The Grupe Company, which had a large net worth and was very liquid. It was a difficult adjustment for him to ask lenders the exact opposite of what he had practiced for so many years. But when reflecting on his years with the company, Don observed that, although I didn't personally guarantee my loans, I was "more honorable than the people who guaranteed."

In my experience I've learned, as our pastor puts it, "truth always demands a response." You will find yourself in situations where it may be tempting to act untruthfully. During the savings-and-loan crisis, our lender could not locate the loan agreements for the $350 million we had borrowed. Can you imagine? We were their biggest borrower, and we received a call saying they couldn't find any of our loan documents! Of course, most of their senior staff had been replaced in the wake of the crisis, but it's still no excuse.

Now, while some could have been tempted to say, "I don't think I borrowed it," we never wavered. We had a full set of paperwork on our end, which we duplicated and sent back to them. Why? Because our integrity is fundamental to who we are, and it can't be bought. As my Bohemian Grove campmate and friend, former Senator Alan Simpson, said, "If you have integrity, nothing else matters. If you don't have integrity, nothing else matters."

Keeping high ethical standards in our business has not always been convenient. Once, when we were the owner *and* contractor for a large apartment complex, we ran into an issue with defective wood siding. We had a lot of investors in the project by that time, and the

LEANING ON YOUR VALUES

obvious solution was to sue the contractor, which was us. So what did we do? We hired two attorneys, sued ourselves, and worked it out.

It was a stressful process, though. As our attorney Nelson Bahler recalls, "I was actually in a deposition. I was sweating bullets. In fact, that might have been the worst day of my life, the day I went to that deposition. What do you say? But, it got worked out. I don't really remember how, but we settled that one. But, that's doing the right thing." It's better to do the right thing than do things right.

Our commitment to integrity extends to all those we do business with. In fifty years of building, we have never stiffed a subcontractor. Once upon completing negotiations on a piece of property with two of my executives, the other party asked if either I or Frank Passadore—who has been with the company since 1966—were available to meet. Frank recounted the land seller's request: "I've been negotiating with your company here, and I think we've reached an agreement. Before I go, I would like to know that you're on board with this. Here's what we've agreed to. I'd like a handshake from you. I know that this company is good on a handshake. So if you can assure me that you're comfortable with it, I'm good with it."

As Frank reflected on the interaction, he concluded, "We shook hands, and I think that spoke volumes about the company and the tradition that it had in terms of never stiffing anybody, always paying our bills, always honoring our contracts."

Our customers also trust in our reputation for being honest and doing what's right. As a builder we have an obligation to take care of the customer and guarantee the craftsmanship of our homes for a certain period of time, usually ten years. As part of our business philosophy, we offer a generous home warranty program. If there's something that goes wrong in a home that is truly our problem—we didn't do something right or one of our subs didn't do something right—we go back and fix it. We don't look at the law (such as the statute of limitations)—we look at the situation. If we made a mistake, we'll fix it even if it's been fifteen years and the warranty has expired. We've found that erring on the side of the customer has been good for business, keeps true to our reputation, and is the right thing to do.

Honesty is at the core of our company culture. It's what we expect from each other. When I invited Nelson Bahler to work for the company as our attorney in 1980, he was both hesitant and nervous. I didn't know this until recently, but he was afraid that if he came to work for us, we would pressure him to form his opinions to whatever *we* wanted, rather than what was right. After almost forty years with the company, he can proudly say that was never the case. "I was never forced," he recalled. "I never felt any pressure. I always felt free that I was independent to say and give the opinion that I wanted. And, there's a lot of pressure because nobody wants to have a legal-problem hang-up. That's unacceptable. You have to find a legal answer."

My company and executives have felt the reward of running an honest business. As Nelson recalled, "One of the things that made my job easy was I never had to apologize. You go in and say, 'I need this,' and people believe you. You go to the bankers when you're negotiating loans; you say something, and they believe you because they know the reputation of the company."

Not all businesses value honesty the way we do, and that has been surprising for some of my executives. I learned that the hard way after Lincoln Village West was already underway, and I was looking to buy some property in Bellota. A neighbor of my parents, who I had

LEANING ON YOUR VALUES

known since I was a kid, had moved to Stockton and wanted to sell his ranch. I had talked to him over the years about it, and, finally, when he decided he was serious about selling, we agreed on a price. I said, "I'll write up something so we have an agreement."

He dissuaded me, saying, "We've known each other for a long, long time. My word's good. You don't need to worry about it. I'll just meet you at the title company."

A couple weeks later, when I called the title company, I was surprised to learn that nothing had come in. So I called him. "What's going on?" I asked. "I thought we were going to get these things closed."

"Oh, I sold it to somebody else," he replied.

"You *what?* We had an agreement on the price. It was *your* price, and I agreed, and you gave this big, long explanation that we didn't need it in writing because your word was good."

I'll never forget his response. "Well, my word is good. But, it's not worth $90,000."

In such times, I can't help but think of the scripture, "For what is a man profited, if he shall gain the whole world, and lose his own soul? For what shall a man give in exchange for his soul?" (Matthew 16:26 KJV)

When you say you're an honest person, is there a level at which you can be bought off? If the answer is no, is it because the price isn't high enough?

As hard as it may be during times of setback or when the other party isn't playing fair, keep to your core values because wrong does not correct wrong. Perhaps you've heard the saying: "Talent wins games; character wins championships." The same holds true for business.

One way I've dealt with injustice is to think, *Well, there's the practical side (what's fair) and the sleep-good side.* As you get old, what do you have? You have memories more than anything. I'm glad I've got happy memories. There are times we were upset and things didn't go right, for sure, but on the other hand, I'm not up at night dealing with guilt because I caved in when it came to my integrity.

A Word on Accountability

Having integrity also means you take responsibility for what's going wrong in your life, rather than blame others. I've focused a lot on that in this book because I feel so strongly that it can make all the difference in your performance and end result. Personal coach Lou Tice—whose "Achieve Your Potential" seminar I used with my company in 1985—captures the very essence of why accepting responsibility is so crucial in the book he wrote with Joyce Quick, *Personal Coaching for Results: How to Mentor and Inspire Others to Amazing Growth* (1997):

> When we take responsibility for our lives, we give ourselves power. Accountability goes hand in hand with confidence and the feeling of controlling one's own life. When we're accountable, it means that we're capable of making rational or moral decisions on our own and that we are answerable to others for our behavior. It means that we can be trusted—that our word to others *and to ourselves* can be depended on.

Do you keep your word to yourself? I've already talked about the confidence that comes from keeping promises to yourself, such as the goal to lose weight or start any new habit. Take a moment (or longer, hopefully) to think about what characteristics define you as an individual. Who do you think you are?

LEANING ON YOUR VALUES

Now answer this: Who do people say you are?

Are those answers in sync?

If not, to me, that equals a stomachache.

As Stephen Covey taught, while we judge ourselves by our intentions, people judge us by our actions. Your actions reflect what you value. If you want to change how you act, start by assessing what you believe and value. As Lou Tice said, "When you change the way you think, the way you behave changes. And when you behave differently, you get different results."

When all else is uncertain, values stay constant. If you are ethical, people will trust and believe in you—even when you're at low points of your journey. And perhaps most importantly, *you'll* still believe in you.

Chapter 16

Keeping Balance

I OFTEN GET ASKED how I deal with the stress that accompanies running such cyclical, diversified companies and how I've dealt with the intense professional setbacks I've experienced, such as the savings-and-loan crisis that began in 1986 and the housing-market crash of 2008.

The best answer I can give is that work is *not* my highest priority in life.

I've always told my executives that business should not be number one. It isn't for me, and I don't expect it to be for them. If you put business before everything else, what will you do if it fails? What about when you retire? If your identity and definition of success can be measured by only one source—such as money, physical appearance, or your dream—what happens if you lose it? When you still have your health, your family, and your faith, and you say you've lost everything—what the hell is "everything"?

We are responsible for the pace, quality, and balance of our lives. As hard as it can be during times of stress, it's important to keep perspective and stay clear on priorities. For me, faith, family, and *then* work are the order of my priorities, with a balance of maintaining good health, which requires diet, exercise, fun, and friends. The stronger and more stable your life is *apart* from your career, the more you'll enjoy life, and the better you'll pull through turbulent times.

> *We are responsible for the pace, quality, and balance of our lives.*

The Time for Happiness Is Now

Happiness is a byproduct of how you live life. You don't wake up and just feel good if you haven't done anything. Happiness should not be contingent on achievement. To say, "When I earn X amount, then I will be happy" is not enough. What if *achievement* is not the end-all, exhilarating experience you had hoped for and, instead, comes with a letdown feeling?

After the goal has been reached, new anxieties might take shape as you ask, *What do I do now?* That is especially true if achievement has been the focus, to the exclusion of all other aspects of a well-rounded life.

On occasion, I have needed to be reminded to be less focused on work. In January of 1986, my dad sent me a postcard for Phyllis's and my 25th wedding anniversary, something he did for birthdays and other special occasions. His handwritten message on this particular card has stuck with me for more than thirty years.

KEEPING BALANCE

Postcard from my dad reminding me of my priorities, 1986.

> At your age [I was forty-eight], it is time to ask yourselves these important questions:
> Who are you?
> Where are you going?
> And when you get there will the bars still be open?

In other words, was I going to spend my entire life focusing on my job?

His postcard arrived during a stressful time in my career. I was in the middle of dealing with the fallout from American Savings and Loan going under. My dad would call to ask if I wanted to go hunting or fishing, and my answer always came back, "I can't. I've got to work this out."

I was in survival mode, and the *unforeseen, unforeseen* had knocked my life out of balance. From my dad's perspective—which put a clear premium on life experiences over business—I'm sure he thought, *My kid's screwed up.*

As I've shared, my father felt uneasy that I was not satisfied just building in Stockton. When he made enough money to cover his needs and leave time to hunt and fish, he was happy. He couldn't understand why I didn't do the same once I had "made it."

That postcard struck a chord with me because he was right. I had been struggling to keep my priorities in order at the time.

I have needed such reminders here and there to get things back in check, but one of the things I'm proudest of is that I *have* balanced family and business. I *have* made time for friendships, in spite of the long hours. That's a real tough one for an entrepreneur who always has more to do than the time or money to do it. But if you keep your priorities balanced—faith, family, friends, health, bliss, and charity along with your career—you get to reap the harvest of time well spent.

Finding Stability

When I need added support in my life, I reassess my priorities and make sure I'm making time for my faith in God, my family, and my friends. Faith reduces my stress and reminds me of the importance of trusting God's timing, which may be different from mine. Family brings me comfort and rejuvenation. Friends bring an outside perspective to my problems and provide sound advice and guidance.

Trials remind me of the power and healing purpose of friendship. As Greek playwright Euripides observed, "Friends show their love in times of trouble not in happiness." At one time, we had a very serious health scare in our family that, as you can imagine, really affected us all. We were distraught and felt helpless.

Our friend and partner of more than twenty years, Fred Franzia of Bronco Winery, came over and invited Phyllis and me to go for a ride as it would "do you good to get outside and do something other than worry." At that same time, close ULI friend Joe Canizaro, who is an extremely successful New Orleans businessman and devout Catholic, made time to reach out and give exemplary spiritual support. He arranged for Sister Briege McKenna, a Catholic nun and author known for her healing ministry, to pray over the phone with Phyllis and me for our grandchild during this extremely difficult time. It's experiences like these that remind me of the importance and meaningfulness of our relationships and our interactions. Fortunately, our grandchild who experienced this illness has survived and is a healthy young adult looking forward to a promising future.

Standing with partner and friend Fred Franzia and Forest Glen, the top-selling Angus bull at our 1990 purebred auction.

The Importance of Self-Care

When there's so much to do, it can be tempting to put yourself last, but controlling stress is imperative. Stress decreases your energy and passion for other things—and makes you feel like you're working harder than anyone else! Most importantly, it can make you insensitive to the feelings of others and drive away the very people you need.

Whether through exercise, humor, or making time daily for the things that bring the highest level of bliss, it's important for all of us to learn how to manage the stress in our lives. There are things I can do alone to give myself peace of mind, such as being in the outdoors, seeking solitude, being with my animals, dreaming, and meditating (fostering a relationship with God).

I've found it rewarding to structure days that allow for relaxation, stress management, and exercise. As The Grupe Company's life coach Dr. Tracy Tomasky teaches in her book *The Conscious and Courageous Leader: Developing Your Authentic Voice to Lead and Inspire* (2016), "If we are tightly wound with our bodies and mind in constant motion, there isn't time or space for creative energy to flow. It is from a relaxed state that we are able to be most productive."

Time in nature is part of my creative process. Phyllis has often said that the further you get away from the land, the more you need it. In fact, whenever our children would say they were bored, our answer—as well as my mother's—was to "go outside." Soon enough, they discovered *something* to do and got a taste for the inspiration that nature can provide.

For me, nature and husbandry have been constant sources of rejuvenation, fun, and fellowship since I was a child. I still enjoy the tradition and fellowship of hunting, and I joined in Phyllis's horse habit full time in the early 2000s, which you'll hear more about in the following Digging In.

Having outside activities that give *quick* feedback (for me, a sport like hunting, fishing, or golf) helps offset the uncertainty of work.

Vocational work can be more rewarding in the short run, as it provides immediate feedback (you can see what you accomplished that day), but managers may have to wait years to see the final result.

Making time for hobbies not only allows you to unwind, but it also puts you in the position to make connections with people who care about what you do. When I reflect on the personal interests I have prioritized, they involve being with the people I hold most dear. That's often what makes the hobbies most fun for me. And I have such good friends and family that they'll join me even if they *don't* share the same passion for some of my hobbies.

Phyllis will tag along as I continue to try to learn golf (a game I picked up for the first time at seventy-eight years old), and Jim will go duck hunting with me. As he sees it, "I duck hunt once or twice a year, and I *always* wonder why I'm sitting out there in the dark, rain coming in, in this little, itty-bitty hole. *Why am I doing this?* I mean,

Duck hunting with Jim Klingbeil at Greenhead, located in Northern California's Butte County, 2000.

I only do it because of Fritz. If Fritz doesn't take me duck hunting, I'm never going to go again!"

Final Thought

As counterintuitive as it might sound, making time for what you *enjoy* improves your resilience and helps you succeed. When my friend (and former advisory board member) Jack McDonald reflected on the more than ten thousand students he had taught in his fifty-year career with the Stanford Graduate School of Business, he concluded that his most successful students—who cumulatively have gone on to earn trillions of dollars—were the happy ones who lived a balanced life.

Even during setbacks, priorities should remain in order. I've never forgotten the Dalai Lama's observation about humanity's struggle to keep life balanced and in perspective: "[Man] sacrifices his health in order to make money. Then he sacrifices money to recuperate his health. And then he is so anxious about the future that he does not enjoy the present; the result being that he does not live in the present or the future; he lives as if he is never going to die, and then he dies having never really lived."

Are *you* happy? Are you finding time for joy and bliss *now*, or are you forever putting it off?

This seems as good a time as any to pass on my father's questions: *Who are you? Where are you going? And when you get there, will the bars still be open?*

Digging In: Our Horse Habit

About two years after we moved to Brookside Farm in 1975, I had an idea while driving down the half-mile lane that led to our farmhouse. As soon as I entered the house, I shared it with Phyllis: "You know, every time I drive up, I think, *Wouldn't it be fun to have a big old draft horse standing in the field?*"

I'm sure you've seen the Budweiser horses and how pretty they are. I thought one would complete our farm.

"Well, we have Quarter Horses and Appaloosas," Phyllis responded. "We have all kinds of animals with 4-H, and I really don't know where we're going to find a big old draft horse to stand in the field."

About six months went by and, being tenacious, I brought it up again. "I keep thinking every time I drive down that lane that I would *love* to see a big old draft horse."

"Well, I think they're extinct," Phyllis said, "but if you *really* want to see a big old draft horse standing in the field, we'll see if we can find you one."

Now, we both share a lifelong love of horses. As kids, Phyllis had saved her nickels to buy Desba, and I'd galloped around my parents' ranch bareback on Babe, with Buster, my dog, loping alongside. While I was getting a handle on the cattle-breeding business as a teenager, Phyllis cultivated her skills as a talented horsewoman. In addition to working at a stable, she had opportunities to learn from the talented people and horses at the W. K. Kellogg Arabian Horse Center in Pomona, California.

Our time as newlyweds at my parents' ranch in Bellota further gave Phyllis a taste of farm life, and she soon had her own horse again, an untamed mustang. This came about when I was shopping at Solari's Inn—the same Solari's of the infamous trailer accident. A man entered the store announcing he had a truckload of wild horses from Nevada for sale at 75 bucks apiece. Intrigued, I walked out to see the quality of what he was selling and asked if he'd haul the horses out to our ranch, which was about four miles away.

I thought this would be the perfect gift for my new bride. After we arrived, I had Phyllis come out and told her she could pick any horse she wanted. Phyllis picked a mustang that took three of us (and a gunnysack over the mare's head) to get her to the barn. I remember asking Phyllis if she was sure she wanted such a wild horse, but Phyllis always had confidence when it came to horses. She named the mustang "Cricket."

While we had Cricket and other ranch horses to work our cattle, our needs changed once we moved to Stockton in 1962. We had one child, with a second on the way, so we sold Cricket. It would be about six years until we bought some horses just for riding and entertainment and boarded them at a stable in town. Not until we moved to Brookside Farm, almost fifteen years later, would we have horses on our property again, when we purchased some Quarter Horses and Appaloosas. But that didn't quite seem like enough. I had the nagging feeling that just one majestic draft horse would make all the difference. Little did I know the quest for that horse would kick off a major era in Phyllis's life and morph into so much more than satisfying my initial desire.

We learned that not only were draft horses *not* extinct but also that there was a strong culture across the U.S. (the Amish) relying on these horses to provide power for farm equipment. In our search, we were pointed toward the Midwest and, in 1978, found ourselves not one but *four* Belgians—a breed we selected for their intelligence, power, and gentleness.

Those first Belgians—two mares, a stallion, and a month-old baby—weren't of the quality we would later seek, but, given time, we learned how to locate the best networks. Seeing those horses standing in the field *was* beautiful and led me to think, *Wouldn't it be wonderful to use our Belgians for promotional events for our company?* I envisioned how we could get a big wagon and go to shopping centers or apartment openings and offer carriage rides. I brought this idea to Phyllis, and she said, "I don't know anything about driving or harnessing horses." But, like before, she was willing to try.

Our beautiful Belgian horses along our tree-lined lane at Brookside Farm.

We bought a decrepit freight wagon and an old harness that was dry, cracked, and well-used. We harnessed the horses, hitched them up to the wagon, and took off. It was only by the grace of God that all ended well, because we really didn't know what we were doing. As Phyllis rode up high in the wagon and drove the Belgians across the plowed field, she felt pure accomplishment. Thrilled by the success of that first drive, her success turned into a passion. She wanted to learn everything she could about draft horses and was willing to make every effort to become as proficient as possible as a carriage driver.

Our old mares and older freight wagon. Company executives were only too happy to exit from this experience, 1979.

We purchased safe harnesses and a beautiful wagon for the horses to pull and hired someone to give us lessons. Phyllis became a marvelous driver. For ten years, she kept a rigorous schedule, entering draft-horse shows all over North America, and she reigned for a time as the female driving champion for single cart with her horse Firestone.

Phyllis with her champion Belgian draft horse Firestone, 1990.

She was committed to doing everything to the highest standard for the Belgians (fifty of them at one point) that lived at Brookside. We made changes on the farm to accommodate our horse habit's growth into a full-fledged business. We had the finest herd of Belgian draft horses in the western United States, and while our horses started out as The Brookside Belgians, they became The Grupe Company Belgians, helping promote our company and developments. And we kept them quite busy. In 1988 alone, they performed more than 140 times. We participated in the Rose Parade four times in the late eighties and early nineties, as well as performed at the Superdome in New Orleans for ULI's annual conference. We competed with the horses all over the United States and won the North American six-horse hitch at the Royal Winter Fair in Toronto, Canada.

While participating in parades and competing in shows brought joy and exposure, one of the greatest joys was sharing the Belgians with children at our farm. We worked especially with children who had mobility or physical disabilities and held events so they could visit the farm. In addition to watching a calf being fed or touching a lamb, the children got to watch the harnessing of the Belgians before riding around Brookside Farm on a special carriage made to accommodate their wheelchairs. Afterwards, we shared a picnic on the lawn. We also developed the elementary school program The Belgians Are Coming, an educational assembly that we took into the local schools, which I described in Part One.

Around this time, we were also dealing with the aftermath of the savings-and-loan crisis and had to cut back on our overhead. As sad as it was, it was time to move on, so we sold our great, gentle giants.

But we didn't last long without horses, or the horse sport, in our lives. Not long after we parted ways with our Belgian horses, we stumbled upon a new equine sport that would become our horse passion for the next twenty years.

While visiting our YPO friends Peter and Ginny Ueberroth in Coeur d'Alene, Idaho, in 1997, we learned our ULI friends Mike and Sigi McCormack, who lived nearby, had recently become involved in combined driving, a sport that neither Phyllis nor I had heard of. As we learned and saw more, Phyllis and I looked at each other and said, "We could do that!" We had no idea of the magnitude of the sport but knew it could be a lot of fun and a new way to enjoy our love of horses.

Once again, we were back to square one, you could say, as we didn't know anything about the sport. As before, we found people who *did* know something, got the proper carriages and harnesses, and sought out the right horses. We'll never forget longtime American Driving Society member Judson Wright taking us to our first driving event at Windsor Castle. Even then, we had no idea where our journey would take us or that I'd return to compete at that very event.

We started driving Haflinger ponies and upgraded to Holsteiner horses in 2002 to be more competitive. But we still felt we were not competing at the level we desired. Again, it came down to upgrading our horses. I spoke with Chester Weber and Tucker Johnson—the two top United States drivers and international medalists—and they recommended I switch to Dutch Warmbloods. I was actually sitting in Chester's swimming pool when Tucker convinced me to turn competitive. They were very influential and helpful to my journey. Chester, who wasn't quite yet thirty at the time, put in the most time with me. Phyllis and I lived for two winters on his family's plantation in Florida to train. It was through Chester that I met Koos de Ronde, who's probably the best marathon driver there's ever been in combined driving. Koos is an excellent coach as well. As recently as 2017, he flew out from the Netherlands to compete with me and helped me find a new horse in 2018.

After finding my Dutch Warmbloods in 2004 with the help of Chester and Tucker, I became extremely competitive. By 2005, at the age of sixty-eight, I won the United States Equestrian Federation National Pairs Championship and won a spot on the U.S. Equestrian team. Phyllis and I took the horses and went to Germany and spent the summer competing and training for the World Equestrian Games in Salzburg, Austria, a one-of-a-kind experience that we will forever remember, especially as more than fifty friends and family flew all the way to Austria to support us.

Winning the U.S. Pairs Combined Driving Championship, 2005.

After that experience, I continued to compete and won the U.S. Combined Driving Championship in the advanced single horse division in 2009. With that award, I made a little bit of history by becoming the first American driver to have a national championship in both singles and pairs driving.

Shortly after my 2009 win, it became apparent that the Great Recession was something none of us had experienced before. As I've mentioned, that challenge brought me back to The Grupe Company as president and CEO to help develop strategies for surviving the Great Recession and for rebuilding the company.

One way I *did* stay involved with horses after my return to the company was through continuing to offer our farm, Shady Oaks, as a venue for the American Driving Society's Combined Driving Event (CDE), a multi-day event consisting of three competitions (dressage, marathon, and obstacle/cones). It was Hardy Zantke, a native of Germany and one of the great horsemen and carriage drivers of our time, who encouraged us to develop a CDE venue at our property. Shady Oaks would become one of the finest combined-driving facilities in the world, due to its quality, size, and ability to accommodate the three competitions in one spot.

From the first year we hosted (2000) until the last (2017), we received a lot of joy from opening up our property to share our love of the sport with others. Hardy officiated at the last event, a nice bookend to our almost twenty years of working together. After announcing that we would be closing our venue, he wrote a letter describing what our journey together had meant to him:

> We set out nineteen years ago to make Shady Oaks a world-class event, and you certainly succeeded with that. Nobody else did as much for the sport of driving west of the Mississippi than the two of you! Well, actually, to be more precise, even as of 100 miles west of the Eastern

Seaboard, and even in that stretch I could think of only about a handful of people who would come close! We all in the West are very grateful to you two—and the rest of your family and team as much as they participated—for that!

As they say, high praise from Caesar!

As the company strengthened, finding its feet again around 2012, I returned to the sport and began to drive four-in-hand, competing in earnest in 2014, and I continued to love having the opportunity to compete.

Phyllis has also competed in combined driving since 2005. She started by driving horses in single competitions—a natural way to prepare horses that I would later drive in pairs competitions. She thought it would be fun to give driving ponies a shot and found an amazing teammate in Cincinnati Shine, a rescue animal that ended up, as is often the case, being the one doing the rescuing.

Phyllis competed with Shine for about eight years before she retired him at the age of twenty-five. Together they were shortlisted for the pony international driving championship twice, and, while she didn't go to Europe, it was nice to know they could have gone. Although retired from active competition, Phyllis's beloved pony can often be seen being led around the farm, with one of our great-grandchildren riding on his back and smiling from ear to ear.

What can a passionate pastime bring to your life?

It's never too late to try something new. When Phyllis began competing with our Belgians, she was a mother of four and forty-one years old. When I started combined driving, I was sixty. A later start does *not* have to limit the possibilities of your journey. If you're passionate about something and can afford it, go for it.

Avocations can be the gateway to unimaginable adventure. When we began with our Belgians and later with the sport of combined driving, enjoying our horses was the purpose—not shows or competition. But, like most humans, you always want to do better if you can, so as we saw opportunities to grow and try new things, we did just that. In the process we were introduced to people, places, and cultures that, otherwise, we may have never experienced.

Making time for passions reminds us of life's potential. Our habit provided an opportunity to be in nature, enjoy the landscape, and spend important time together as a family. We've gained a lot from keeping physical exercise, sport, and competition in our lives.

Pastimes mean more if they're shared. For more than forty years, we have become great friends with many of the wonderful people we have met while indulging in our love for horses. Sharing the strength and beauty of the Belgian draft horses or the speed, endurance, and versatility of the combined-driving horses with others has heightened our enjoyment and overall experience.

Balance and peace bring bliss. Although we were blessed to be able to compete domestically and abroad, bringing home many ribbons and awards, we often felt the greatest fulfillment was found in the simple things, like driving home every night and seeing those magnificent animals grazing in the field—our farm complete.

Chapter 17

Banding Together to Bounce Back

*W*HATEVER SETBACK I'M withstanding, I've learned that someone else is usually struggling with it, too. I've had a lot of success creating networks with like-minded people dealing with the same issues. When The Tax Reform Act of 1986 hit me, it hit Jim Klingbeil, too. He lost about 40 to 45 percent of his net worth in twenty-four hours. When asked how he dealt with such a loss, he responded, "You have to have a lot of enthusiasm and a bad memory."

When times get tough, the networks we create and the people we partner with can give us the boost we need to keep plugging along.

Before YPO had forums, six of us put together a group called The Advisory Group (TAG). This was

> *When times get tough, the networks we create and the people we partner with can give us the boost we need to keep plugging along.*

before any of us had an outside board of directors for our companies. Dino Cortopassi, Jiggs Davis, Walt Hogan, Paul Foster, Albert "Bo" Raisch, and I would get together at each other's headquarters and spend the day talking out issues facing our companies. We were all in YPO and presidents of Northern California companies. Although we had different businesses (agriculture, high tech, steel manufacturing, poultry, heavy construction, and real estate development), we faced similar issues and benefited from being able to talk strategy. We each were heading up a start-up company, growing fast, and finding barriers we didn't know even existed. To have this ad hoc board of directors helped us keep moving forward, despite setbacks.

As an extra benefit, we developed strong friendships. Jiggs, for example, is also a Bohemian Grove campmate of mine and another friend who never misses the opening of dove season. Hogan once lent me a significant amount of money on the spot so we could complete a deal. The bank we depended on for the loan needed more time to complete paperwork, but the seller refused our request for an extension. If we didn't close on time, we'd have lost our deposits and the right to buy. While I did not ask for a loan in the meeting, and financial help was not the purpose of the group (in fact, this is the only loan that ever happened), this story reminds me of the strong commitment we had to help each other succeed and bounce back.

Likewise, in 1987, I saw a need to forge a relationship with other leaders in the community to help improve the quality of life in San Joaquin County—specifically focusing on infrastructure, education, and land use. I formed the San Joaquin Business Council, Inc. by joining CEO leaders in the business and education sector. We have been able to coordinate and tackle economic issues that impact all of us. And, like YPO, it has allowed me to get to know people I might not otherwise

BANDING TOGETHER TO BOUNCE BACK

have had the chance to meet and, therefore, has broadened my overall perspective about the resources, needs, and issues within the county.

The Business Council is made up of 120 local CEOs, is 100 percent privately funded, and has done a tremendous amount of good for San Joaquin County. Since its inception, the council has secured funds for transportation projects such as the rebuilding of Highway 99 and Interstate 5, efforts that have raised billions of dollars in matching funds. In 1991, the council formed the nonprofit San Joaquin A+, which among its several goals has worked to improve school readiness among children, especially those in high-risk areas. The Business Council also formed and helped get the San Joaquin Partnership—a public-private partnership with the county and five cities—off the ground. The sole mission of the San Joaquin Partnership is job formation.

Monthly meetings take an educational approach. We bring in experts to speak on topics that affect us all—education, infrastructure, land use, and any other major issues facing our county (e.g., homelessness, public-safety policies, etc.) One of the main draws is the fellowship it provides—any member can feel comfortable calling another member for advice or experience on a particular issue. One of the advantages of local committees and councils is the element of proximity, which can result in viable local networks.

Councils and committees are only as strong as their members, and the Business Council has had excellent leadership. After working on the Brookside development, Ron Addington, former vice president of Grupe Development Company, helped us with Fresno's Woodward Lake and then moved to Stockton to help me with the Business Council by becoming its chief executive, a position he held for twenty-four years. I am still chairman after three decades (despite my many attempts to relinquish that position to someone else).

My relationship with Jim Klingbeil in particular has helped me bounce back for the past forty years. In a lifetime, how many friends does a person have to whom he or she is willing to expose heartache, concern, and sensitive issues? One must have a lot of trust and confidence to become that vulnerable.

Jim and I have a lot in common. He was raised in a small town in Ohio and went to Ohio State, where he is now a trustee. He went on to Stanford Medical School to please his father. While in medical school, he started building apartments; later, he quit medical school to be a full-time apartment developer. Before he was forty, he'd sold 49 percent of his company to the television broadcasting company CBS, which was delving into the real estate business and had promised to help him become the largest apartment builder in the United States. Ultimately, the relationship with CBS did not work out, but he persevered and became one of the largest apartment developers in the United States on his own. He has had a ride similar to mine, so we've had a lot to share.

Our personalities are similar, too, proving the old saying: "Birds of a feather flock together." Neither of us is risk-averse, and we're both tenacious. We have a vision for our futures, want to get through setbacks, and are generally positive. We place a high value on ethics and don't waste time placing blame. As Jim will say about partnerships, "In many cases, it's the pursuit of whose fault it is. And I'm just not like that, and neither is Fritz. Most of the time, it isn't anybody's fault. It's the cycles of life."

We have served on each other's advisory boards and developed multiple real estate projects together—more than $100 million invested. Jim was president of ULI not long after me. In the years between us, Smedes York acted as ULI president. Smedes is a great leader, former mayor of Raleigh, North Carolina, and chairman of the board for York Properties, a construction company founded in 1910. Jim and I were in the same YPO forum as well and enjoyed traveling with our wives to ULI conferences across the country and YPO universities around the world.

Phyllis and I have enjoyed many adventures with Jim and his wife, Sally. In addition to traveling together often, we owned homes next to each other in Snowmass, Colorado, and enjoyed hiking and skiing the mountains of Colorado for more than thirty years. Jim has joined me on countless hunting trips and has been a regular at my annual dove hunt for the past forty years.

Skiing in Snowmass, Colorado, with Jim and Sally. Maroon Bells mountains in the background.

But perhaps most of all, we have suffered through misfortunes together. It's very therapeutic to be able to joke with someone who's also had a lot of setbacks and understands what you are going through. It's an advantage that comes with being older and having a lot of different experiences. Part of the special sisterhood that Sally and

Phyllis share is supporting Jim and me through the many ups and downs in the real estate industry.

So how can you make sure those helping you are also benefitting from the relationship?

- Collaboration works best in an atmosphere of respect, openness, and honesty. You're going to need to be able to admit your mistakes and be okay with it. In my case, I've had to get used to some friends' "helpful input" not being as sensitive as it could be, or friends reminding me of my mistakes. Once when I asked Jim, "How could I do something so stupid?" he didn't mince words: "Because you're stupid!" Harsh and exaggerative, of course, but refreshing to have someone who'll be honest. And, the bold overemphasis helped deflate the situation I was feeling bad about. As Jim will say, "No shot is too cheap to take," but it's always followed with help. Jim is great at helping me spot potential and "see a lake in a drop of water," as he puts it.
- Take and act on their information! Let them know how it worked out for you. Make sure they know you'll listen to them.
- Make sure they're getting something out of the relationship, too. There needs to be take-home value for all. For the advisory board I formed for our company in the 1980s, I wanted to make sure they got as much *from* the relationship as they gave. I wanted to provide an opportunity for an expert in one area to get an inside view of another expert's processes, successes, and trials. I think they all looked forward to the times our "think tank" met because they didn't have an opportunity to meet with each other otherwise.

Part Three

Life Is Better When It's Shared

*O*VER THE YEARS, I've enjoyed handing my executives wooden plaques with well-known quotes engraved on the brass plate. I've picked the sentiment based on the needs of my team and specific to issues we were facing at the time. I enjoy distributing advice I believe can uplift, motivate, and inspire my team in a fun and unique way.

I love sharing what I learn, especially wisdom that's stood the test of time. Some of the principles in this book date back more than two thousand years. Some came from the minds of friends who have built billion-dollar companies, while others came from religious leaders, ancient philosophers, politicians, scientists, and even a humorist. There is much we can learn in this life if we open up and share.

So how do these concepts apply to working in teams? How can leaders use these lessons to manage more effectively? Which principles can help us make a more visible difference in our community?

The answer will sound familiar. Put people first. Our company thrives on putting people before business and *making* the time to give back and have fun.

It's one thing to make a good living; it's another to change and improve the lives of others. Best of all, though, is succeeding *together*.

Chapter 18

Building Teams That Execute

ONE OF THE FIRST THINGS you learn as a real estate developer of master-planned communities is that it takes a big team with diverse skills to turn an idea into a marketable product. If your team doesn't have the ability to execute, all you'll ever have is a paper development. In other words, you'll be promising something but never delivering.

As people buy into your vision, how will you build productive and successful teams—teams that don't just talk about what should happen but also have the ability to execute?

It's not easy, but it is worth the effort. An effective team begins with finding compatible members who respect each other and can build on each other's expertise—and then giving them the trust, autonomy, mutual respect, and purposefulness to execute for the greater good.

A Leader's Role

If you're like me, building a team to implement your vision may be one of the most satisfying parts of your journey. There's nothing like creating something greater than its individual parts. That's the reason for a team, isn't it? To do a job together that none of us could do alone.

Teams require a leader. Even if you're not the president of a company or an executive at your workplace, you are the leader of your dream. A leader can set a vision but cannot set the strategy alone. A leader without a team isn't a leader.

I see a leader as a person with a vision who is a risk-taker, and as a consummate opportunist who is innovative, charismatic, and tenacious. A leader keeps focus on the goals while shaping ideas, creating excitement, unleashing energy, and inspiring commitment in others. A leader picks good people and sees team members for what they *can* become and enables them to grow. In chaotic times, a leader keeps overall perspective and can discern if the difference makes a difference.

> *In chaotic times, a leader keeps overall perspective and can discern if the difference makes a difference.*

Why do people want leaders? Because they lack the confidence or knowledge to get where they want to go, or won't take the risk involved in going after it on their own.

While some people want a leader because they question their own ability or lack the necessary discipline, others prefer to work in an organization because a big success shared is better than a limited success. As one of my executives confided, "I could have never been this successful on my own. I do not fit the leadership model. I want to be part of a company."

> ### Thoughts from the Team
> #### JOHN DINKEL
>
> "Fritz is very inspirational. He was obviously a big-picture visionary kind of a person that you knew was looking out ahead just by the product he put on the table for people to buy. He was focused on what he wanted to do. He was people-oriented. He was very honest, and if there was a problem, he would bring it up."

The Importance of Choosing Compatible People

We've all been on unsuccessful teams, where the team's job was to design a horse, but it came up with a camel. As I've said, a team is only as strong as its members. Pick people who accept responsibility and have the ability to recognize their weaknesses and mistakes, work hard, take action, make decisions, think creatively, have tenacity, and communicate with compassion, humility, and trust—all the principles covered in this book.

The more deep-rooted the relationship, the more selective you need to be. There is a difference between a partnership (an ongoing relationship) and an investor (a one-time decision).

As you decide who to partner with for the long haul, pick the person over the deal or opportunity. Why? Because if the deal doesn't work out, you want to make sure you are partnered with somebody who will stick with you through tough times. When I form a partnership, I always look for the following:

- The other player is clear on the rules of engagement and our purpose.
- The other person is willing to compromise. As my friend Alan Simpson says, "If you cannot compromise you should not be in politics, and for sure you shouldn't get married." That's my philosophy, too, when partnering for business.
- The potential partner has enough character not to leave me high and dry.

Whoever proposes the deal is responsible for the structure and outcome. After doing all your due diligence and giving suggestions, let the other party run with it, and don't second-guess them when things go wrong—you had your chance for input. One of the benefits of trust is that it speeds up the process and eliminates a lot of things that you don't have to put into legal contracts.

As I've shared, I have been fortunate to have partnerships with several of my closest friends that have lasted decades. I don't think it's a coincidence that these friends, along with myself, have all been married almost sixty years. I'd say we take our commitments seriously.

I've mentioned the partnerships I've had with Dino and Jim, and Ed Rasmuson is a third example of a trusted friend and business partner. From Anchorage, Alaska, Ed's grandfather was an early missionary to Alaska and later started the first bank in Alaska, the National Bank of Alaska, which is now part of Wells Fargo. Ed and I met at a YPO conference and hit it off from the get-go, as did our wives. We shared similar interests: faith, family, business, hunting, and fishing. Phyllis and I have been Ed and Cathy's guests in Alaska many times. Over the years, Ed and his family have partnered with us in more than twenty real estate projects. Most have done very well, but we have hit unexpected cycles. He is always there asking, "How can I help?" rather than, "Why didn't you see this coming?" Even though he, like his father, went to Harvard, that hasn't seemed like much of a handicap!

One of the most costly business mistakes is a bad hire; it carries serious economical and emotional consequences. Dr. Pierre Mornell, author of *45 Effective Ways for Hiring Smart: How to Predict Winners and Losers in the Incredibly Expensive People-Reading Game* (2003) and whom I hired to work with The Grupe Company on several occasions, spent more than a quarter of a century screening applicants for a wide range of companies. From his experience, he concluded, *"If you make a mistake in hiring, and you recognize and rectify the mistake within six months, the cost of replacing that employee is two and one-half times the person's annual salary. . . .* The wrong executive making $100,000 will cost you a quarter of a million dollars *if you rectify the mistake within six months.* And this economic estimate doesn't even consider the emotional costs." As my friend Gary Rogers, put it, "Very few companies *really* hire smart. In my experience you have choices when you put a team together. You can either hire smart, or you can manage tough. It's a lot easier to hire smart than to manage tough."

Before hiring individuals for key positions at The Grupe Company, I ask myself several questions:

- Does the person buy into the company's overall vision?
- Does he or she share my values, compassion for others, and commitment to hard work?

- Does he or she also believe in putting the customer first? Or, are they of the mindset, *Business would be great except for the damn customer*?
- Do they have integrity?
- Am I confident in this person? Can I delegate to this person?
- Does the person fit with the culture of our workplace?
- Has the applicant shown the ability to adapt and be flexible?
- Do I like the person? Don't underestimate your gut reaction.

If the applicant checks out, knows his or her business, and I feel good as I run through the above questions, I get a second opinion.

In the early years of the company, I never hired anybody without Phyllis's input. This wasn't something where I would give her a resume with the assignment to follow up by making calls to the applicant's former employees. This was after due diligence had been done and the applicant had checked out. Phyllis and I would take the applicant out for dinner. I wanted Phyllis's sound judgment, her women's intuition, if you will, to size up the person. I've learned that gut feelings are as important as the resume. In my experience, 99 percent of the time, a hire will not work in the long run if he or she does not fit in with the existing work culture, regardless of how qualified the person may be on paper.

This isn't to say that your team is going to be made up of only perfect people. You don't have to be perfect to be a winner. Everyone has weaknesses. Good management, as taught by renowned management educator Dr. Peter Drucker, is building on a person's strengths and making their weaknesses irrelevant. It's the leader's, or manager's, responsibility to figure out how best to leverage people. As I've said, if the weakness is covered by a solution, then it's no longer a problem.

That said, there are some weaknesses you cannot tolerate in business, such as: non-performance, dishonesty, indecisiveness, or bad work habits that drag down the workplace. Life is too short to do business with jerks or people who are unwilling to adapt. As Jack Welch, former chairman and CEO of General Electric, expressed, "I've always believed that when the rate of change inside an institution becomes slower than the rate of change outside, the end is in sight."

If you make the right hire the first time, every time, as Mornell put it, your company will be stronger for it.

> ### *Thoughts from the Team*
> #### DON BENIOFF
>
> "Fritz reviewed and understood and hired people based on: they are strong enough to run their own companies (so someday, they could be doing their own thing), but for one reason or another, they needed the support of a good company."

The Attributes of a Highly Productive Team

With people in place, a highly productive team is made up of members who:

- understand the vision
- believe in the vision
- know their *specific* role in turning that vision into a reality
- feel trusted and free to act
- collaborate with mutual respect and purposefulness
- pull in the same direction

- take joy in success, regardless of who brings it to the team
- have fun

How does a *healthy* team function?

It has clarity. Members know the goals and objective of the team. Team members need to have a purpose within the team; they need to feel needed and to be given opportunities to strengthen their confidence. Team members should be delegated measurable tasks and held accountable for the execution of those tasks.

It provides safety. In healthy teams, ideas are exchanged, mistakes revealed (and fixed), and disagreements resolved. Mistakes are not a problem as long as they are learned from and not repeated constantly. A team is not a place for members to be shamed or humiliated. It's a place for people to find support, encouragement, and solutions.

It reflects diverse talent. Wise leaders surround themselves with people possessing different talents, especially strengths differing from their own. Part of a leader's job is recruiting people who normally wouldn't be together. Despite the different skill sets and personalities, the team is connected by common goals and a shared culture.

It requires collaboration. The team should be a hub of knowledge sharing. A company shouldn't have silo thinking (withholding of knowledge). It interferes with the free flow of information, thwarts creative thinking, slows down action and progress, and impacts trust and harmony. Collaboration is *fun*; holding cards close to your vest, not so much.

It is cohesive. No individual on the team is more powerful, or important, than the rest. Everyone is in alignment (I'll talk about this more later). Internal fighting can be more detrimental than outside competition. Everyone needs to be going in the same direction. Most people don't grasp the reality that five people working on a task are reduced to one if two are pulling in the opposite direction. Many will ask, "Aren't there still three members on the team making progress?" They forget that two members pulling in the *wrong* direction negate the efforts of two members pulling in the *right* direction.

It handles mistakes. Team members are going to make mistakes. When you have a team, they all have to feel part of the defeat. A strong team knows how to rebound and doesn't use the misstep of a team member as an excuse to hurt others or to give oneself an advantage. One of my favorite quotes by a fellow YPO'er is: "When things go right, I don't want all the credit because when they go wrong, I don't want all the responsibility." The team that sees mistakes as something to fix together rather than evidence to hold over others is a team that will go far.

Thoughts from the Team

JERRY ABBOTT

"When a member of Fritz's team makes a mistake, especially one that could be costly, rather than berate that person, Fritz will ask, 'What can we learn from that, and what can we do differently next time?' I think that really empowers people."

JOHN DINKEL

"I loved the way the company was set up. It was a team atmosphere. If there was a problem, we brought everybody in, and we'd talk about the different things we could do to fix it. They gave you room to do what you needed to do in order to utilize your talent. It wasn't over-managed. You had the flexibility to come up with ideas."

Giving the Authority to Act

Delegation is a powerful and essential tool for getting the most out of your team. When you delegate, you trust someone else to complete a task with the understanding that he or she will keep the lines of communication open if any problems arise. You are not absolved of *all* responsibility. Delegation is not abdication. I can assure you that, if one of our employees makes a serious-enough mistake, our partners or customers are going to come to *me,* too, not just the person who made the mistake. The buck always stops at the top.

> *Delegation is not abdication.*

When you delegate, it's fair to set parameters. When are you going to get back to me? What will you have accomplished? Is it measurable in regard to time, quality, quantity, and cost? Those are legitimate questions. It doesn't do any good to delegate more than a person can handle.

Raising children is a perfect way to learn the skill of delegation. You start small, check in frequently, and don't set them up for failure. You wouldn't let them go off a cliff to show them it wouldn't work. If results are good, you delegate more and, in the process, build confidence.

Sometimes, as the leader, you'll feel that confidence and see a person's potential before they do. I'll never forget when I was delegating to one of my key guys and encouraging him, "You can do this. You *can* get this thing done."

"I'm not sure," he admitted.

"I know damn well you can get it done. Just get out there and get it done."

"Well, *you* think I can get it done," he said. "But *I* don't know if I can get it done."

And, as I predicted, he got it done.

Part of a leader's responsibility is to see others as they could be, not as they are. I call that having a Pygmalion attitude. That's key, and a point I'll expand on in the next chapter.

If the individual does not follow through and fails to ask for help, then you have a career discussion because they're not keeping with the boundaries that have been set.

Another pitfall is when individuals delegate up. Team members should know more about their role and job than their boss. I can remember one time when I was working with executives in the company during a time of rapid growth. "There are a lot of challenges in this company," I admitted. "Every problem in The Grupe Company will have somebody's name attached to solving it. Somebody is going to be given responsibility for solving each problem. And that name will never be Fritz Grupe."

If you're the leader, you cannot be tasked with solving *every* problem. There are just too many. Does that mean I won't help? Be a participant? When I have time, I will. But does that mean it's my problem? No. That's delegating up. While the boss is not absolved of all responsibility, that doesn't mean he or she should solve delegated responsibilities to show the "genius at work." It's a disservice not to let team members learn on their own how to solve problems.

Breakout: How Delegating Allowed a President to Speak to His Nation

I have often marveled at what can be done when people pool their individual talents and knowledge. For example, in February of 1983, I served as chairman of a week-long educational conference for YPO in Phoenix, Arizona. YPO had been holding conferences since 1952, and I had been attending them since the 1970s. The theme of this national "university," as they are called, was, "Mastering Change in the '80s," and it was a fitting title for the Herculean behind-the-scenes effort that went into coordinating the opening ceremony. In addition to a performance by the University of Arizona marching band and an address from the governor of Arizona, we had also arranged what would be the third live teleconference with the then-president of the United States, Ronald Reagan, who had been to our home at Lincoln Village West in Stockton when he was running for the governor's office.

It was my first experience with this kind of two-way communication via satellite, projected onto a twelve-by-sixteen-foot screen. I delegated much of the preparation to my assistant Ann Quinn, who I would promote to vice president of public relations and community services some years later.

Two weeks before the conference was to begin, the executive director of YPO called Ann, saying that they had a problem. They didn't have the staff to figure out *how* to make the two-way communication work. Ann came to me and explained the situation. I advised her to call Karen Munro at Continental Cable, someone I knew by her reputation in Stockton, confident that she would know what to do. Karen told Ann to call a contact she had in Denver, explain the momentousness of what we were attempting to do, and say, "If you do this for free, you'll make history and get a lot more jobs with this kind of technology."

Ann made the call to Karen's contact, and he was game. He arrived with three semi-trucks full of equipment and hooked everything up so that President Reagan's warm welcome to our conference attendees came through loud and clear at the opening ceremony:

> It's a pleasure and a privilege to join such an accomplished group of producers and achievers. . . . you all became presidents of sizable corporations by the time you were forty. That says a lot about your energy, drive, and vision—some of us take a little longer.
>
> You're the people most able to lead the coming economic recovery, increase its momentum, and bring renewed prosperity to America and the world. By definition, you are risk takers, capitalists, and entrepreneurs. Your comparative youth also indicates you're open to new ideas, ready to try new ways of doing things. And that's just the kind of attitude we need to guide America into her next period of economic greatness.

After his remarks, the president went on to take questions from YPO members in the audience. It was an exciting, exhilarating, and proud moment. In 1983, almost no one in the world had ever witnessed teleconferencing, let alone with the president of the United States. By working with others who had the expertise and resources we needed, we achieved more than we could have alone.

To pull off such an important event, delegation was *key*. Delegation not only got the job done, but it also allowed people to grow. As Ann said looking back, "I think that was probably the scariest thing that I ever had to coordinate. But, I learned a lot from it, too. You can get a lot done if you are willing to tell somebody, 'I can't do this alone. I need your help.'"

Success hinges on trusting those you work with and having the ability to network.

Pulling the Same Way

Have you ever heard of the Abilene Paradox? It's a principle developed by a professor of management science, Jerry B. Harvey, based on a spontaneous trip he took with his family to Abilene, Texas, some fifty miles away, for dinner. The trip does *not* go well. As things unravel, each family member reveals that he or she never wanted to go to Abilene in the first place. So, even though nobody wanted to go to Abilene, they all went because they thought everyone else wanted to go. How often does that happen within a family or a business?

I often check with my team and use the phrase, "Is this a trip to Abilene?" Are we all headed somewhere we really don't want to go but we're not comfortable in saying it? It's a good idea to check in, in other words, to make sure things are on the right track.

For a team to maximize progress, it has to be in alignment. Once the team has agreed to a plan, we all *must* pull the rope in the same direction. We can't have members of the team subsequently decide, "I don't like this plan, so I'm not going to help." Worst of all is what I call *vicious compliance*, where a person pretends to help, but the real goal is to prove you wrong.

Does this mean a team needs to always agree?

No. Alignment and agreement are not the same. I've got no problem with people questioning something we've decided on. In fact, I once had badges made that said, "That's the way we've always done

A Letter from a Fellow Chairman
SMEDES YORK

"Fritz, I often think about the change in direction of ULI back in the 1980s, which you led....One especially significant process which you put forward was strategic planning....I have often used that process when other strategic plans are discussed.

I clearly remember that our leadership group first identified issues, concerns, and initiatives. We then put each on a piece of paper and put them in a pile in the middle of a table. We then went through all of them and put them in categories. We ended up with 14 different areas of focus.

Next we took each area of focus and assigned it to either a standing committee, a council, a task force, or to management. Measurable parameters were determined, along with a timetable and a budget. Each task area was 'assignable, measurable and had a budget.' So in effect we had 14 separate strategic plans.

To my recollection, we accomplished all 14 tasks which was positive for ULI. As I sit on boards and the subject of strategic planning comes up, I say 'we need objectives that are assignable, measurable and with a budget attached.' In other words, an objective would not be to 'improve morale.' It would need to be perhaps a measurable goal related to retaining a certain percentage of employees.

Fritz, I think about this process at least once a month. Actually I'm not sure I've seen any other strategic planning effort really work."

it," with a big line through it. I had everybody in the company wear the badge as a visible reminder that there were changes we needed to make, and, just because we'd done it one way before didn't mean we were always going to do things that way. Therefore, it is always legitimate to ask, "Are we on a trip to Abilene?"

It's a lot more enjoyable when people agree with you—we all know that. But, sometimes, when people disagree, it turns out to be a better stew. We view positive disagreements as good and healthy. They help us improve our products and give better service to our customers. One of the sure paths to the death of an organization is the absence of differences of opinion, a "yes mentality." When the members of an organization have respect for each other's ideas and abilities and are in general alignment, new concepts, products, market niches, and services will flourish.

I don't claim to have all the knowledge in the world, so I'm always open to other people's input. After you listen, compromise if needed, and build avenues of agreement. You'll be back on track.

Thoughts from the Team
NELSON BAHLER

"When a person is given responsibility and authority, they are allowed to grow."

FRANK PASSADORE

"I never once felt like I was stifled from creating something or coming up with an idea. And then again, I was never

> criticized for making a decision and not having it work. You know, 'That didn't work. Fine. Let's learn from it and go from there.' So it was a culture that Fritz had created within the framework of the company that let you use your creative talents and didn't make you feel like you were going to be bullied if you made the wrong decision. And I think that's what got everybody constantly moving to the next level in terms of their talent, their creativity, and in the people they hired, and why we were able to stay ahead of the typical builder."
>
> ANN QUINN
>
> "And the thing that was great about Fritz and Phyllis is that they gave me a chance to make mistakes. They trusted me to come up with a plan but to check with them before I went out on a limb and chopped myself off at the end of it."

Building Camaraderie

I have always enjoyed scheduling events away from the office to promote teambuilding. Giving teams opportunities to work together, or bond, leads to better business decisions and improved performance.

One of my favorite events that we've held over the years was the annual Mariposa Roundup that I'll describe in detail soon. It was a great event for the entire family, and it allowed our employees to work on transferable skills and concepts in a fun way.

We also built camaraderie through encouraging Grupe employees to work together in our big fundraiser, The Country Fair, an event that provided a lot of satisfaction for our employees as they enjoyed working together to give back to the community.

We continue to schedule retreats so employees can enjoy leisure time together away from the office while strengthening their ability to work together.

Handing out awards to children attending the Mariposa Roundup.

Final Thought

In writing this book, I gathered a dozen of my executives, past and present, to ask for help identifying what has been rare and consequential during our journey together. We spent a good amount of time reminiscing on different projects and efforts, but often the conversation turned to discussing what being part of the team had meant in the long run. Many expressed appreciation for being given autonomy and the freedom to create and take risks.

"I've never felt like I've had a boss," Nelson Bahler shared. "I've always thought I was working for myself for the last thirty years."

"Interesting! That's the way *we've* all felt," I said.

We all got a laugh out of that.

"I said the wrong thing there, didn't I?" Nelson admitted. "But it's true. No one pounds anybody. They just let people do their job."

It's amazing what a team can accomplish if egos and personalities don't get in the way and if team members feel they can rely on each other, complement each other's strengths, and make up for any weaknesses. As one of my financial executives, Paula Tarantino, said, "When you put the right people in the right spot, great things can happen."

Digging In: Teaching Teamwork

Teamwork is learned at a very early age when you're part of a ranching family. As soon as our grandchildren and great-grandchildren are walking, they're fascinated by our cattle brandings and eager to watch the action through pipe corral fencing. By the age of five, they start to feel they're an important part of the team. From feeding the cattle to branding the calves, work around the ranch is made lighter (or sometimes is possible *only*) when it's shared.

For more than forty years, we have enjoyed using our 8,000-acre working cattle ranch—the G Ranch in Mariposa—to help teach teamwork to our children, grandchildren, great-grandchildren, and employees of The Grupe Company. Our ranch is located in the foothills of the Sierra Nevada Mountains. Its elevation ranges from 1,000 feet, where the Chowchilla River runs through the east side of the property, to 2,000 feet, at the top of Horse Mountain. During the winter months, our cattle roam the range, relying on their own instincts. About five

Our daughter Sandy Huber with our great-granddaughters, Evelia Joy (in arms) and Clara Belle Baker, watching as calves are branded, 2017.

BUILDING TEAMS THAT EXECUTE

hundred calves are born in the winter without any human assistance. Then, every spring we hold roundups where cowboys on horseback drive in about a thousand head of cattle from the range so we can brand the calves and attend to the healthcare of the entire herd.

After the cattle are herded into one of our big corrals, riders on horseback separate the mothers from the babies, which are between one and three months old and weigh between 150 and 250 pounds. This is the first time the calves and mothers have ever been separated, so there's a lot of mooing and bawling as both walk up and down the fence that now temporarily divides them.

We move about twenty calves at a time into a smaller 100-by-100-foot corral. There, cowboys and cowgirls on horseback rope a calf by its rear legs. The roper pulls the calf across the corral to a crew that then pins it to the ground. These "calf wrestlers" have to keep the calf as still as possible so that the others can complete their jobs without causing injury or harm to the calf (or to anyone participating). If a calf gets loose, it can knock you over and trample you, and with little kids in the arena learning the ropes, it's important for everyone to be focused and pulling the same way so no one gets hurt.

The team of cowboys and cowgirls wait on the edge of the arena to jump in and do their jobs as soon as the calf is secured. The different steps that make up a branding take place in rapid succession. The brand is applied to the calf's left hip. Other team members give a series of vaccinations and a vitamin shot. If the calf is male, he is castrated. And finally, the calf's ear is tagged. All of that needs to happen in less than two minutes!

And the conditions are challenging—the calf is bawling and kicking, dirt and the smell of burnt hide are in the air, and a cloud of dust and smoke can make it hard to see. In the crucial seconds of the branding, such challenges are overcome through teamwork and a lot of detailed preparation ahead of time—the branding iron is kept red hot, so it need be applied for only seconds. The syringes have already been properly filled and refilled. All of this is done in service of our goals: to keep everyone safe and get the calf back up and reunited with its mother as quickly as possible.

Over the course of the morning, we brand about seventy-five calves. We end the day's work at lunchtime and celebrate what we've achieved together over a delicious feast of steak, beans, salad, and pies that has been prepared by yet *another* team.

As tradition has it, I apply the first brand
at the Mariposa Roundup, 2017.

BUILDING TEAMS THAT EXECUTE

It's a day of celebration for us, but it's also a day of tradition. We use the G̲ brand, the same brand used by my great-grandfather John Carsten Grupe, who raised Durham cattle in the late nineteenth century. He obtained one of the first cattle brands in the state of California, and his branding iron was handed down to his son George (my grandfather). It's also become tradition that I brand the first calf.

To keep brandings fun, efficient, and less stressful, we position ourselves in the various necessary roles by strengths and interests, but all of our individual efforts have to coalesce so as not to let the team down. A lot of the work happens *behind* the scenes, but regardless of whether the job is inside or outside of the arena, *every* job counts. The straightforwardness of the goal of the branding and its fast pace give immediate feedback to the team, making it a wonderful exercise in teamwork.

Since we feel that the Mariposa Roundup epitomizes teamwork (and is a *great* way to spend the morning), we've used the branding as a way to work on teambuilding with our Grupe Company family. For a time, we'd bus the employees' families up for a fun-filled day of teambuilding opportunities.

But we held more events than just the branding. We'd have competitions throughout the day—BB gun shooting, archery, Jeep rides, fishing, horseback riding, watermelon seed-spitting, and pie-eating to name a few. A favorite was "calf mugging," where team members had to untie a ribbon off a calf's tail. We'd reassemble the families so that it was a mom and a dad, but they couldn't be married to each other, and they had to pick somebody else's kids. The teams always turned out fairly equal, and once we turned the calves loose, the goal became to rope the calf, catch it, and remove the ribbon. Meanwhile, as one executive remembers, "little kids are just tumbling in the air." Think of the liability nowadays!

We had prizes for the various events, but all of the kids got a ribbon just for showing up. We even had an award for the person who racked up the least amount of points—a pen holder in the shape of a cow pie that the winner got to display on his or her desk for the coming year. For the man and woman who racked up the *most* points, they received big, silver belt buckles engraved with "Senior Cowboy," or "Senior Cowgirl." For the kids, we had a "Junior Cowboy" and "Junior Cowgirl."

Participation in the branding has helped build camaraderie among our family and business partners and has been a wonderful teaching tool, as it allows those we love to feel the great sense of satisfaction that comes from achieving as a team.

Chapter 19

Helping Others Succeed

ONE OF MY GREATEST REWARDS as a manager has been helping individuals achieve more together than they could alone. My go-to pitch for recruiting team members has always been, "I think you would be better as part of our team than doing your own thing." Part of being a *good* manager is to help team members reach their potential.

To be a successful manager requires a lot of different skills working in sync—the discipline to manage one's self, the willingness to see the good in others, the capability of relating with empathy, the courage to give trust, and the ability to see and appreciate the contributions of others. This all takes time, patience, and persistence.

What does it take to be an effective manager—one who inspires individual performance? And, how can performance be evaluated in a way that's motivating?

The answer is really quite simple: When people are treated with respect and appreciation, they *want* to do a good job.

The Role of a Manager

There's a saying: "Businesses don't compete; managers do." Have you ever thought of why being a manager is so difficult and why many people just don't like it? Managers need to know how to manage not just themselves but others as well. As any text on management will tell you, a good manager should:

- focus on the important, not the urgent
- not require constant positive feedback or reward
- be a good coach and supporter
- be receptive and prioritize listening and understanding
- provide resources within the workplace to help offset stress
- give credit and acknowledge and appreciate good work, big or small

Setting an Example

My father used to say, "If you see somebody in front of the store sweeping the sidewalk, it's either the owner or the janitor. There's nobody in between who will do it." That may be true, but we try to create a culture where every employee is all in. No one should feel above certain tasks—that's an important principle for the manager to model.

In my office, I have a two-foot-high bronze statue of a cowboy with his hands on his hips and an attitude that matches the title, *I Ain't No Fence Tender*. Cowboys ride the horses and don't tend fence. But, if you're out on your cattle ranch in the middle of nowhere and see a fence down, you'd better fix the damn thing and not wait.

It is just as important to acknowledge work performed by employees and team members. Here again, leaders and managers set the example.

One day, one of our stable hands (an immigrant who had about a sixth-grade education) approached Phyllis and complained that his supervisor was "stealing my ribbons."

Confused, Phyllis asked, "'Stealing your ribbons'? What do you mean?"

He explained, "I do something. I work hard. I make something happen in the barn or with the horses, but when you come over to the barn, he says that *he* did it. He's stealing my ribbons."

In other words, he was stealing the credit which, to him, was probably of equal value to his pay. All he wanted was credit to be given where it was due. When possible, team members need to be credited for their work and acknowledged for their achievements in front of others.

Seeing Potential

Respect starts with how you see those around you. You've chosen to bring team members onboard because you had confidence in them and respected what they could bring; it only makes sense to ensure that respect continues in the interactions that follow. I have found that it helps to have what I call a Pygmalion attitude, seeing others as they *could be* rather than as they are. I don't see an executive, or a bare piece of land, or a business deal just for what it is *now*. I try to think ahead and see potential. This is especially useful when dealing with difficult people. As my grandmother "Mama Lou" used to always say, "There's no one so bad that you can't find a little good."

I appreciate those who saw my potential, such as my high school ag teacher, Chet Pierce, seeing a budding entrepreneur behind the mischief of a consummate prankster. My mother was also determined to focus on the good. Phyllis was surprised to learn my nickname had

ENJOY THE RIDE

been "Good Boy" growing up because of some of the stories she had heard, such as the time I drove my motorcycle up the steps of my old fraternity house, through the front door, and into the dining room just to provoke my old football buddies.

Eventually, Phyllis asked Luanne, "Why'd your mom call him 'Good Boy' if he was so mischievous?"

Luanne replied, "Well, he was so full of mischief my mom thought if she just called him 'Good Boy,' he'd be better."

That's the power of positive thinking!

Throughout my journey I've benefited from the faith others have put in me. When developers Bob Nahas (president of ULI 1965–1966) and Roy Drachman (president of ULI 1970–1973) asked if I would take the position of president of ULI, I was taken aback. I was young compared to past presidents, and it was going to be a tough time for the real estate industry. The savings-and-loan crisis was upon us. I went to my advisory board for counsel. Did they think I could balance all that was going to be required of me? They all said, "You can do it."

And it was a great experience. Our team, Smedes York, Jim Klingbeil, Charlie Shaw, and Joe Canizaro, all went on to be future presidents of ULI. With all those Type A personalities, challenges, and hardships, we still had a lot of fun together, and we became lifelong friends.

Breakout: Focusing on the 80 Percent—University Park

One of our most unique projects is University Park, a 102-acre, mixed-use development in midtown Stockton. It's an example of how a project's or person's potential often is limited by our own perceptions.

The site dates back to the early 1850s, when the location was chosen to become The Insane Asylum of the State of California—the first hospital in California exclusively for the mentally ill and the first of its kind west of the Mississippi River. After closing the facility (by then known as the Stockton Developmental Center) in 1996, the State was left with the task of figuring out what to do with the site. The following year, the State transferred the site to the California State University (CSU) system to serve as a home for the CSU Stanislaus Stockton Center. After a couple of years and struggling to make it work financially, the CSU system partnered with the City of Stockton to find a company to take over development, operations, and management of the site.

There was a lot of hesitancy among my associates about whether or not to pursue the project. Many of my associates thought it wouldn't work because it *hadn't* worked. If the CSU system couldn't operate it successfully with their budget, how could we do it for half the existing annual operating fee provided by the State and make money on top of that?

It's easy to see why there'd been doubts.

But my curiosity was piqued—how could you go wrong when you control that many acres and they'll pay you to figure it out? Where others saw trouble, I saw potential. For example, there were a number of functionally obsolescent buildings that had to remain due to their historic designation, and that appeared, to many, to be an imposition and liability. I saw an opportunity. I imagined those historic buildings acting as a backdrop, much like a movie set, to the bigger picture, serving nothing but an aesthetic purpose but bolstering the *perceived* value of the campus.

As I continued to look, I realized that, under the right circumstances, we *could* do it if we focused on the property's *potential* rather than its issues. There were a lot of problems, but they were only 20 percent of the picture. I chose to focus on the 80 percent that *did* work. So we chased after it. My son-in-law Kevin Huber made the pitch by juxtaposing pictures of the site next to images of how we did things in our developments and what elements of design and style we'd bring to the property. In October of 2002, we began to develop and manage the property.

With the input, creativity, and dedication of the company, University Park has transformed into a thriving, relevant, and innovative educational and healthcare hub. It's a one-of-a-kind resource—local students can go from preschool through a university degree right on the campus. And those historic buildings? We highlight them along a "discovery trail" that encourages the public to enjoy the beauty and history of the site. Significantly, thanks to efforts spearheaded by our daughter Sandy (Kevin's wife), University Park became home to the University Park World Peace Rose Garden in 2015, furthering the site's mission to educate and inspire.

Measuring Performance

When I started implementing standards of performance thirty years ago, we were in our fast-growth period. It was a tool I had learned at a YPO meeting, and I was eager to integrate it. If you're growing rapidly, how do you manage outcomes for a lot of people and do so efficiently?

I think it works best if employees set the standards by which they are judged.

It doesn't have to be an overly detailed process. Simply put, employees list the five to ten things they will take responsibility over. Then, in a couple of sentences, explain the purpose for each duty.

From there, expectations are filled in: When are duties supposed to be done? What is the dollar and time commitment? What are the expected results? Brevity, clarity, and measurability are key, and everything should be captured on one page (a timesaving element you'll appreciate at follow-up meetings).

Once the boss has approved the standards, the employee has total freedom to act within them as long as communication lines stay open. What a boss hates most is a surprise. All of this is done with flexibility. Responsibilities can be added, dropped, and changed as needed and agreed upon.

The rule that makes this arrangement work is that the employee agrees not to fall below the standard they have set without immediately bringing it to the boss's attention. Failure should not be seen as something going wrong but as the team member not letting the boss know that a problem exists. If you conceal bad news, nobody can help you improve, change, or solve the problem.

When it's time to evaluate, it's easy. There is no grade (A – F). Each duty is either passed or failed. And if team members slipped below the set standards, it was *their* expectation, not yours, that wasn't met.

Standards of performance inspire responsibility and action. It's the employee setting the bar. That subtle shift is actually a substantial one, and it leads to personal empowerment *and* adds to the achievement of the whole.

Embracing Empathy

The biggest step toward compassionate management is embracing the attitude, "I care about you, and we're in this together," a sentiment I learned from friend and campmate Rev. Alan Jones.

How do you communicate care?

By seeing others as multidimensional people and trying to understand the complexity of their lives.

At our company, executives don't have to punch the eight-hour clock. All I care about is that the job gets done. I don't care what time of the day it gets done. I know from my own experience that my most creative times often don't happen in the office. I also know from experience how pressing demands can be outside of the workplace, and I don't expect work to be number one.

The Grupe Company has never had policies about maternity or family leave—all employees have to do to get time off is say they need it, and they get it. That's not something that was created after the company grew and developed; it's been that way since day one. That's just being a nice human being—looking out for other people.

It's a two-way street. If those you hire feel like team members rather than "employees," they won't shut off when they punch out. Work crosses into their personal lives, too. Employees offer loyalty to the company and stick with it during good times and bad, and we do the same with our employees. As Doug Unruh said when he retired after three decades of working for The Grupe Company and was interviewed by the local paper, "Raising my family was the highlight of my life. Being a member of The Grupe Co. was certainly another highlight. Grupe allowed me the flexibility to do things the right way."

A good manager, or person for that matter, sees the best version of others and recognizes there is *much* more to them than what happens solely in the workplace. We once had an employee who had decided not to return after giving birth, but changed her mind as the reality of dire circumstances for her extended family—refugees trying to escape a postwar environment—began to set in. She talked to her manager about her need to return so she could send money to her family overseas. In that meeting, her manager wrote her a check for $2,000, saying, "This is an advance for you." At that time, she was making only $18,000 a year, and the money really helped two of her extended family. In that moment, she said she knew, "I'm an employee for life."

When you respect and support the other responsibilities in an employee's life, everybody wins.

Giving Trust

I talked earlier about the power of delegation and trust in building effective teams, and I want to restate that: It is vitally important for the people you work with to feel your trust in them. Given enough opportunity, people will succeed or self-destruct on a team. As I learned from my friend Gary Rogers, "The two most important words in the English language are: *You decide.*" As Gary once explained in a lecture at UC Davis, giving others the power to decide removes excuses and increases a person's responsibility for the outcome. Gary then shared a story of putting the "You decide" principle into action. It was the day before Thanksgiving, and one of his receptionists wondered if she could leave early, as surely no one would be calling so close to a holiday. "You decide," he encouraged cheerfully as he walked passed. He didn't follow up with her directly to see what she decided, but as you may have guessed, when trusted with the decision, she opted to stay.

Trust and freedom are huge motivating factors. For some, it's the ultimate reward of success.

One of my closest friends, George Brown, recently reminded me of the value *we* placed on freedom and autonomy as we were building our own careers. Phyllis and I met George and his wife, Marilyn, at a YPO meeting in the early 1970s, and we immediately struck up a friendship. Although he was the president of a major insurance company's San Francisco offices (and handled all of our insurance), he's another friend who made sure he never missed the annual dove hunt at our ranch in Mariposa over the past forty years. In fact, at the first dove hunt in 1978, he helped me build a temporary septic tank for the mobile home that was our interim house. Talk about a good friend!

George is also a great fly fisherman, and we've enjoyed fishing together all over the West, from Mexico to Alaska. I was the first among my closest friends to get a jet (to help me stay in close contact with regional offices as we expanded, as well as maintain the work-life balance I wanted), and we were all excited by the prospects of that. Once, while Dino, George, and I were flying to Canada for a fishing trip, we started to get a little philosophical. We started brainstorming what we would do if we "had it all." We agreed that taking off the entire month of October—perhaps the best month for hunting—would mean we had *arrived*.

Our first jet, a Cessna Citation with Grupe logo on tail, flying over Yosemite, 1980.

As George recalled looking back at that exchange, "Imagine taking a whole month off—if you could do that, you'd have really arrived. Forget the money. Forget the jet. To be able to take the month of October off—even then we weren't measuring ourselves in net worth at the time. We were measuring ourselves in freedom, even then, as a goal."

For many, it's freedom, flexibility, and autonomy—not dollars—that motivate performance.

Showing Appreciation

Through the years, I've enjoyed rewarding good work. And I've been blessed to be able to do it. I've mentioned how indispensable Ann Quinn was as my executive assistant during a stressful time of immense, rapid growth. One summer, I pulled her aside and said, "Ann, you've been working really long hours. You've been traveling with Phyllis and me for ULI, and I think you and your husband need a vacation. We know you love Italy, and so we've put together a package for you both." Ann had gone to school in Italy, and I knew that she wanted her husband, Tim, to see it. So, we sent them to Europe for three weeks and were thankful we could express our appreciation at a level that matched our gratitude.

Of course, that was a rare situation. You don't have to give trips to Italy to make it clear that you're grateful and that you care. It's not about *how* you show appreciation, but that you make it a priority to do so.

We thank employees in a number of ways at our company that have been really effective at improving morale and communicating our commitment to manage with compassion:

- We still ring the gong at our corporate office to acknowledge good work, continuing the tradition that my daughter Michelle and The Grupe Company president, Mark Fischer, started during the Great Recession. Our vibrant gong committee continues to motivate and lift spirits. And as I said before, we celebrate accomplishments big and small. The littlest chip at the problem—that deserves acknowledgment, too.
- We've always had a form of in-house communication (these days produced by COO Jeremy White) to profile promotions, recognize good work, and acknowledge successes people experience inside *and* outside of the workplace.
- We give annual bonuses. At times we've gifted not just the employee but also their significant other as a token of our appreciation for their support. We recognize that our employees'

loyalty, performance, and productivity require support from home. We want our appreciation for those efforts to be visible. In good years, we've been thankful that we could be a little extravagant with gifts to be on par with our appreciation.

- We set aside a couple of "employee fun days" where, on company time, our team and their families enjoy fun outings, like the Mariposa Roundup, which was a favorite event for many years. Today, our employees enjoy outings such as bowling, bocce ball, and the annual Christmas party.
- We have a life coach on retainer so employees can meet with her on a regular basis to work on issues they're having. Since the mid-1970s, I've brought in outside consultants to make sure employees are happy in and out of the office. We all know that, if you're not happy at home, the workplace suffers. Through YPO, I became aware of some outstanding consultants such as Stephen Covey, and I *still* apply their advice in my own life. I often prioritized bringing in consultants with a background in psychology, such as Dr. Pierre Mornell, who could help us pull together the different personalities we had in our office so we could work better as a team. We've offered seminars and workshops on a variety of topics. For example, we once offered a seminar titled, "Kids, Kids, Kids!" to equip working parents specifically with skills to connect better with their children.

Extra-mile work deserves extra-mile appreciation, and that extends to the people behind the scenes (the family) who support the employee. The goal of each of these efforts is to communicate that we *care* about our employees' general happiness and that we're a team.

In my experience, if you help somebody beyond what you are required to do, they won't forget it. As one of my former executives, Niem Dang, recalled, "My needs changed over time, and I always felt this receptivity to find a slot for me to do things." She added, "I never felt that I was being set aside. I was given plenty of opportunity, sometimes more than I thought I could handle, even. There's a lot of recognition when you do something good. It was really a great place to work. I was very lucky."

Chapter 20

Giving Back

I'VE DESCRIBED THE SAFETY and comfort of the ranch I grew up on, but it didn't take me long to learn it's not an equal world and that I have been very blessed.

By 1940, the San Joaquin Valley had an influx of eighty thousand poverty-stricken individuals from states ravaged by the Dust Bowl. Referred to disparagingly as "Okies" (although they were also from states other than Oklahoma, such as Arkansas, Missouri, and Texas), these now-itinerant farmers came in search of work and opportunity.

I didn't have to look far to see stories representative of the Dust Bowl's devastation—masterfully depicted in my campmate Ken Burns's documentary *The Dust Bowl* (2012)—unfold around me, such as seeing illiterate workers camp on my parents' ranch, or knowing individuals like "Bam" Hayes from Alabama, who drove around in his Ford Model A pickup without a driver's door and the passenger door held shut by baling wire. Seeing examples of such need, as well as how hard some people fight to improve their situation, left a lasting impression.

Phyllis and I feel very fortunate for the opportunities we've had and for the life we've led. We feel privileged to have been born in the United States of America and to grow up in homes with loving and supportive parents. We are likewise thankful for our health and the success of our business endeavors. We believe sharing what we have is a way to express our gratitude. As Jesus taught, "Every one to whom much is given, of him will much be required." (Luke 12:48 RSV)

Phyllis and I have enjoyed giving back to San Joaquin County, the very community that has believed in us since I first pitched Lincoln Village West in my mid-twenties. We started giving back in small ways, and, as our means increased, we gave more, focusing particularly on supporting educational programs. For example, in 1982 we built a high school store and classroom to support a Retail Sales Program that allowed teenagers to learn hands-on marketing and management skills and prepare them for life after high school.

Phyllis and I never wanted our charitable contributions to be made public (and we still do not disclose our church giving). We didn't want the attention. But in the late 1970s, when a member of the Board of Supervisors voted against one of our projects because, as he said, "Fritz Grupe doesn't give money to the community," we began to think about being more transparent about our giving.

Around that same time, organizations were starting to ask us if they could use Brookside Farm as a venue for their respective fundraisers. We obliged but soon grew uncomfortable with that structure, as some of the organizations operated in ways that did not keep to our standard. We realized that if *we* sponsored and ran one big event, not only would we be more comfortable opening up our home and farm, but we could more

GIVING BACK

effectively raise funds to benefit multiple organizations. It would also provide a fun and natural way to make our dedication to community giving public. With those goals in mind, The Country Fair was formed.

Since 1981, we have hosted and fully funded The Country Fair twelve times (the first six fairs being held at Brookside Farm). Underwritten by The Grupe Company, the fairs raised close to $5 million. It truly was *the* event of the year. For an entrance fee that went directly toward charitable causes, guests had access to food from the best restaurants in San Joaquin County, carriage rides with our Belgian horses, live entertainment, and even a full-size Ferris wheel one year. We had a number of booths and displays from art and handiwork to beautiful, collectible automobiles from Ken Behring's Blackhawk Museum, farm animals, or traveling museum exhibits that embraced the theme of country life. Guests, decked out in boots and rhinestones—their finest country fashion—added to the atmosphere and overall excitement. As Phyllis puts it, "We had all the original cowboy bling."

It was a family affair (with daughter Bonner taking over management of the event in the early 1990s) as well as a company effort—each department had a specific role to play, and on the day of the event, it was all hands on deck. One year, that meant about forty Grupe employees moving 120 lineal feet of fence at the last minute to accommodate unforeseen rains.

The highlight of the event was the performance by a major country music star. Guests covered our front lawn, sitting on plastic cushions we provided, as they enjoyed the special headliner performing on stage, which the construction division of The Grupe Company assembled. We opened that first year with Roy Rogers and Dale Evans, and the Sons of the Pioneers, and have since welcomed Helen Reddy, Kenny Rogers, the Oak Ridge Boys, Reba McEntire, the Gatlin Brothers,

Glen Campbell, Marty Stuart, Clint Black, Clay Walker, and Broadway stars Teri Bibb and Dennis McNeil.

The night concluded with dancing around the pool (line-dancing lessons had usually been given earlier in the day on the tennis courts), a meet-and-greet for VIP guests in the house, and a *great* fireworks display. While guests arrived around four o'clock in the afternoon, they often stayed until two or three in the morning, dancing and laughing the night away.

Even after we moved from Brookside Farm in 1995, we continued to host the event in Lodi until 2013. The Country Fair was a way to unite people together to make a *visible* difference and to raise millions of dollars for education. Phyllis and I strongly believe you can judge the health of a community by the well-being of its children and that you can stop generational poverty (one of our community's biggest challenges) by improving people's access to education.

Phyllis's passion and commitment to improve the lives of children has been a wonderful example of the difference personal involvement and leadership can make when it comes to service. When I became president of ULI in 1987, Phyllis spearheaded a one-of-a-kind program for spouses of ULI members to give heightened purpose to their conference attendance. Wanting to bridge the realms of business and education, Phyllis developed the Project for Excellence in Public Education (PEPE), a knowledge-sharing effort that identified notable educational programs throughout the United States (at a time before the convenience of the Internet), and created a database of successful projects that educators could tap into. If a teacher had issues in his or her community, that teacher could learn from another community that had addressed that very issue. In time, the effort grew to outline a process by which business and education could design rewarding partnerships.

GIVING BACK

Phyllis worked on that effort for eight years before it evolved into San Joaquin County A+, the educational thrust of The Country Fairs. The primary goal of A+ was to improve school readiness and literacy among children, and Phyllis looked across the nation to locate programs that dealt with high-crime, low-income areas. Once again, her dedication and passion inspired her to go further in terms of implementation. In 1998, she helped found the Community Partnership for Families of San Joaquin (CPFSJ). A spin-off of San Joaquin A+, CPFSJ is an agreement between all the social services and nonprofits in San Joaquin County to bring services to individuals in high-risk areas. By working together, the partnership and its affiliates offer the support and opportunity families need to become stabilized and get out of their troubled predicament.

I've learned from Phyllis that giving of your time can have an even greater impact than the gifting of money. For the silent ones who write the check, we'll always thank you, but for those who jump in the middle and try to work on projects themselves—they deserve double thanks.

Here are eight lessons Phyllis and I have learned through the years as we've tried to make a *visible* difference to the Stockton community:

1. **Everyone has a duty to give back.** Giving increases awareness of other people's needs, heightens gratitude, and gives life new meaning. As Phyllis puts it, giving "lightens our souls and relieves the burdens of a complex world." Even if a person can give only a nickel, everyone should give what he or she can. What value do the assets you temporarily possess have if they're not shared?
2. **There are many ways to make a difference.** Money, time, experience, leadership—there's more than one way to *give back*. The patriotic service of Phyllis's father in World War II

and the volunteer efforts of her grandparents (who housed boarders during the war) are examples that linger in her life. Giving back is something we expected of our children from a young age. We encouraged them to start their day by asking, *What is one thing that I will do for somebody else today?* It's intent that matters most—and any small act will serve. As Mother Teresa said, "There are few great things. There are only small things done with great love."

3. **Charity begins at home.** The best service you can give is helping your own community, neighborhood, and home. When our granddaughter Meredith wanted to be an international journalist (she's now the executive director of CPFSJ), I gave her this advice: "Before you save the world, save your country; before you save your country, save your state; before you save your state, save your city; before you save your city, save your community; and most importantly, before you save anyone or do anything, save your family and yourself." Give back to the very community (and home) that helps you succeed.

4. **Giving requires action but no invitation.** As Phyllis once shared in an address recognizing the charitable contributions of women, "Giving is doing, not wishing. Giving is leadership, capacity, energy, foresight, and effectiveness. All of these words are synonymous with service." Have the will and courage to start giving back *today* without waiting to be asked.

5. **Work with the willing.** There are a lot of people who need help in this world, and it is impossible to help everyone. So, where do you start? Who do you help? As Jesus Christ instructed the Twelve Apostles before they went out to minister, "And if any one will not receive you or listen to your words, shake

off the dust from your feet as you leave that house or town." (Matthew 10:14 RSV) When you are trying to be a do-gooder, zero in on those looking to change to maximize your efforts.

6. **Gifts of *time* matter as much as money.** Phyllis's tireless effort on behalf of education is a wonderful example of the impact someone's time and leadership can make, a contribution that can be more valuable than money. Her involvement has had a bigger impact on us, the *giver*, than if we had just written a check.

7. **Follow your passions to avoid burnout.** Taking up somebody else's cause when you really don't have a passion for it might *seem* like a good idea, but I have found that can lead to burnout. As you try to exemplify the giver you want to be, focus your efforts in an area or subject matter that interests you so you stick with it for the long run and feel motivated to work hard enough to see outcomes.

    My sisters have made a lasting impact on their respective communities by pouring *years* of energy into issues they're passionate about. Luanne developed a program to reduce hunger in East Palo Alto—a community many mistook as free of such troubling issues—and ran that program for twelve years. Likewise, Sue has provided leadership for the literacy program San Joaquin A+ for more than twenty years and has been an inspiring and familiar face in the effort to improve local education. As they say, do what you love, and you will never work a day in your life.

8. **Making a *visible* difference requires tenacity.** In 1986, Phyllis and I had the opportunity to travel to India, meet with Mother Teresa, and visit some of her missions. Of all her remarks, I was

most impressed by her answer to this question: "With India's population and disease problems, your challenges seem almost insurmountable. How do you deal with this?" To which she replied, "It's not my problem; it's God's problem. I'm just here as a helper to do what I can by loving those whom others find unlovable." It's easy to get overwhelmed by the level of need in the world or to underestimate the impact your efforts can make. As I shared in Part One, the most *important* things in life take time and constant effort; they can't always be solved overnight but rather must be chipped away at one day at a time.

Charity, or giving back, rewards both giver and receiver. When done with purposefulness and passion, it provides self-improvement for both. Carve out time to give back, and you'll enjoy the byproducts of happiness, confidence, joy, and gratitude. As American poet Edwin Markham (1852–1940) penned in his poem, "Man-Making":

> We are all blind until we see
> That in the human plan
> Nothing is worth the making if
> It does not make the man.
>
> Why build these cities glorious
> If man unbuilded goes?
> In vain we build the world, unless
> The builder also grows.

GIVING BACK

Breakout: Learning about Charity from the King of the Cowboys

When we decided to have our first fundraiser at Brookside Farm in 1981, American singer and western film actor Roy Rogers (1911–1998) had not done any commercial entertaining for years. He came out of retirement because of the creative idea to reunite him with the Sons of the Pioneers.

THE BLUEPRINT

A GRUPE COMPANY PUBLICATION
SEPTEMBER / OCTOBER 1981   THE GRUPE COMPANY P.O. BOX 7576 STOCKTON, CALIFORNIA 95207

1981 COUNTRY FAIR

The 1981 Country Fair sponsored by Phyllis and Fritz Grupe netted in excess of $50,000 to benefit Easter Seals' new Therapeutic Center to be located at the corner of Bianchi and Claremont Streets in Stockton. Pictured above are Roy Rogers and Dale Evans with party hosts Phyllis and Fritz Grupe.

Phyllis and I drove down to the airport to pick up Roy and his wife, Dale Evans (also a singer and actress), me in my Chevy Blazer and Phyllis in her Mercedes. We didn't know what they were like or what they might want to ride in. We got to the airport, introduced ourselves, and I said, "Do you want to ride with me, Roy, and Dale can ride with Phyllis?"

Roy and I got in my Blazer. In the cup holder between the front seats I had a can of chewing tobacco. We had a ranch, and all the cowboys chewed tobacco, and at the time I indulged in it on occasion when we were up there riding horses or working cattle.

Seeing the can, Roy said, "You use this stuff?"

"Yeah," I told him. "Once in a while."

"Can I use it?" he asked. "Dale made me leave mine at home. She said, 'Don't take that in this man's airplane.' You mind if I have some?"

"Help yourself," I said.

And that's how Roy Rogers and I shared a can of Skoal.

We started talking about hunting, and I learned he was a competitive shooter (and later learned he was a hell of a shot) and enjoyed the ride out to Brookside Farm.

After the show, Roy and Dale came into the house. Dale put her feet high up because her legs were bothering her from being on stage that night and performing for the five hundred guests. I mean, it was just like your grandparents being there. By then you could say we had really hit it off, and Roy asked, "Where's the money going for this fundraiser?" We told him it was going to construct a swimming pool for children with disabilities. Roy said, "Well, you know how we are about children. I don't know how much they're paying me, but just keep it."

That's the one and only time we had the headliner donate their fee.

Touched by his generosity, on the drive back to the airport, I asked, "That was pretty generous, Roy. Is there anything I can do for you?"

"I don't think so," he said.

"Do you have plenty of places to hunt?" I asked

"Actually, I'm not doing so well on my dove hunting."

I told him about our annual dove hunt held the first of September every year. "Do you want to come? I'll send a plane for you."

He liked the idea and came to our hunts until his health no longer permitted him to make the trek. Roy visited the ranch so many times, we even named one of the roads "Happy Trails" after him.

Roy Rogers, "King of the Cowboys," joined me for many dove hunts starting in 1982 and beyond.

One year, he and Ken Behring (former owner of the Seattle Seahawks) had come out to go dove hunting, and they were riding back for breakfast with my son-in-law Kevin in the very same Blazer I was mentioning. We had just done some work on the dam, and the dirt on it was softer than usual. Kevin was looking at a deer up on the side of the mountain and started to drive off the edge of the dam, but thankfully got stuck. As the SUV tipped precariously on the edge of the dam, Roy climbed out, put his hands on the side of the vehicle and shouted, "Okay, Ken! Get out! I have it!" So here you have this old man who thinks he's going to hold up the weight of this huge SUV, but it shows you a lot about Roy's selfless nature and willingness to put the welfare of his friends first.

I was right ahead of Kevin when it happened. I saw him go over the edge, so I came back, and they were already bailing out. "I've got to take a picture of this," I said.

"Don't take a picture of this!" Kevin pleaded. "It's so embarrassing!" He was barely out of his teens at the time and didn't quite yet see the humor. Now, he really loves to talk about the time he ran the King of the Cowboys *and* the owner of the Seattle Seahawks off the road—yet they all lived to tell the tale without a scrape.

We had Roy back and forth enough times that Phyllis and I were invited to the celebration of Roy and Dale's 50th wedding anniversary. Phyllis and I sat at their table. That night, as all these old movie actors, and some current ones, too, came up to congratulate Roy and Dale, Phyllis and I just soaked it in.

You never know what'll happen when you put yourself out there to do good. Sometimes good things, like great friendships, come right back at you.

Chapter 21

Having Fun and Being Thankful

WHEN OUR CHILDREN WERE YOUNG, we had the opportunity to go to London for a family trip. Our flight arrived late to the busy O'Hare International Airport in Chicago, so we were in the desperate predicament of trying to make a connecting flight.

As the seven of us ran through the airport, I held on tightly to our youngest daughter Michelle's hand as I basically dragged her alongside me. Despite the pandemonium, I smiled at her and exclaimed, "Isn't this fun!"

Michelle still remembers that exchange as a life lesson—the adventure of running through an airport as a family, at its core, *was* fun—even though we *did* miss our flight.

> *It's amazing how fun life can become with quick shifts of perspective or, sometimes, revised expectations.*

It's amazing how fun life can become with quick shifts of perspective or, sometimes, revised expectations. As I've said, my ground rule for almost any project is that it has to be fun. And that always applies to those I work with—if we're not having fun as a team, it's time to reassess what we're doing or how we're going about doing it. When a process is no longer fun, it's healthy to ask why and might even be cause for pulling the pin.

Enjoyment and fun aren't just the end reward for being able to execute your dream with success. They're the very *way* I think a dream should be chased. While some may be motivated by the promise of admiration, wealth, or power, I've found that nothing replaces the euphoria of having fun while doing good work.

If you need to improve your outlook and find levity, "Give thanks in all circumstances." (1 Thessalonians 5:18 RSV) In 2013, *The Wall Street Journal* ran a piece by Diana Kapp showing how "concrete benefits come to kids who literally count their blessings," such as feeling more satisfied, doing better in school, having a more positive outlook, and feeling less envious. Who wouldn't want more satisfaction and positivity in their life?

At our family dinners, we invite everybody to take a turn giving thanks and have found it to be a rewarding and educational exercise. It allows Phyllis and me to learn more about what those closest to us value and provides an opportunity for us to reflect on our own list.

Sometimes I reflect on all I have in my life that took zero effort on my part, such as free will or Jesus Christ dying for my sins. Other times, I'm amazed by how much I have gotten to choose in my life, such as who I married, the number of children I have, my profession, or my faith. I don't take any of those for granted.

Regardless of where you are at this moment—be it laying your foundation, rebuilding after a setback, or enjoying and sharing your successes—be grateful. Your vision and dream will be better for it.

In Conclusion

This has been my journey thus far, filled with dreams, great successes, major setbacks and comebacks, always with Phyllis at my side. What a different life it would have been without my family, my many great friends, business partners, and hunting buddies.

How grateful I am to my great-grandfather John Carsten Grupe, who at age sixteen left Germany to pursue his dreams, crossing the Atlantic and then coming by schooner in 1849 from New York City to the California Gold Rush, before California was even a state.

Because of his courage, I had the privilege of being raised in the United States. As a sixteen-year-old boy, I dreamt of my future while irrigating fields on my father's farm, and I thank God every day I have had the freedom this country provides me to pursue my many dreams.

I have learned many lessons over the past eighty-one years. The tried-and-true principles I have shared in this book have been valuable to me in both good and bad times, allowing me to create a life of balance, fulfillment, and joy.

I have witnessed many doors opening, but I have learned they open only if I knock. There are still so many doors out there! I plan to keep on knocking on them—and to enjoy the ride along the way.

In closing, I'd like to offer a poem I wrote a couple of years ago that I periodically share with friends and family.

Life on earth is a finite gift from God!
How will I invest my remaining days?
Will I separate the urgent from the important and focus on the latter?
Do I accept the premise that happiness is a choice?
Will I let today bring joy to my life?

— Fritz Grupe

"All I have seen makes me trust the creator for all I have not seen."
— Ralph Waldo Emerson

An evening toast to the sunset from our beloved hilltop home at Mariposa, California, 2017.

Acknowledgments

I HAVE BEEN BLESSED to share my life with many wonderful people, quite a few of whom helped me write this book.

First and foremost, my wife, Phyllis, has been a tireless co-writer, editor, and champion. She has been beside me as a partner, friend, and collaborator through every accomplishment. Without her, this book would not be what it is—and neither would I.

My children and their families are among my life's greatest joys, and I thank them for their love, input, and support.

In sixty-some years as a businessman, I've been fortunate to work with talented and dedicated people, many of whom took time to help with this book. Thank you for your encouragement and enthusiasm.

I've been blessed that many business acquaintances and work relationships turned into treasured friendships. It's been rewarding to reflect on those who have come along on the ride, bumps and all. My greatest appreciation goes to my friends who I've mentioned throughout the book.

Tory Swim Inloes worked tirelessly to research, write, and perfect every page of this book. Veronica Rossi assisted with developing and editing it, and ushering it through the production process. It was a pleasure to create this book with them.

Finally, I thank God for all the blessings I have enjoyed in my life.

Notes & References

    A variety of primary sources were of instrumental value in cementing dates and details: oral history interviews, personal papers, government publications, newspaper coverage of our projects, and The Grupe Company in-house publications, promotional materials, and website.

I am grateful for the family members, friends, business partners, and company executives who participated in interviews and contributed their time and memories to this endeavor:

> Phyllis Grupe, Mark Grupe, Sandy Grupe Huber, Bonner Grupe Murphy, Michelle Grupe Jaques, Kevin Huber, Jim Klingbeil, Dino Cortopassi, George Brown, Gene Gini, Sunne Wright McPeak, Frank Passadore, John Dinkel, Ann Quinn, Nelson Bahler, Niem Dang, Don Benioff, Ron Addington, Jerry Abbott, Paula Tarantino, and Michael Kristoff.

My appreciation extends to the following friends who submitted written reflections: Congressman John Garamendi; The Very Rev. Dr. Alan Jones; Professor Ken Jowitt; former president of Applied Materials, Jim Morgan; and past president of ULI, Smedes York.

ENJOY THE RIDE

Additionally, I am grateful for those who have shared their knowledge and expertise with me through the years and for the research that I reference in the notes that follow:

Introduction
        Back then, it wasn't yet a state: Eric Foner, *Give Me Liberty! An American History, Volume 1: To 1877* (New York: W. W. Norton, 2006), 407.

Chapter 1
Daring to Dream
p. 5   **At that time, a dozen eggs sold for 75 cents:** Scott Derks, *The Value of a Dollar: 1860–2004,* 3rd ed. (Millerton, NY: Grey House Publishing, 2004), 280.
p. 9   **This was at a time when a public school teacher:** Ibid., 355.

Digging In: John Carsten Grupe
The Legacy of a Nineteenth-Century Entrepreneur
p. 12   **My great-grandfather John Carsten Grupe:** Information about John Carsten Grupe (1828–1889) is based on genealogical research compiled by my sister Sue in our family history, *How Are the Camellias?* (self-published, 1994) as well as a number of primary sources: *Illustrated History, San Joaquin County, California* (Chicago: The Lewis Publishing Company, 1890), 268–269; Leigh H. Irvine, ed., A *History of New California, Its Resources & People, Volume II, 1828–1889* (New York: The Lewis Publishing Company, 1905), 844; the United States Census (1860, 1870, and 1880); the 1866 California Voter Register; John Carsten Grupe's 1852 U.S. Passport; and, the September 12, 1883 land patent between John Carsten Grupe and the County of San Joaquin and State of California.
p. 12   **In 1844, great-grandfather Grupe:** There are mixed reports of when my great-grandfather arrived to New York. I have chosen the year 1844, the same year used in my family's history, *How Are the Camellias?*

NOTES & REFERENCES

p. 12 **He was one of the two million people:** Roger Daniels, *Coming to America: A History of Immigration and Ethnicity in American Life,* 2nd ed. (New York: Harper Perennial, 2002), 124, 146.

p. 13 **He would be one of the eighty thousand prospectors:** Andrew C. Isenberg, *The California Gold Rush: A Brief History with Documents,* The Bedford Series in History and Culture (Boston: Bedford/St. Martin's, 2018), 8.

p. 13 **In 1848, the indigenous population:** Foner, *Give Me Liberty!,* 409.

p. 13 **The non-indigenous population:** Ibid., 407.

p. 13 **Ideologies grounded in domination and racism:** Ibid., 409.

p. 14 **Stockton had already developed:** R. Coke Wood and Leonard Covello, *Stockton Memories: A Pictorial History of Stockton, California* (Fresno, CA: Valley Publishers, 1977); Daniel Kasser and Amanda Zimmerman, *Stockton Then & Now* (Charleston, SC: Arcadia Publishing, 2011); Raymond W. Hillman and Leonard A. Covello, *Cities & Towns of San Joaquin County since 1847* (Fresno, CA: Panorama West Books, 1985).

Chapter 2
Values Worth Their Value

p. 23 **"In the years to come":** W. Fred Ellis, "Principal's Message," Stockton High School, *The Guard and Tackle* annual (Stockton, CA: The Associated Students of the Stockton High School, June 1929), 8.

p. 26 **I recently read a statistic**: Zig Ziglar, letter to John C. Maxwell, 15 April 2002, as quoted in John C. Maxwell, *Ethics 101: What Every Leader Needs to Know,* 1st Center Street ed. (New York: Center Street, 2005), 28; Zig Ziglar, *Over the Top: Moving from Survival to Stability, from Stability to Success, from Success to Significance,* rev. ed. (Nashville: Thomas Nelson, 1997), 297.

p. 30 **"Trust is the highest form":** Stephen R. Covey, *The 7 Habits of Highly Effective People: Powerful Lessons in Personal Change* (New York: Simon & Schuster, 1989; New York: Free Press, 2004), 178.

p. 35–6 **Many can't write a check to cover a $500 emergency:** Maggie McGrath, "63% of Americans Don't Have Enough Savings to Cover a $500 Emergency," *Forbes,* January 6, 2016, https://www.forbes.com/sites/maggiemcgrath/2016/01/06/63-of-americans-dont-have-enough-savings-to-cover-a-500-emergency.

Chapter 3
Learning Financial Responsibility

p. 42–3 **Millennials particularly like the trend:** Bernard Marr, "The Sharing Economy—What it is, examples, and how big data, platforms and algorithms fuel it," *Forbes,* October 21, 2016, https://www.forbes.com/sites/bernardmarr/2016/10/21/the-sharing-economy-what-it-is-examples-and-how-big-data-platforms-and-algorithms-fuel.

Chapter 4
Getting Curious: Learn How to Ask the Right Questions

p. 58 **Central to that organization's culture:** Urban Land Institute/Los Angeles, "Partnership Forum," accessed September 13, 2017, https://la.uli.org/get-involved/young-leaders-group/partnership-forum/.

p. 58 **Likewise, my involvement in YPO**: More can be learned about the Young Presidents' Organization at https://www.ypo.org/.

Chapter 5
Becoming a Lifelong Learner

p. 69 **The chaos and uncertainty of the Great Depression:** See Kriste Lindenmeyer, *The Greatest Generation Grows Up: American Childhood in the 1930s* (Chicago: Ivan R. Dee, 2005).

p. 72 **Although the motto of the Bohemian Club:** "Weaving spiders, come not here" comes from Shakespeare's play *A Midsummer Night's Dream*, Act 2, Scene 2.

NOTES & REFERENCES

Digging In:
Learning to Create Solutions —My First Big Deal

p. 76   **"The secret to success":** See Robert H. Schuller, *Success is Never Ending, Failure is Never Final: How to Achieve Lasting Success Even in the Most Difficult Times* (New York: Bantam Books, 1990).

Chapter 6
Listening and Communicating Effectively

p. 81   **I think how people want to be treated:** I have since found that these sentiments are shared by bestselling author John C. Maxwell in his book *Ethics 101*, 29–40.

p. 84   **"Seek first to understand":** Covey, *The 7 Habits of Highly Effective People*, 235.

p. 85   **"Bad news is good news":** Jim's full "Morganism" on this principle is as follows: "Always listen for and even seek out signs of trouble. Bad news is good news if you do something about it." James Morgan with Joan O'C. Hamilton, *Applied Wisdom: Bad News Is Good News and Other Insights That Can Help Anyone Be a Better Manager* (Los Altos, CA: Chandler Jordan Publishing, 2016), 186.

p. 95   **As you might imagine:** For information on The Metropolitan Water District of Los Angeles, see http://www.mwdh2o.com/. For the Westlands Water District, see https://wwd.ca.gov/.

Chapter 7
Having the Courage to Take Action

p. 101   **"Faith and fear are polar opposites":** Johnson is profiled and quoted in Andy Galloway, "The Marvelous Mentor," *Comstock's Magazine,* November 17, 2015, https://www.comstocksmag.com/article/marvelous-mentor.

p. 103   **"The cost of perfect information is too high":** Morgan, *Applied Wisdom*, 29.

p. 105   **…the urgent from the important:** Covey, *The 7 Habits of Highly Effective People*, 150–151.

p. 105 **I've found success with the ABC System of Prioritization:** Alan Lakein writes about the ABC System of Prioritization in his book *How to Get Control of Your Time and Your Life* (New York: Signet Books, 1973), 28–29, 70, 103–108.

Chapter 8
Building Confidence and Trust Through Action

p. 112 **ULI was still in its infancy**: Julie Stern, "Timeline—Overview of 75 Years in ULI History," *Urban Land,* December 13, 2011, https://urbanland.uli.org/uli-day-december-14-2011/timeline-overview-of-75-years-in-uli-history/.

p. 121 **…the City of Stockton approved an ordinance**: "City's 1st Planned Unit Ok'd for Cluster Housing Project," *The Stockton Record*, February 25, 1967.

p. 121 **By 1970, we were introducing this entirely new housing concept:** Maury Kane, "In Lincoln Village West: A New Housing Concept for the Stockton Area," *The Stockton Record*, October 24, 1970.

p. 121–2 **Our approach drew attention from** *California Builder:* "Lincoln Village/West Aquatic Community Hits Jackpot," *California Builder* (September 1968): 6–8, 19.

Chapter 9
Digging In: From Sharing to Selling the Dream
A Closer Look at Creating a Sense of Urgency and Marketing a Master-Planned Community

p. 140–1 **As a headline in** *The Stockton Record* **read:** Julie Schmit, "Grupe project changes face of Stockton," *The Stockton Record,* April 8, 1990. *The Stockton Record* ran a multipart series chronicling the development of Brookside titled, "Development of a Development."

p. 141–2 **We spent three years of research:** "King Ferronite Comes to Brookside or: The Lights Went on at Brookside," *Brookside Reflections,* Fall 1990, 4; Janice Fillip, "Finishing What He Starts: Fritz Grupe, Jr., puts his considerable resources behind

NOTES & REFERENCES

efforts to stimulate San Joaquin County's economy," *Comstock's: The Business of California's Capital Region,* July 1993, 25.

p. 143 **To keep that excitement up:** In the early 1990s, I wrote about those efforts in my article "Marketing the Dream," *Urban Land,* April 1992, 10–14.

p. 144 **My mom was especially excited:** "Brookside's First Lot Closes," *Brookside Reflections,* Fall 1990, 3.

p. 145 **"Figure out what they're going to want before they do":** A direct quote from Steve Jobs in Walter Isaacson's *Steve Jobs* (New York: Simon & Schuster, 2011), 567.

p. 151 **We contributed $18.3 million:** Dianne Barth, "Development of a Development," *The Stockton Record,* August 27, 1990.

Chapter 10
Valuing Relationships

p. 153 **In fact, a recent article in *The New York Times* showed:** Tara Parker-Pope, "The Power of Positive People," *The New York Times,* July 10, 2018, https://www.nytimes.com/2018/07/10/well/the-power-of-positive-people.html.

p. 159 **When it comes to relationships, studies suggest:** Emily Sohn, "More and more research shows friends are good for your health," *The Washington Post,* May 26, 2016, https://www.washingtonpost.com/national/health-science/more-and-more-research-shows-friends-are-good-for-your-health/2016/05/26/f249e754-204d-11e6-9e7f-57890b612299_story.html?utm_term=.025f1b246764; Liz Mineo, "Good genes are nice, but joy is better," *The Harvard Gazette,* April 11, 2017, https://news.harvard.edu/gazette/story/2017/04/over-nearly-80-years-harvard-study-has-been-showing-how-to-live-a-healthy-and-happy-life/; Tara Parker-Pope, "What Are Friends For? A Longer Life," *The New York Times,* April 20, 2009, https://www.nytimes.com/2009/04/21/health/21well.html.

p. 165 **My daughter Bonner was a full-time Grupe employee:** Debra Lee, publisher, "The Grupe Companies: Creators of Lakeside Lifestyles," *Builder Digest of Northern California,* Nov./Dec. 1995.

p. 167   **See his very-well-written book**: Dino writes about "Berenda Blues" on pages 153 to 166 of *Getting Ahead: A Family's Journey from Italian Serfdom to American Success* (Stockton, CA: Black Hole Press, 2014).

Chapter 11
Prioritizing Relationships

p. 170   **This was at a time when, according to an article:** Urie Bronfenbrenner, "The Disturbing Changes in the American Family," *Search* (Fall 1976), 7 as quoted in Pierre Mornell, *Passive Men, Wild Women* (New York: Simon and Schuster, 1979), 185.

p. 170   **During this time, *The Nielsen Television Report* stated:** *Nielsen Television Report*, 1977, pp. 4, 7 as cited in Mornell, *Passive Men, Wild Women*, 20.

Chapter 12
Accepting Consequences

p. 208   **Dr. Julie Logan…has found that:** The research of Dr. Julie Logan is referenced in Brock L. Eide and Fernette F. Eide, *The Dyslexic Advantage: Unlocking the Hidden Potential of the Dyslexic Brain* (New York: Hudson Street Press, 2011), 158.

p. 212   **"Those who don't fall short every once in a while":** Norman Augustine and Kenneth Adelman, *Shakespeare in Charge: The Bard's Guide to Leading and Succeeding on the Business Stage* (New York: Miramax Books, 1999), 149.

p. 215   **It's probably no coincidence**: Referenced in Eide and Eide, *The Dyslexic Advantage*, 17–18.

p. 216   **Augustine and Adelman suggest companies compile a "worry list":** Augustine and Adelman, *Shakespeare in Charge*, 182.

p. 221   **"Stay between the cones and go faster":** Phyllis to Claudia DeLorme in DeLorme, "Singer Secures Another Selection Trial Victory at Southern Pines CDE," *The Chronicle of the*

NOTES & REFERENCES

Horse, May 25, 2005, https://www.chronofhorse.com/article/singer-secures-another-selection-trial-victory-southern-pines-cde.

Digging In: Dealing with the Unforeseen, Unforeseen with Integrity and Confidence
Rebounding from the Savings-and-Loan Crisis

p. 231 **Copley chose partners following a formula:** "Grupe/Copley Partnership," *The Blueprint: A Grupe Publication,* Fall 1990, 7.

Chapter 13
Embracing Change

p. 236–7 **Although I didn't realize it at the time:** Pearl Janet Davies, *Women in Real Estate: A History of the Women's Council* (Chicago, 1963) as quoted in Kathy Peiss, "'Vital Industry' and Women's Ventures: Conceptualizing Gender in Twentieth-Century Business History," *The Business History Review* 27, no. 2 (Summer 1998): 239.

p. 237 **Today 80 percent of our agents are women:** "Quick Real Estate Statistics," National Association of Realtors, accessed December 9, 2017, https://www.nar.realtor/research-and-statistics/quick-real-estate-statistics.

p. 242 **"It is not the strongest":** This quote has long been misattributed to Charles Darwin and in recent years it has been confirmed by the Darwin Correspondence Project out of the University of Cambridge that it is *not* an original quote of Darwin but originates from an article written by Leon C. Megginson, a professor of management and marketing who paraphrased Darwin in his research.

p. 243–4 **In December of 1974:** Stanley P. Klevan, "Massive Busing: An SUSD Integration Plan," *The Stockton Record,* Dec 11, 1974; William Trombley, "Desegregation Goes Smoothly in Stockton: Months of Planning Eased Way for Schools Program," *Los Angeles Times,* September 19, 1977.

Chapter 14
Making Difficult Decisions: When It's Time to Pull the Pin

p. 260   **"A decision is a judgment":** Peter F. Drucker, *The Effective Executive: The Definitive Guide to Getting the Right Things Done*, rev. ed. (New York: Harper Business, 2006), 143.

Digging In: When Surviving Is Success
Withstanding the Great Recession

p. 263   **In fact, between 2000 and 2006, median home prices nearly quadrupled:** Sydney Evans, Bohdan Kosenko, and Mike Polyakov, "How Stockton Went Bust: A California City's Decade of Policies and the Financial Crisis that Followed," May 24, 2012, a publication of California Common Sense, available at http://uscommonsense.org/research/how-stockton-went-bust-a-california-citys-decade-of-policies-and-the-financial-crisis-that-followed/ (site discontinued).

p. 263   **In the spring of 2005, the median price of a new home:** Bruce Spence, "New house means digging deep," *The Record* (Stockton, California), May 6, 2005.

p. 264   **"financial institutions loaded up on them":** The Financial Crisis Inquiry Commission (FCIC), *The Financial Crisis Inquiry Report: Final Report of the National Commission on the Causes of the Financial and Economic Crisis in the United States* (U.S. Government Printing Office, January 2011), xx.

p. 264–5   **This was a major blow:** Ibid., xix.

p. 265   **From Wall Street to Main Street**: Ibid., xvii.

p. 265   **In 2011, the FCIC produced a report:** Ibid., vi.

p. 265–6   **"The crisis was the result of human action":** Ibid., xvii.

p. 266   **…wiped out nearly $11 trillion in household wealth:** Ibid., xv.

p. 267   **Just to illustrate, construction permits fell:** Jed Kolko, "Just the Facts," The California Economy: Crisis in the Housing Market," Public Policy Institute of California, March 2008, https://www.ppic.org/content/pubs/jtf/JTF_HousingMarketJTF.pdf.

NOTES & REFERENCES

p. 269 **As he explained to *The Sacramento Bee:*** Jennifer K. Morita, "New homes save on energy—West Roseville to become the largest solar-powered community in the area," *The Sacramento Bee,* May 18, 2006.

p. 270 **As Mark said in 2009:** Leora Broydo Vestel, "Energy—Capital area a trendsetter—Young firm builds modular homes that make as much power as they use," *The Sacramento Bee,* November 29, 2009.

p. 272 **Stockton had the highest foreclosure rate:** Les Christie, "California cities fill top 10 foreclosure list," *CnnMoney.com,* August 14, 2007; Matthew DeBord, "California and Stockton top foreclosure statistics nationwide," *Southern California Public Radio,* August 8, 2012.

p. 272 **...prices came crashing down by 70 percent:** Evans et al., "How Stockton Went Bust."

p. 273 **By the fall of 2009:** Alejandro Lazo, "California mortgage defaults drop 24.3%," *Los Angeles Times,* January 28, 2010.

p. 274 **As *The Record,* Stockton's local newspaper, reported one participant saying:** Kevin Parrish, "Starting over with a rent-to-own program," *The Record* (Stockton, California), November 4, 2013.

Chapter 15
Leaning on Your Values

p. 282 **"If you have integrity, nothing else matters":** Former Senator Alan Simpson to graduating class of 1986 of Big Horn High School in Sheridan, Wyoming; see Donald Loren Hardy, *Shooting from the Lip: The Life of Senator Al Simpson* (Norman: University of Oklahoma Press, 2011), 158.

p. 286 **"When we take responsibility for our lives":** Lou Tice with Joyce Quick, *Personal Coaching for Results: How to Mentor and Inspire Others to Amazing Growth* (Nashville: Thomas Nelson Publishers, 1997), 27.

ENJOY THE RIDE

p. 287 **…while we judge ourselves by our intentions:** Stephen R. Covey, *The 7 Habits of Highly Effective Families* (New York: St. Martin's Griffin, 1997), 40.

p. 287 **"When you change the way you think":** Tice, *Personal Coaching for Results*, 27.

Chapter 16
Keeping Balance

p. 294 **"If we are tightly wound":** Tracy Tomasky, *The Conscious and Courageous Leader: Developing Your Authentic Voice to Lead and Inspire* (Tracy Tomasky, 2016), 100.

Chapter 18
Building Teams that Execute

p. 323 **One of the most costly business mistakes:** Pierre Mornell, *45 Effective Ways for Hiring Smart! How to Predict Winners and Losers in the Incredibly Expensive People-Reading Game* (Berkeley, California: Ten Speed Press, 1998), 5.

p. 323 **"Very few companies *really* hire smart":** T. Gary Rogers, speech, "Lessons Learned in 40 Years of Business Building," Dean's Distinguished Speaker Event, UC Davis Graduate School of Management, February 19, 2015, https://www.uctv.tv/shows/Lessons-Learned-in-40-Years-of-Business-Building-with-T-Gary-Rogers-29449.

p. 324 **Good management…is building on a person's strengths:** Drucker, *The Effective Executive*, 71.

p. 325 **"I've always believed that when the rate of change":** Jack Welch with John A. Byrne, *Jack: Straight from the Gut* (New York: Grand Central Publishing, 2003), 432.

p. 331 **"It's a pleasure and a privilege":** Ronald Reagan, "Remarks and a Question-and-Answer Session via Satellite to the Young Presidents' Organization," February 14, 1983, The American Presidency Project, accessed September 6, 2018, https://www

NOTES & REFERENCES

.presidency.ucsb.edu/documents/remarks-and-question-and-answer-session-via-satellite-the-young-presidents-organization.

p. 332   **Have you ever heard of the Abilene Paradox?:** See Jerry B. Harvey, "The Abilene Paradox: The Management of Agreement," *Organizational Dynamics* 3, no. 1 (Summer 1974): 63–80; Jerry B. Harvey, "Abilene Revisited: An Epilogue," *Organizational Dynamics* 17, no. 1 (Summer 1988): 35–37. I became aware of the paradox because McGraw-Hill made a training video.

Chapter 19
Helping Others Succeed

p. 347   **The site dates back to the early 1850s:** Neal L. Starr, "Stockton State Hospital: A Century and a Quarter of Service," *San Joaquin Historian* Volume XII (July–September 1976); Angela Suzanne Hawk, "Madness, Mining, and Migration in the U.S. and the Pacific, 1848–1900" (Ph.D. diss., UC Irvine, 2011); *History and Closure of the Developmental Center*, produced by California Department of Developmental Services, DDS Television Center, 1997, videodisc; "Campus History," *Stanislaus State*, accessed September 6, 2018, http://www.csustan.edu/about/campus-history.

p. 350–1   **As Doug Unruh said when he retired:** Joe Goldeen, "Stockton business, community leader leaving," *The Record* (Stockton, California), August 22, 2002.

p. 351   **"The two most important words":** T. Gary Rogers, "Lessons Learned in 40 Years of Business Building."

Chapter 20
Giving Back

p. 357   **By 1940, the San Joaquin Valley had an influx:** "Dust Bowl Migration," *Rural Migration News* 14, no. 4, October 2008, https://migration.ucdavis.edu/rmn/more.php?id=1355.

p. 364   **"We are all blind until we see":** "Man-Making," *Poems of Edwin Markham*, selected and arranged by Charles L. Wallis (New York: Harper & Brothers, 1950), 6.

Chapter 21
Having Fun and Being Thankful

p. 370   **In 2013, *The Wall Street Journal* ran a piece:** Diana Kapp, "Raising Children with an Attitude of Gratitude; Research Finds Real Benefits for Kids Who Say 'Thank You,'" *Wall Street Journal,* December 23, 2013, https://www.wsj.com/articles/raising-children-with-an-attitude-of-gratitude-1387839251.

Scripture Quotations
Scripture quotations are taken from the Revised Standard Version (RSV) of the Bible, The Living Bible (TLB), and the King James Version (KJV) of the Bible.

Photo Credits
I am grateful to the many family members and friends who contributed images for this book. Specifically, I'd like to credit the following organizations and photographers:

Page 14   **John Carsten Grupe Freight Line**: Courtesy of San Joaquin County Historical Society and Museum.

Page 15   **My great-grandparents and their first home:** Courtesy of The Haggin Museum.

Page 135   **Our home at Brookside Farm**: Photo by Josef Kasperovich.

Page 147   **Beautiful Brookside Country Club:** Restored by Keith Burgad.

Page 159   **Grandchildren and great-grandchildren:** Photo by Keith Burgad.

Insert   **One of our favorite photos from Phyllis's 70th birthday party:** Photo by Keith Burgad.
      Poppies in the spring at our home at Shady Oaks: Photo by Stephanie Rodriguez.
      Driving my champion team: Photo by Angelina Gervast.
      Surrounded by my grandkids and great-grandkids at my 80th birthday party: Photo by Angelina Gervast.
      Celebrating the G Centennial: Photo by Angelina Gervast.

NOTES & REFERENCES

          One of four appearances in the Tournament of Roses Parade: Courtesy of Pasadena Tournament of Roses.

          Phyllis driving her pair of Belgian draft horses: Courtesy of Pasadena Tournament of Roses.

Page 374   **An evening toast:** Photo by Jeff Davis.

Index

A
Augustine, Norman, 212, 216

B
Bohemian Club, 71–72
Business Council of San Joaquin County, 310–311

C
cattle, 3, 5–6, 5–10, 19, 22, 31, 34, 42, 44–49, 59–66, 79, 86, 124–125, 131, 155–156, 158, 166, 172, 182, 217, 227–228, 268, 297–298, 338–342, 344, 366
Cortopassi, Dino, 55, 108, 165–166, 310
Covey, Stephen, 30, 84, 105, 287, 355

D
dyslexia, 68–69, 208–209

F
faith, 101–103, 131–132, 154, 158, 178, 183, 220, 227, 240, 279–281, 290, 292
family
  branding and cattle ranching, 5–6, 8–10, 18–22, 31, 34, 38–40, 42, 44, 47–49, 52, 61–66, 63–64, 68, 86, 155–156, 160–162, 166–167, 172–173, 177, 180–183, 191, 203, 227–228, 240, 297–298, 338–342, 352
  childhood memories, 4–5, 19–24
  devotion to, 153–159, 168–169
  education of, 69–72
  Grupe children, 27, 32–33, 40, 66, 124, 154–159, 168–171, 173–175, 177–178, 183, 191, 280, 294, 362

Grupe grandchildren, 40, 66, 158–159, 168, 171–173, 182–183, 187, 191–192, 219, 293, 338
Grupe great-grandchildren, 43, 66, 158–159, 306, 338
history and heritage of, 12–27
importance of, 27, 48, 154–159, 158–159
parenting tips, 338
partnership with Phyllis, 6, 154
raising children, 169–178
success and, 4
support of, 154–159, 227, 292, 355
farming, 3, 5–6, 8–9, 15–16, 19–22, 27, 29, 37, 39, 43, 45–46, 55, 69, 71–76, 114–115, 132–137, 148, 155–158, 167, 172, 180, 183, 208, 211, 214–215, 240, 268, 297–308
friendship, 159–161, 222
annual dove hunt; hunting, 155–161

G

Garamendi, John, 85–87, 94, 196
Grupe, Phyllis, 4, 6, 8, 27, 31–33, 37, 40–42, 47–48, 52–53, 61–66, 67, 77, 89, 92, 132–136, 141, 146–147, 154–156, 158–160, 163, 165, 168–174, 176, 178, 180–183, 186–187, 189, 193, 196, 198–199, 205, 207, 221, 227, 236, 248, 259, 263, 271, 290, 293–295, 297–304, 306, 313–314, 323–324, 335, 345–346, 352, 354, 358–363, 366, 368, 370, 373
Grupe Company, The
history, 209–211, 214, 224–231, 263, 266–275
masterplanned communities
Brookside, 77, 118, 136–137, 138–148, 150–157, 168, 230–231, 253
Carsten Crossings (zero energy), 269–270
Lincoln Village West, 53–54, 58, 111–131, 135, 139–140, 142–143, 148, 151, 154, 169, 195, 209, 216, 224, 243–245, 254, 330, 358
The Peninsula, 248–249
Quail Lakes, 174, 209, 243, 245
philanthropy, The Country Fair, 150–151, 158, 174–175
programs and projects
apartments, 119, 224, 230, 240, 256, 261, 268, 282
Bank of America redevelopment, 93–94, 188
Bear Valley Ski Resort, 216, 253
flipping houses, 272
the Gong Committee, 271, 354
Green Home Solutions, 211–214, 272

Grupe Cabinet & Door Company, 254–255
Grupe Commercial, 158, 188, 267
Grupe Real Estate, 256–257
Hawkeye Security Service, 252–253
Home Warranty Program, 144, 283–284
Investment Condo Program, 224
Kirkwood Meadow Ski Resort, 217–218, 253
Rent-to-Own program, 224, 273–275
Self Storage (Mister Space), 229–230, 240, 259–260, 267, 268
shopping centers, 108–114, 165, 245, 267, 268
Topanga Canyon, 212
University Park, 158, 263, 267, 347–348
public school outreach
The Belgians Are Coming, 149, 302
Grupe Hard Hats, 149

H
Holt, Benjamin, 53, 112, 115, 123
horses
combined driving, 3–4, 71, 158, 182, 197, 221, 263, 302–308
Shady Oaks Combined Driving Event, 182, 197, 305
Tournament of the Roses Parade, 170
U.S. Equestrian Team, 4, 198, 263
housing bubble, 43, 216, 249, 264–266

J
Jones, Alan, 81, 350
Jowitt, Ken, 168

K
key concepts
ability to execute, 10, 42, 57, 101, 110, 319–342, 370
accepting responsibility, 22–25, 203, 216, 221, 223, 286, 321, 328–329
achievement vs. achieving, 31–32, 138, 203, 220
alignment, 326, 332–334
creating solutions, 73–78, 272
decision-making, 11, 29, 33–34, 40, 45–46, 103, 240–242, 247–262, 278, 280–281, 286
deferred consumption, 5, 9, 37–38, 41, 65, 108, 133, 257, 267–268, 280, 281, 286
delegation, 32–34, 39, 45, 208, 328–332, 351
diversification (multiple streams of income), 43, 211, 268

entrepreneurship, 12, 156, 208–209
gratitude, 24, 103, 137, 358, 361
handling mistakes, 22–23, 57–58, 85, 95, 102–103, 171–172, 220, 222–223, 249, 281, 314, 321, 323, 326–328
hiring smart, 323–325
how to ask good questions, 54–57
investing, Rule of 72, 46–47
marketing strategies, creating a sense of urgency, 46–47, 138, 147–148
negotiating skills, 80, 87, 90–97
opportunity cost, 45–46, 48, 60, 100, 214, 215, 240, 247, 251, 252–254
overcoming fear, 103, 216, 219, 260
planning
   beliefs, strategy, tactics, 16, 100, 101, 103, 107–110, 241
   establishing priorities, 87, 104, 105–106, 169–179, 289–292, 296
   list-making, 32, 40, 103–105, 216, 228, 349
positive thinking, 220–223
pulling the pin, 247–262, 277, 370
Pygmalion attitude; seeing potential, 329, 345–346
qualities of a healthy team, 326–327
role of a leader, 320–321
role of a manager, 324, 343, 344, 351
standards of performance, 348–350
success, definition of, 99–100, 183
time management, 28, 32–33, 105
tipping points, 8, 17, 70, 112, 133, 169, 180
traits of a good listener, 84–86
the *unforeseen, unforeseen*, 44, 135, 216, 218, 224–232, 266, 291
visualization, 10, 102, 227
work-life balance, 168, 169–170, 183, 290, 292, 352
Klingbeil, Jim, 46, 177, 196, 222, 249–250, 261, 281, 295, 309, 312, 346

M
McDonald, Jack, 261, 296
Mondavi, Robert, 193
Morgan, Jim, 85, 103
Mornell, Pierre, 323, 325, 355

N
Nahas, Bob, 162, 346
Newsom, Sr., Bill, 242–243

INDEX

R
Rasmuson, Ed, 194, 322
Reagan, Ronald, 195, 222, 330–331
Rogers, Roy & Dale Evans, 189, 359, 365–368
Rosen, Ken, 261

S
Savings-and-Loan crisis, 43, 92, 163, 216, 222, 224–232, 260, 266–267, 281–282, 289, 291, 302, 346
Schwab, Charles, 56, 208
Simpson, Alan, 282, 322
Stockton history, 5, 8–9, 14, 18–19, 22, 47, 52–53, 63, 72–74, 83, 107, 112–113, 116, 118–123, 125, 127, 129–130, 133–136, 140–142, 146, 148, 155–156, 158, 162–163, 167, 188, 207, 233, 235, 242–244, 263, 267, 272, 274, 278, 285, 292, 298, 311, 330, 347, 361

U
Urban Land Institute (ULI), 56, 58, 72, 112, 116, 136, 140, 145, 174, 180, 293, 302, 312–313, 333, 346, 354, 360

Y
Young Presidents' Organization (YPO), 56, 58–59, 71, 85, 89, 93, 105, 136, 144, 156, 174, 180, 190, 208, 256, 279, 302, 309–311, 313, 322, 327, 330–331, 349.352, 355

www.ingramcontent.com/pod-product-compliance
Lightning Source LLC
Chambersburg PA
CBHW052008070526
44584CB00016B/1662